12|13

ASF

D0260589

Books should be returned or renewed by the last date above. Renew by phone 08458 247 200 or online www.kent.gov.uk/libs

796.334092

ADDED TIME

Surviving Cancer, Death Threats and the Premier League

Mark Halsey
with Ian Ridley

Foreword by José Mourinho

Published by Floodlit Dreams Ltd
www.floodlitdreams.com

Published by Floodlit Dreams Ltd, 2013.

A CIP catalogue record for this book is available from the British Library.

ISBN 978-0-9926585-1-9

Floodlit Dreams Ltd
5-6 George St
St Albans
Herts AL3 4ER.

www.floodlitdreams.com

Front cover and inside pictures by Alex Ridley
Cover design by Mike McMonagle

For Michelle and Lucy,
my saving graces

*'The trouble with referees is that
they just don't care which side wins'*
Tom Canterbury, US basketball coach

ADDED TIME

CONTENTS

ADDED TIME

PROLOGUE

Mark Halsey asked me to write his story because he knew what I did. My fascination came in collaborating on the autobiographies of some fascinating, flawed but outstanding characters in football, most notably Tony Adams, the captain of Arsenal and England, whose searingly honest stories transcended their sport – in Tony's case, his alcoholism and recovery from it – and appealed to a wider public. Mark also knew that, like him, I had had cancer and was in recovery from it. He reasoned that I could produce the sort of book, through experience and empathy, that he wanted the public, footballing and beyond, to read.

In turn, I agreed to work with him because he had a vivid story that could not fail to appeal to a writer who believed that sports books had to be more than sports books; they had to be about life. His tale worked on two levels. Not only had he reached the top of his profession of refereeing, to become a well-known figure in the Premier League – on first-name terms with the biggest managers and greatest players in English football – but he had also come through an aggressive throat cancer to return to the top.

What sealed the working relationship for me, though, was the answer I seek from all I write with: yes, he would be honest and self-searching, delving within himself for his true feelings and the detail that might both interest and help other people.

Unfortunately, honesty seems to both offend and threaten some people.

In the winter of 2012, news that we might be working on a book reached Mark's employers at the Professional Game Match Officials Ltd, (PGMOL) overseen by the Premier League, and they appeared to grow worried about what it might contain, knowing that Mark had plenty to say on the state of refereeing and the way it was being administered.

Mark was summoned to their headquarters to explain. They subsequently made his life difficult in the latter part of the 2012-13 season, as will be seen in the book, and pointed out to him some confidentiality clauses in his contract. I had been unaware of them, Mark had overlooked them, never thinking they would try to deny him freedom of speech after he had quit. The PGMOL, and the Premier League, made it clear to him, however, that they believed the clauses should preclude him from telling his story at any time, even after he retired, which he decided to do as the end of that season approached and events on and off the field depressed him.

Sadly, the publishers of the book declined to proceed when presented with the prospect of any pressure from the PGMOL and the Premier League. Mark and I, however, were not ready to be cowed. We both believed that Mark's story should be in the public domain, for two reasons: First, his was an inspirational account of being struck by cancer, the surgery, the gruelling chemotherapy and radiotherapy treatment for it, and his recovery from it. Mark returned to the top of his game, despite the obstacles placed in his way by his employers, and he wanted fellow sufferers to see how it could be endured and survivors to see how there was successful life after it.

Second, he recognised that the public pump huge fortunes into football through ticket prices, merchandising, sponsorship and TV satellite subscriptions. He himself had made a good living for more than 20 years through their largesse. In return for their goodwill accorded to him, he reckoned, they had a right to know about the politics, personalities and economics that inform the game. His views on incidents and internal machinations, along with the game itself and the way it was run, were a matter of public interest.

And so we, two cancer survivors, decided to stare down the powers that be and go it alone – with the support of both of our wives, Michelle Halsey and Vikki Orvice, who had also themselves both been through cancer, theirs controllable but not curable. We decided to publish the book ourselves and rely on natural justice, with faith that a good story well told, one that entertains and informs, offers help and hope along the way, will prevail.

I write this after six difficult, stressful months for both Mark and I, six months of attempts to stop this book and us. If you enjoy it, feel that it has achieved the aims we have for it, then it will all have been worthwhile.

Ian Ridley
St Albans, August 2013

FOREWORD
BY JOSÉ MOURINHO

The relationship between a football manager and a referee normally starts and ends with a match. We have different lives, different positions in the game. In my culture, you are not very open to a personal relationship with opponents, other managers, with referees.

But it was different with Mark Halsey. Early in my time as manager of Chelsea we won a Premier League match 1-0 at Middlesbrough and I had a good feeling with him during the match. He was very polite, very open and strong when he needed to be strong. He would admit the mistake if he made one and apologise to the players. I felt him to be very human, so I had a talk with him after the match.

The next match I had with him was Newcastle v Chelsea in the FA Cup, where we lost 1-0 and I think he made a mistake against us, missing a handball. But because of the feeling he left with me previously, I found myself sad with the decision and the result but accepting the mistake. I realised that the referee also wants to do well but he saw it another way. It was a new feeling for me. I was always against referees after a bad decision.

Mark was not what I call the 'police ref', which is a guy who goes to the game and says: 'I have the whistle. I have the power. I am the boss. You are the player and you are the coach and I am the only one that is correct and I am the only one that has the law in my hands.' Mark was like the 23rd player on the pitch.

I saw with him for the first time that a relationship between a manager and a referee was possible, not by being on opposite sides of the game but by being in the game together. It was special the way he ran a football match. He kept discipline by being a very nice guy.

The guy is special, as I am. He loved to referee the same way I love to coach – with passion, with emotion. I go to the match very happy. He went to the match very happy. I felt we belonged in the same game and so I say that with him, I learned to look at referees in a different way. I am not saying I look at them in the perfect way. Sometimes you lose a match because of a refereeing mistake and it is difficult to accept, but I learned from Mark.

After those early games, I kept the same professional relationship with him. Maybe we would talk in my office if he was referee for a game at Stamford Bridge. I was always admiring him but never a close friend, never went for dinner with him. I was in London, he was in Bolton but now and again he refereed Chelsea matches. I win, I lose, I draw. I remember the Community Shield at Wembley against Manchester United, which was for him too a special day.

Then I went to Milan to coach Internazionale and I heard he was ill with cancer. It was like a big friend of mine was ill. One day I go to Manchester with Inter to play a Champions League match and he brings to the hotel his wife Michelle and his daughter Lucy to meet me. When he brings them, it is because he has the same kind of feeling for me that I have for him and from that moment we were definitely friends.

After that, we were always in contact. Since that moment, I felt free to have a different kind of relationship with him because we were not in the same championship, we were in different leagues. After I was in Italy, I went to Spain with Real Madrid and during the time when he had to stop refereeing for some months due to his illness, we became even closer friends.

I invited him to Portugal for a holiday and then to Spain to visit me. My objective was to give him another light. When you are in this kind of trouble as he was, you need light. The biggest, strongest light is of course the family. It is the love for the wife, the love for the daughter.

But you need to know as well that you have friends, you have people who admire you. They are the little lights that can help you to keep going. I was very positive to him in the fight against his illness.

Mark has been a champion in the way he fought against it and he has also given me the honour to participate in some of his actions through charity against the cancer, and to help others to fight against it.

He has made me a better guy and a better person. He is a good friend and a top referee. He is a special one.

1

THE END GAME

I had slept only fitfully, drifting in and out, the pain in my throat excruciating. I had taken my hot bath, as I always do on match day but that didn't help with the fear and worry either. Only when I was training, running, out in the middle of a football field did I feel any respite from the anxiety, as footballers will tell you they also do when beset by their own life problems.

That was one reason why I was so desperate to referee this Everton v Arsenal televised match this August Saturday. Another, after the shocking news delivered to me the previous day, was that I thought it might well be my last.

The morning was dragging. It was a tea-time kick-off on the ESPN television channel and I had too much time to ponder my state and whether I should really be doing this game. It was a big one after all. There would be no hiding place from 40,000 people in the ground and millions more on TV not just in England but around the world given the phenomenon that the Premier League had become.

Calm down, Mark. Get your kit sorted. Pack your bag. Actually, it is more a suitcase than a bag these days, and one that requires wheels, given the weight of it, what with all the paraphernalia of the modern referee it has to carry. I take less on holiday.

Mind racing about the future, and whether I even had one, I went through my mental checklist as I pottered from room to room gathering up my equipment. Have I got everything...?

OK, let's start where you normally do. The stuff that goes in the side pockets...

- 2 bananas for three hours before the game.
- Energy drink – to be drunk 90 minutes before the game
- 2 caffeine gel tubes and caffeine tablets, for instant energy just before the game and at half-time
- Protein shake for after the game
- 1 packet of Jaffa Cakes
- iPod, for music in the dressing room

Right, now my 'box of tricks' that goes in the bottom of the bag. Come on Mark, keep it together....

- 2 flags (the referee being expected to provide them for his assistants)
- 4 headsets (for myself – the earpiece moulded for me – assistants and fourth official, supplied by the Premier League.) The mechanism for the headset straps to my right arm
- Buzzer, to be strapped to my left arm. It connects with my assistants' flags and I charge it up the night before the game
- Yellow card
- Red card
- 2 whistles
- Pencil
- 2 watches
- Heart-rate monitor, to be strapped around my chest
- Coin (it used to be a FIFA issue but now I was using a Respect campaign commemorative coin)

Now the kit. One piece at a time, in the usual order...

- Boots
- Socks
- Sports underpants, known in the trade as sloggies
- Cycling shorts
- Training top for the warm-up
- Training shorts for the warm-up
- Sweatshirt
- Wet weather jacket
- Vest
- Refereeing shirt – and today I had chosen green as there would be no possible colour clash with the players, though in other weeks it could be either black, yellow or red as well
- Shorts

Yes, shorts, always the last in. Got everything now...

At 12.30, it was finally time to go. I said goodbye to my wife Michelle, who was having a down day herself, which could often happen around this time given her own problems, and would not be coming to the game today. Little Lucy, our then three-year-old daughter, was not her usual bubbly self either. After what had happened with her Mum, she sensed now there was something wrong with Daddy.

It was a wrench to leave the sanctuary of my family but I couldn't just sit at home that weekend, just waiting and worrying about the events of the forthcoming Monday that were bound to be traumatic.

I then drove from our home in the village of Little Lever on the outskirts of Bolton to the meeting place with my two regular assistants, Trevor Massey and Andy Garratt, and fourth official Mike Jones at the Suites Hotel in Knowsley on the edge of Liverpool.

Even the 45-minute drive didn't bring respite from a troubled mind. It was a hotel used often by Premier League referees for Merseyside games and I knew the route so well after ten years on the list of Premier League refs, called the Select Group, so my concentration on the road did not have to be so sharp.

I wasn't going to say anything to Trevor, Andy and Mike but I could see how taken aback they were when I arrived around 1.15pm, the scheduled four hours before kick-off that we are supposed to meet up, on the opening day of that 2009-10 season. I had seen for myself how ill I looked when I stared at myself in the mirror as I had a shave that morning. I recognised their look. It was the same shocked expression I had seen in my reflection.

I told them that I was going to need their help that day. I had a tumour in my throat. I had cancer. I was going in for an operation in 48 hours' time.

They listened intently and there was a silence. It was broken by Trevor.

'Tax,' he said, using the shortening of my nickname of Taxi, after my occupation to make ends meet in my early days of refereeing. 'We are always bloody baling you out, so what's going to be different today?'

We laughed and that was another reason why I wanted to be there. The camaraderie of football and its dressing rooms can help people through the most painful, difficult times, which may be why so many players have trouble adjusting to life after they leave them, or why they are so keen to stay in the game in some capacity. I wanted to feel the fun one more time.

I hadn't had much of that all year. I had felt ill most of the time, but passed it off as simply being under the weather. In the January, I went to my GP with a sore throat and big yellow ulcers in my mouth and lips. My teeth looked constantly stained and twice

I went to a dentist, who polished them and asked if I smoked or drank a lot of tea, neither of which I did.

The doctor could find nothing much wrong with me, he said, and put me on some antibiotics. By the March, I was not feeling much better, though still refereeing every week and getting by well enough despite frequently feeling tired. I went back to him with an ear infection. He gave me a balloon and told me to stick it up my nose and blow down through each nostril, one at a time, to inflate it. It would clear any fluid in the inner ear, he said.

But it still didn't feel like it was working. Troubled also with a nagging throat infection, I was constantly run down. From the end of March right through the summer, I was continually put on antibiotics – seven courses of them. That included one episode in Spain where a doctor told me that if I had been a dog, I would be a candidate for being put down. I didn't know the Spanish for, 'Charming, thanks pal'.

Michelle and I had bought a small villa with access to a pool at Caba Roij on the Costa Blanca not far from Alicante in Spain back in 2004 as respite from the rigours of football and the English weather, especially in the North, which this southern-born softie had never taken to. We could get cheap flights there for little midweek breaks and half-terms with Lucy and even spend whole summers there between football seasons.

Come the end of the 2008-09 season, we promptly took off for warmer climes, looking forward to a well-earned rest after a season that had seen me referee 44 games, including 28 in the Premier League. Michelle also deserved it. She had received a bombshell that shook us all just before the New Year when she was diagnosed with a cancer of her own, chronic myeloid leukaemia, a disease of the blood. Without all my stuff to contend with as well, she had been through her own ordeal as the doctors tried to control her condition with medication. There would be no cure for Michelle; they could only control the disease. With her blood test results so up and down, these were anxious, uncertain times.

But I just couldn't enjoy the down time. I struggled to eat and I was in a lot of pain when I had a drink, with the back of my throat feeling like barbed wire. I would ask Michelle if she could see anything there but she couldn't. By now, though, I did have cold sores and massive ulcers the size of 5p pieces in my mouth.

Michelle got fed up with me at times as I frequently would not want to go out for dinner or a drink and we would argue a lot. I also fell out with her parents, who were with us, amid a lot of family tension. I was just so miserable and didn't want to speak to anyone, and went walking on my own some of the time. In fact, I didn't speak to my mother-in-law for four weeks. It was not like me but I felt so tired all the time. I mostly put it down to the strength and conditioning training regime that I had to keep up ahead of a new football season and which was getting harder by the day.

I flew back to England for a week's pre-season training camp in Cornwall with the other referees who made up the Select Group administered by the Professional Game Match Officials Ltd, which is the governing body of referees who look after the Premier League and Football League officials. Although I was still capable of doing all the running and training, having been keeping fit in Spain, I knew I was not up to my usual standards.

In late July, I was asked to referee Tottenham v Barcelona in the Wembley Cup pre-season tournament and came back from Spain again, staying at Sopwell House hotel in St Albans the night before. I struggled to get through the game, though, with my performance off the pace, even if I managed to cover up with my experience. As soon as I landed back in Spain the next day, I asked Michelle to take me to a local clinic.

That was when the doctor tried to joke about my appearance and how ill I looked. But then I knew that. I had recently seen a picture of myself on my 40th birthday and compared how well I was then with how I now appeared, eight years on, on my birthday this July. He gave me three very strong antibiotic tablets – which cost me an extortionate 30 Euros – for the ear infection and told me if I still didn't feel better after those, to come back and he would refer me to a vet about being put down.

I suppose he was trying to lighten my mood but this now felt serious and I was getting extremely worried. I had lost over a stone and a half in weight, dropping from 83 to 72 kilograms.

In early August, it was time to return to England for the impending new season and my annual fitness test at the Pingle's Leisure Centre athletics track in Nuneaton. I went to my GP almost immediately after I got back and Michelle came with me as she was now very concerned as well. The doctor wanted to put me back on antibiotics but Michelle intervened and said no, that I had now had seven courses in as many months and nothing had improved.

She wanted me to have a scan instead and said we would go private, having checked that we had health insurance through the Premier League. An appointment was then made for me with an ear, nose and throat specialist, Mr Christopher Lobo, at the Beaumont Hospital in Bolton for the following Tuesday, five days before the start of the Premier League season.

In the meantime, I travelled down to Warwickshire for our referees' fitness test day. The requirement was to get through six 40-metre sprints in under 6.2 seconds each, with 90 seconds recovery time between them, then 20 runs over 150 metres inside 30 seconds each one, 35 seconds rest between each. I managed it, but quite how I got through it I will never know. Sheer willpower, I suppose; I had never failed a fitness test in my life and was not going to start now. My colleagues wondered what was wrong with me. Their guess was as good as mine.

At the Beaumont, the specialist, Mr Lobo, took one look in my mouth and throat before sticking a tube up my nose. He concluded there was something there but he couldn't properly see the extent of it. I would need a scan the next day, the Wednesday, he said, and should come back on the Thursday for the results.

Then came the shock. When I returned that Thursday, he told me that the scan revealed that there was a tumour in my throat. It was cancerous, but he didn't yet know what type, nor how wide-spread it was. He wanted to operate to remove it the following Monday and if I came back tomorrow, the Friday, he would talk me through the procedure. Tumour. Cancer. The words made me feel numb.

I got in my car and sat there dumbstruck for a while. When the phone rang and Michelle's number came up, I could not even ring her back for a while. She had not been able to be with me at the hospital because she had to run the Italian restaurant called Sottovento in nearby Farnworth we had invested in back in 2006 but she was clearly thinking of me and worried.

I just didn't know what to tell her though. On top of her own illness, she had been suffering from a heap of stress caused by running the restaurant that had become a millstone round our necks with its trail of staff problems and financial losses. When I did ring her, I told her about the tumour, the cancer, and that the specialist wanted to see us both the next day to explain in detail the procedure that would be involved from now on.

She would be there, she said. I could tell the fear in her voice but she was a strong Lancashire lass as she had already shown and I was grateful that she was in my corner. She phoned my Mum and my brother Paul, as well as my best friend Fred Barber, who was goalkeeping coach at Bolton and godfather to Lucy, to tell them that I was ill. I just couldn't face it. She didn't tell Mum how ill I was at that point, though, not wanting to worry her unduly.

I don't remember the drive back from hospital to home at all, a thousand thoughts feeding my worst fears. A tumour. Cancer. In my throat. Bloody hell, is this it? Was I going to see our toddler

Lucy grow up? This, after all we had been through to have her —
me having two painful operations in 2004 to reverse a vasectomy
so that I could produce sperm for IVF treatment, which would
cost us £13,000.

By the time I got home, my mind had cleared enough to realise
I needed to ring Kelly Wright, personal assistant to the PGMOL
general manager Keith Hackett, to tell her what had happened.
After the Everton v Arsenal game, I was due to be fourth official
at the Sunderland v Chelsea match on the Tuesday, August 18th,
and Burnley v Manchester United on the Wednesday.

'Kelly, it's Mark Halsey,' I said. 'I've got a problem. I'm going to
need an operation on Monday. I can't go to Sunderland or Burnley
next week.'

'Oh no,' she replied, perhaps thinking it was something less
serious like a hernia, 'Can't you postpone it? We're really short
next week...'

'Kelly,' I said. 'I have a tumour in my throat. It's cancer.'

I could feel her shock and embarrassment in the long silence
that followed. Later she would tell me that she was in Clinton
Cards in Oxford Street in London when she took the call.

'Oh Mark, I'm really sorry,' she said. 'I think you need to have
that operation.'

She must quickly have told my line manager Keren Barratt,
second in command to Keith Hackett, because I found myself
taking a call from him very soon after. He suggested I might want
to pull out of the Everton game but would leave it up to me. I am
sure he was being thoughtful but I wondered if they might have
wanted me off the game.

'I want to do it and I'm going to do it,' I replied. 'It could be
my last game.' Tears came to my eyes as I said it.

I was stunned that Thursday night. I had always been really
fit having played and been involved in sport from a very young
age, had never smoked, hardly drank apart from a nice glass of

red wine now and then, and was baffled how this could have happened to someone like that. I did use a lot of mouthwash; was that anything to do with it? Surely not. But that was the kind of illogical, racing, thought I was having.

Though I had a sleepless night, I was thinking straighter the next day after the consultation with Mr Lobo, which this time Michelle was able to attend. The tumour, he explained, was on a tonsil, the right one of two, and that tonsil would be removed. After that, I might need radiotherapy to mop up any cancerous cells around the area affected. The surgery would tell him more. He made it sound simple and achievable. Well, we thought, that's good, isn't it? That's more encouraging. The worst of this crisis could even be over by Monday night.

The problem was I felt anything but good the day after when the time came to walk out of the tunnel at Goodison Park and on to the pitch.

The dressing room pre-game had been sombre, though my colleagues were very supportive of me. I had good relationships with the match delegate, John Bramhall from the PFA, and assessor Joe Worrall, who told me to enjoy the game. I doubted I would be doing that. Only much later did I find out that Mike, Trevor and Andy had made plans when I was out of the room. They didn't think I was going to last 15 minutes and Mike was mentally preparing himself to referee the game.

I did tell the Everton kit man, the Scot Jimmy Martin, what was going on with me as we had become friends down the years. His family once came out to Spain with us and ended up buying a property just down the road. He was naturally stunned. But I didn't want to tell anyone else involved in the match, certainly not the two managers David Moyes of Everton and Arsene Wenger of Arsenal, even though I was on good terms with both of them.

Despite my worried and weary state, I still reckoned I had enough fitness and experience to perform adequately and not let anyone down. My biggest fear was that I would miss a key match incident or get a big decision wrong because if I did, and once my illness inevitably became public, everyone would have been talking about how I should never have done the game.

And, in the honesty of hindsight, I never should have done it.

Everton 1 Arsenal 6
Barclays Premier League
Goodison Park
Saturday, August 15th, 2009

Sometimes players can annoy you with their tackling or elbowing. Sometimes they can exasperate you with their diving and cheating. Today, though, I would be grateful to one of them – the Everton defender Joleon Lescott.

The home supporters were furious with him as he was angling for a big money move to Manchester City, talk of which had dominated the build-up to the game, and Goodison Park made its feelings known loudly as David Moyes insisted on selecting him.

It meant that any struggles I may have had were not, initially at least, going to be the centre of attention. I always knew that could change, though, with just one controversial decision. Don't cock up Mark, I kept telling myself. If you do, they'll find out you went into the game finding out about your cancer and everyone will say your performance was sub-standard and you should have been taken off the game.

I didn't really think about being ill and the imminent surgery during the match, certainly not the way I had been so disturbed with worry during an FA Cup tie I took at Hartlepool some eight months earlier after Michelle had been diagnosed. It was different with myself, pre-occupied me less, at least during the freedom of the 90 minutes. Instead, I used all my powers of concentration to make sure I did not cock up. My mind was working properly, at least. Not my body, though. I hurt when I ran and only willpower and adrenalin kept me going at times.

It was an even sort of game for the first 25 minutes or so, with the midfields crowded, but after Denilson curled home from distance and Arsenal's new signing, defender Thomas Vermaelen, had headed home from a free kick, it was all but over as a contest. Before half-time, William Gallas headed home a third from another Robin Van Persie free kick.

Along with Everton, I was grateful for the breather at half-time, but just as there was no respite for me in the second half, so there was none for the home side as Cesc Fabregas scored twice and Eduardo added the sixth on his debut. Goodison was too busy booing Lescott and his defence when Louis Saha scored for Everton in added time. There was not a yellow card in the game, nothing I could become the focus of attention for, which was how I wanted it.

When I blew the final whistle – in relief – I thought I was going to collapse but was determined not to. Not now Mark, I kept telling myself, not after getting through the game, not out on the pitch in front of all these people here and watching on TV.

I called to my two assistants through my headset into their earpieces.

'Quick lads. Get to the centre circle,' I said. They rushed to my side and escorted me off the field, virtually propping me up to make sure I did not stumble. Game over. Thank God.

In the sanctuary of the dressing room, I slumped on a bench with my head in my hands, a towel over my head, and wept. Nobody said much until Joe Worrall arrived to tell me that his assessment would say that I hadn't run wide enough today, as I normally do, that I was too narrow in my movement up and down the pitch.

That, I thought, was the least of my worries. If only you knew, Joe, if only you knew. But I wasn't going to voice that. I didn't want to make excuses to my assessor. I was too proud to be shown any favouritism. Some time later, having found out what I was going through that day, Joe would email me with his best wishes.

I wanted to get out of there straight away. Often, I would have a glass of wine in David Moyes's office but this was not the day – either for him or for me. We four officials all got back into the people carrier to go back to the hotel where we had left our cars and barely a word was spoken, not even about what was an amazing result that would get plenty of media coverage over the weekend. The game passed satisfactorily enough for myself and the three other officials but it was as if we had screwed up. Such can be the gloomy post-game mood for referees and assistants as well as losing teams.

As I drove the three quarters of an hour back to Little Lever, exhausted, I was glad it was all over. In a strange way, I was also relieved about the cancer. Now we knew what it was that had been making me so ill and now we could do something about it. In fact, I was almost looking forward to having the tumour removed. It would be sorted. I wanted that potentially fatal lump in my throat out of my body and in 48 hours it would be. We had a break for international games coming up and I even reckoned that I could be back refereeing straight after that if the surgery went well.

How naïve I was – and how grateful am I now that I was so naïve given how much I might have panicked had I known quite how serious it was and the dangerous times that were to come. I lay on

31

the sofa awaiting *Match of the Day* that night unable to eat, though that was not unusual when so agitated after a game. I had been able to get down and past that thorny throat only a protein shake and two bananas. Even the Jaffa Cakes went uneaten. I was weary but suddenly optimistic again, having survived the day's ordeal. My naïvety stemmed from not having an inkling that night that far from being sorted, it was going to get much, much worse.

I did not realise that the refereeing career I had fought so hard for – through the internal politics of the job and football's organisations that can get you down, through battling the many prickly personalities in the profession and among those running it – could be finished. And that some of my enemies would want that.

In reflective mood that Saturday night, I also thought beyond all the many controversial incidents and episodes on and off the pitch at every level of the game in England and abroad that I had been party to, the back-biting that comes with the territory of making it to the top as a referee.

I remembered, too, all the adversity in a life that had included growing up without my real father, who left us when I was a small boy, leaving my mother to struggle to make ends meet at times. Then I thought of my own bitter divorce that involved fierce rows with my two sons from my first marriage and estrangement from one of them.

And I recalled how through it all, even if I had never encountered anything with the same seriousness as the fatal threat of cancer, I had been toughened by it all and become such a survivor. I was certainly going to need all the toughness and resolve I could discover deep in my mind, body and soul from all those formative experiences if I was to survive this crisis.

2

LOSING MY SPURS

eafy Hertfordshire and the new town of Welwyn Garden City, around 25 miles north of central London, may sound like a nice place to grow up, and it was. It also produced its fair share of well-known people despite a population of just over 40,000, such as the golfer Nick Faldo, England goalkeeper David James, *Britain's Got Talent* judge Alesha Dixon and former Rolling Stones guitarist, Mick Taylor.

A decent environment doesn't mean you can avoid a tough upbringing, though.

My father Richard left my mother Shirley when I was about three and he was never a part of my childhood after that, apart from one time early on when there was a wrangle between the two of them over looking after me and my younger brother Paul. Mum was in hospital with a stomach problem and Dad came to take us off a family friend where we were staying to his home in East Acton, West London. According to Mum, he couldn't cope with us and tried to get us put into a home but she came and took us back from social services once she got out of hospital. They were both young and making mistakes, I suppose.

I was born when Mum was just 18, in 1961, and Paul arrived on exactly the same date, the 8th of July, two years later. She had it tough being a single mother in those days. The King's Road in Chelsea may have been just a short train journey away but the so-called Swinging Sixties would still have been a long way removed from Welwyn Garden City. Every day, she would walk us the half-hour to nursery school and then go on to her job in a chocolate factory before collecting us again, taking us home and feeding us and putting us to bed.

Football quickly became a huge part of mine and Paul's life. Rather than being my little brother, who I looked after when he was young, he soon grew into a big old lump and like me, he loved his football, becoming an Arsenal fan after changing from Chelsea. He would go on to have a decent career in non-league football before becoming manager of nearby Ware Town then assistant manager of Essex club Billericay Town in Conference South.

I played for my primary school team – Creswick – but was not much good as an outfield player. I was then put in goal and when I went on to my secondary school, The Howard, I stayed there. Paul would also become a goalkeeper. Sport developed into a respite from what would become a difficult home life as I also represented the school at cricket, Rugby Union, basketball and athletics. I was always a pretty good runner at both middle distance and sprints.

Quite often I would be jealous of other lads who had their parents coming to watch them play. Mum had one or two boyfriends who came and went before meeting a man called Danny when I was about ten and after they married he became my stepfather until I was about 21, when they divorced.

Danny took no interest in my sport, though, and I had a volatile, uneasy relationship with him. During my teenage years Paul and I often came home to an empty house, with Danny also working, at the local Polycell factory, and we would have to fend for ourselves. I remember being hungry sometimes and on occasions we took coins from a jar that my stepdad used to save silver in and we bought crisps and sweets. When he found out, we got a bit of a smacking.

A low point came when I was 13. I was late home one day, we

got into an argument and he gave me a fearful crack. I exploded and went to hit him back. After that, I left the house and went to live at my Auntie Rita's nearby for six months or so, never speaking to my Mum and stepdad during that time. I was upset with her as well as him as she always took his side. Looking back, it can't have been easy for either of them dealing with two teenage boys but at the time, I just felt so angry with them.

My mother came from a large West London family, of five sisters – one of whom, Lorraine, she lost to cancer at the age of 28 – and two brothers. I used to love visits to my Grandmother Ivy and Grandad Archie, a big Charlton Athletic fan, in East Acton on a Saturday. It was on one of those visits that I was first taken to watch Queens Park Rangers, by my Uncle Len, at the age of eight. It was against Swindon Town in the old Second Division and QPR won 2-0.

I was immediately hooked on the Super Hoops and mesmerised by Loftus Road. I guess I felt a mixture of awe and excitement like every young boy who is developing a liking for football does at such occasions in the company of the men in the family. The roar of the crowd, the green of the grass, the glare of the floodlights, and all that. On the way, we would pick up my other uncle, Brian, who lived a few doors away from the main gate to the ground in Loftus Road, and walk into the Ellerslie Road stand at ten minutes to three.

Afterwards it was round to Brian's for a cup of tea before going back to Nan's where we would wait for the newspaper man, who would walk the surrounding streets shouting 'Standard, News' with London's two Saturday night football papers. Then sandwiches before being allowed to stay up and watch *Match of the Day*. Great times.

In those days, my first hero was the marvellous maverick talent of Rodney Marsh, who would go on to play for Manchester City and England. He had led Rangers to winning the League

Cup in 1967 as a Third Division side but I was just too young to remember it. My personal highlight was probably that of most older QPR fans, the time that Rangers finished runners-up in the old First Division to Liverpool in 1976, still their best ever finish.

I was at our game when we beat Leeds 2-0 to go top of the table on the last Saturday of the season and delightedly thought we might even be champions of England for the first time. Due to postponements or European commitments, Liverpool had a game in hand, though, and ten days later went and beat Wolverhampton Wanderers 3-1 to overtake us and leave this poor lad heartbroken.

I can still reel off the team from that Leeds game, starting with the man who became my hero, as a goalkeeper – Phil Parkes. In those days, England had so many great goalkeepers and he found himself behind Peter Shilton and Ray Clemence. Nowadays he would be number one, I'm sure. After that, it was poor old Dave Clement, who took his own life, Ian Gillard, John Hollins, Frank McLintock, Dave Webb, Dave Thomas, England captain Gerry Francis, Don Masson, the great Stan Bowles, and Don Givens.

Perhaps I loved the crowds and the escape as a haven from being a quiet, shy teenager who found it hard to communicate with people close to me and who would remain in later life someone who would often bottle up his feelings. I desperately wanted a father figure who would encourage my football and a mum I could talk to but I was just too angry with her.

I also became surly and stubborn at school, especially with my head of physical education, Mike Evans. If I didn't want to do something, such as the hated swimming when I preferred to play football, I would just refuse. He usually called my bluff by saying that nobody would be going swimming and so I gave in under peer pressure. It was strange, just a sign of my unhappiness at the time, as I would later end up getting on well with Mike and he became a bit of a mentor for me.

There were good times at school as well, such as a skiing trip to the Cairngorms in Scotland and another jolly to the Isle of Wight, though some of the local lads didn't take kindly to a group of cocky kids from the London area and chased us, throwing stones and bottles at us.

I also recall a kindly teacher at the school, Alan Kirby, who taught geography and who was a Portsmouth fan. Knowing my love of football, he took me and a cousin, Gary, to a night game at Fratton Park, though I got a telling off from my Auntie Rita, with whom I was living at the time, when I got back at 1am. Years later, Alan would write to me when I became a referee.

Then there was another PE teacher in Phil Mowbray, who helped me a lot with my goalkeeping from the age of 12. Phil was also a scout for Tottenham Hotspur, one of a network that clubs retained in those days to monitor local talent with a view to recommending them to the club.

He got me in at Spurs for a trial at their old training ground at Cheshunt when I was 13 and I did well enough to be asked to start going for training. Uncle Len took me to White Hart Lane for my first session in the indoor gym there but after that, I was on my own. It was a train to Finsbury Park, then the old 279 bus to the Spurs ground. I had to be there for 6pm and would not get home till 11. Food would usually be a bag of chips in Tottenham High Road.

When I was offered associate schoolboy forms, I was delighted to sign and for a while, all looked rosy as I did well in the age-group teams. These were happier days. I was also playing for the school team and a Sunday youth club team named Walnut Wanderers, my brother Paul and I were close, looking out for each other, and I had no need to work hard at school. I could gaze out of the window in the certainty that I was going to be a professional footballer.

And that was the trouble: I thought I had made it. I started not to work as hard and would miss training at Spurs now and then, due partly to having got a part-time job stacking shelves in Tesco. I also got fed up with travelling on my own by train and bus on those long, cold winter nights.

These days it probably wouldn't be allowed and parents would drive their kids there and back. I just felt I had no back-up and was doing everything alone. I can't blame anyone else but it would have been nice to have had a proper father figure to be there all the time and get hold of me when I needed a talking-to. I remember reading David Beckham once talking about what he had to sacrifice in his teenage years to become a pro, watching his mates go out on Saturday nights while he stayed in, but I guess I never quite had his dedication nor the support system. Or, to be honest, his talent.

Although I never really drank, I went off the straight and narrow and I discovered girls, went out instead of staying in, even though it mostly involved hanging about on street corners. Still in my mid-teens it didn't occur to me that I was going to be anything other than a footballer. That was until I received a rude awakening at the age of 15.

Peterborough United juniors 7
Tottenham Hotspur juniors 0
South-East Counties League Division Two Cup
London Road
September 11th, 1976

All through that long, hot summer, I had been looking forward to the new season and playing for Spurs under-16s and there was eager anticipation as I travelled by coach up the A1 with the team this Saturday morning, I was nervous but excited to be playing at a big stadium, the Posh's London Road ground.

This was proper. This was big time.

It turned into a nightmare, though. I had a shocker, no getting away from it. The defence might have let me down now and then but mostly the goals were down to me. I could almost hear the lads around me saying: 'What have we got here?'

To be honest, I remember very little about the game itself except my embarrassment as I kept picking the ball out of the net. I guess I have blocked out the details down the years.

Afterwards, I sat in the dressing room holding my head in my hands and I did well not to drop that. My team-mates were embarrassed for me and it was a quiet atmosphere. The only one I remember, the only one who went on to play for the first team, was Garry Brooke, the little right winger with a powerful shot.

On the coach home, all I recall is the feeling of deflation at odds with the eagerness I felt on the way up. I did my best to avoid eye contact with the team manager, a man by the name of Peter Shreeves – who would not only go on to become the first team manager but later a refereeing delegate I would meet often.

Come the next Tuesday after training, Peter asked to have a quiet word with me in private. He was respectful but firm.

Peter told me that I hadn't been performing as I once had and did not look as if I had been applying myself properly.

He had, he said, asked himself whether I was going to be good enough to make a player for Tottenham Hotspur and the answer was no. He would be letting me go. He also told me to question what I wanted to do with my life.

The next week the *Tottenham Weekly Herald*'s match report read: 'Goalkeeper Mark Halsey from Welwyn Garden City was making his debut for the juniors – and what a nightmare start for the youngster!' In the following week's club programme, the details were there for all to see in black and white underneath those for the first team's 1-0 home win over Leeds, the Spurs team featuring Glenn Hoddle and Steve Perryman.

I guess now they would call Peter Shreeves's words to me tough love. Then they just felt tough. The South East Counties League registration I signed on August 15th was cancelled on September 22nd. I didn't want to tell anyone for a while, kept it to myself out of embarrassment at my humiliation. I was devastated.

Looking back, though, I can hardly be surprised if I am honest with myself. I had wasted a golden opportunity through taking too much for granted, not working hard enough and resenting my family circumstances rather than using them as motivation.

I seemed to spend my last nine months at school gazing out of the window, infused with resentment and feeling sorry for myself at the death of the dream that had been a release from my worries at home. I left with CSEs in just English, cooking and PE and had had no experience of working beyond the job at Tesco. I had thought that football was going to take care of all that.

It seemed serious, as life does in your teens when sometimes you can't see where you are going wrong yourself and look to blame other things. The country is full of shelf-stackers who could have been professional footballers – or so they will tell you as they bore you down the pub. Was I going to be one of them? What on earth was I going to do now?

3

GOALKEEPER TURNING GAMEKEEPER

That summer of 1977, the year of the Queen's Silver Jubilee and the Sex Pistols, I turned 16, signed on the dole for the £30 every fortnight it paid and started going out with a girl called Jackie Armstrong. She would later become Jackie Halsey. We had been at school together but only now did any relationship blossom and it was fortunate for me at that time that it did.

I worked in the warehouse at Tesco for a few months but got bored with it. Luckily Jackie's father Jim, a local businessman with a taxi firm, offered me a way out. Jim also owned a burger van and offered me a job running it. He would drive me out to the van, which he would set up at various Hertfordshire locations, mainly the A414 Hertford by-pass, until the police closed us down and he would have to come and get me. I often had to wait hours for him to arrive. After that became too regular an occurrence, Jim gave me a job in his taxi business when I passed my driving test.

The job sometimes involved taking parcels to a big local company called Polypenco, an engineering plastics company, and I got to know people well there.

Soon after I turned 18, I was offered a job with them in the warehouse for a more than handy sum to me at the time of £200 a week, including overtime. I would go on to spend 12 years working there, rising to supervisor on the factory floor.

I stayed so long because another couple of chances to become a full-time professional footballer disappeared through my fingers.

The first came with Watford in a little spell when I travelled over to train with their youth team, then managed by Tom Walley and captained by Kenny Jackett. I even played the odd South-East Counties League game for them.

Again, though, the travelling got too much as I took the 724 Greenline bus that came through Welwyn and went through Watford to Heathrow Airport. If I had felt they were going to take me on, I would have kept going, even though I was only getting my bus fares, but it became clear that I wasn't going to get offered anything.

I then had a stint playing for Welwyn Garden United on Saturdays in Division One of the South Midlands League but got picked up by Hertford Town of the old Isthmian League, a level up in a competition for decent and decent-sized semi-professional clubs in the south-east. I did well for them, too, in what would prove to be a great season for the club in 1979-80.

We didn't think all that much of it when we beat Chelmsford City 2-1 in the preliminary round of the FA Trophy that season but soon we were embarking on quite a run. After beating St Albans City 3-0 in the first qualifying round, we then beat Sudbury Town 1-0 away, where the referee was a man called Peter Foakes, who would go on to become a Football and Premier League official and refereeing coach. We followed that up with a 1-0 home win over local rivals Ware.

That took us into the first round proper and a 3-0 home win over Slough Town, which brought us an away tie at Dulwich Hamlet. It was a cracking match but we went out 2-1. It was almost unheard of for a club of our size to get that far and the last 32 remains the furthest Hertford have been in the competition.

That season, we were also drawn against Norwich City in the old East Anglian Cup and I had a stormer of a game, despite a 2-0 defeat. Afterwards, the Hertford manager Tommy Barnett sang my praises and offered me a contract on £25 a week. I was happy to sign and the money was handy. I was young – just 18 – naïve and open to flattery.

Not long after, though, I found out that the Norwich manager John Bond had made enquiries about signing me. He was told, however, that with me now on a contract, it would cost a transfer fee and he was apparently quoted a sum of £20,000. Naturally his and the Canaries' interest quickly cooled.

I was upset with Hertford and though I stayed for a while – even enjoying a Herts Senior Cup tie against Barnet, when the great old Spurs and England striker Jimmy Greaves was in their line-up – I was never really happy there again.

I drifted across to nearby St Albans City and played a few reserve games at their nice little leafy Clarence Park ground before moving to Cambridge City, playing under their old manager Bill Leivers, legendary in non-league circles, for an acceptable £50 a week and travelling expenses.

It was never about money for me, though, and sadly I was falling out of love with football.

After a couple of seasons with Cambridge City, I knocked about various clubs. I had one game for Barnet in the Alliance Premier League, the new national competition for the bigger non-league clubs that would become the Conference, when I was doing a favour for an old mate I had played with at school and now playing for the Bees, Ian Ferguson, as they had an injury crisis. I hoped something would come of it but nothing did. Losing 4-3 at home to Kidderminster Harriers was not the best self-advertisement I suppose. Being a professional at a decent level continued to elude me, contributing to my disaffection with the game.

I played some Sunday League football for a local team called Wellingborough, managed by an old mate called Russell Foster, who I had played with for Welwyn Garden United. He was still playing, and with his customary, shall we say, physical approach. In fact, he was a dirty player was Russell, a big old boy of a centre half who was fond of a bit of kicking and butting.

I also played for another old mate in Ray Sullivan at Welwyn Garden City in the South Midlands League Premier Division on a Saturday on occasions and also switched on Sundays to play for the Smith, Kline and French pharmaceutical company's works team, managed by an old cricketing pal Dave Lawrence, who was captain of Potters Bar when I played for Hatfield Hyde. I was a left arm over, military medium bowler and a middle order batsman.

After my failure to make it as a pro, I fell out of love with football for a while and fancied a change of sport. So, at the age of 22, I turned to Rugby Union, joining the Welwyn club and starting life in their fifth XV but making my way through to the firsts within a month or two. I loved it. I was a quick full back who enjoyed going on runs and getting stuck into the tackle.

My stag do when I was 21 had been at the rugby club before my wedding to Jackie on March 12th, 1982. Uncharacteristically, I got very drunk and my brother Paul had to get me home after I ran down a street naked. I was seriously ill the next day and have never been drunk again since. In fact, it would be in my mid-30s before I developed a taste for a glass of wine with dinner.

We couldn't afford a house in Welwyn and so, with the help of Jackie's parents, bought a house in Stevenage and put our names down for a council house in Welwyn. Our first son, Michael, was born in the April of 1984 and our second Jason in January 1986 but I have to admit I wasn't a great husband or father in the early years of our marriage. During our courtship, I was training for football twice a week and often playing up to three times a week, and then came the rugby. In the summer I played cricket as well. I would also, after three years of the rugby, go back to football.

We got our council house, which we would go on to buy, after the boys were born but we were never really settled. Jackie and I argued a lot, and I confess I lived my life selfishly during my 20s. Perhaps my devotion to sport at that time – although it is not an excuse – was because I had messed up my sporting career in my teenage years. After being annoyed with myself over the lost opportunities, there was still a feeling that I might yet get back what I had lost, thinking that one day I was going to be spotted all over again. But it was never going to happen. Time had moved on and professional sport was not missing me. Anyway, I was often too tired after work to train properly or perform to as good a level as I wanted.

In my third season playing rugby, I dislocated my shoulder and had to take four or five weeks off. Very soon after I came back, though, it popped out again. Then again. Very soon I could not make or take a tackle. In fact, by now the shoulder would pop out if I just sat up too quickly in bed.

It meant I needed an operation and, what with all the rehab, several months on the sidelines. And it was literally on the sidelines. About the only thing I could do was act as a linesman on a Sunday morning for Smith, Kline and French just to get some exercise without any physical contact.

I decided to go back to football, thinking it would offer less chance of getting injured. I reasoned that although you still had to fling yourself about, in goal there was not so much physical contact. Little did I know.

I had a spell back at Hertford Town and in a reserve game against Finchley, I took a stud in the leg as I dived at the feet of a forward and my leg began to swell up as the match wore on. I carried on playing, however, which was daft. I bled internally, the leg became poisoned and I had to go to the accident and emergency at the Queen Elizabeth II hospital in Welwyn. I then had to spend two and a half weeks bed-ridden on a ward there, having antibiotics injected into the leg four times a day.

Then I went and broke my jaw and lost five teeth playing for Hertford – at the time managed by Paul Fairclough, who would go on to manage Barnet and the England Non-League team – in a game at Letchworth Garden City, ending up in casualty at the Luton and Dunstable Hospital. When Hertford refused to pay the £50 for the dental work, I moved again, this time back to Welwyn Garden City.

We were a decent side and reached the final of the Herts Senior Centenary Trophy, in which we played Pirton. It would be my first encounter with a young referee from Stevenage, who would go on to be better associated with another town in the county where he later settled. His name was Graham Poll, the thing from Tring.

I didn't notice too much about Graham at that time, certainly wasn't able to recognise him as a man who would go on to be England's leading referee. The only thing that really struck me was how friendly and chatty he was with the opposition. Not that it did Pirton too much good. We won 2-0 after extra time.

I was still playing Sunday League football as well and, not that I could have known it then, it would sow the seeds for my own refereeing career. In fact, though a humble game, it was to have a huge impact on what I would do with the rest of my life.

Smith, Kline and French 0 Wrestlers 4
Welwyn and Hatfield Sunday League
Premier Division Cup semi-final
Lemsford Village Hall ground
May 4th, 1986

A shocking result that was entirely down to poor officiating, which saw Wrestlers reach the final with four breakaway goals against the run of play, at least two of them offside. At least that was the way I saw it.

The culprit? One Russell Foster – yes, my old player-manager at Sunday side Wellingborough, the bloke who had been fond of a bit of kicking and butting. Now he was the classic case of the poacher turned gamekeeper.

I could not believe that Russell did not put his flag up at least those two times and the second time, I let him know in no uncertain terms what I thought of him and what he might like to do with his flag. Being a mate, I thought I might get away with it but he called over the referee, who threatened to send me off before I quietened down, though I seethed on right through till the final whistle.

Afterwards, when I had calmed down and realised that both my own and the team's performance might have contributed to the defeat a little bit more than the officials' display, I went to apologise to Russell for losing my temper. He was a good guy and would go on to become a linesman in the Isthmian League, though it stopped there for him as he failed the fitness test to become a referee. He always was a bit on the burly side.

Russell was gracious enough to accept the apology and as we got chatting, he said that I should try refereeing myself to see just what it was like on the other side of the fence. He told me that it would involve an eight-week course, at the end of which there was an exam to be passed.

No thanks, I said, I had finished with exams at school, was rubbish at them. Refereeing was not for me.

And that, I thought, would be that. I kept playing for another year, with Hertford Town reserves on a Saturday and SKF on a Sunday. I even helped win the Welwyn and Hatfield Sunday League President's Cup with SKF in a dramatic final against a team called Smith and Nephew. At 3-3 after extra time, it went to penalties. I saved their fifth, scored with our fifth and we lifted the trophy.

But Russell was still always on to me about refereeing: 'Go on, have a go,' he would say whenever I saw him. I was reaching my

47

late 20s and beginning to feel that my playing career was winding down largely due to the injuries that had taken their toll on me. When I thought about it, I did reckon I might be a decent referee. Couldn't be worse than some of the clowns I had seen. And there was also a bit of pocket money to be made.

A seed had been sown in that losing semi-final. If Russell was the poacher turned gamekeeper, I could be the goalkeeper who turned gamekeeper.

4

REFFING HELL

The Mid-Herts Referees' Association were good to me. If I could pass the exam, they said when I inquired about becoming an official, they would waive the eight-week course as I had played the game to a reasonable standard for a while. I think also they were short of referees – as everybody, everywhere always is.

And so, that summer of 1987, I read up on the laws of the game and took the exam, passing on August 1st with flying colours. I was a Class 3 referee, the lowest classification in those days compared with nine, for trainees, now. Next stop was the supply officer for the Mid-Herts RA to buy full kit, linesman's flags, whistles, yellow and red cards, pencils and a pad to write the teams down on. Clubs did not supply their own team sheets at that level then.

It cost around £50 for the lot, or actually nearer £100 for me as I needed two sets of kit because I wanted to do Saturdays and Sundays as often as I could. It was a fair old whack back then, especially when you were getting just £15 for a Sunday League game or a Herts County League reserve match.

My refereeing debut, if anything so raw can be given such a formal description, was on the playing fields at Old Welwyn – a Welwyn and Hatfield Sunday League meeting between Arctic Lites, named after a lager popular at the time, and Welwyn. It was pub football between two teams of boozers, some of whom had played to a reasonable standard, and I was assailed by the nerves that would plague me forever in my refereeing career. I was taking

49

charge of blokes I had played with and I was a bit worried about them taking the mickey out of me.

Of course, I had not a clue what I was doing, though I was certainly keen. I just ran around like a headless chicken, not knowing where to stand for game situations. But my concern about them taking the rise soon disappeared as I relaxed and I thoroughly enjoyed it. As a well-known figure in the area through my goalkeeping career, I had the blokes' respect straight away. I got no abuse, and had no need to caution anyone, though I probably should have done. At least, that's what an assessor or evaluator later in my career might well have said.

Man management came easy to me. Football is a working-class game and uses industrial language on the field. My style then was as it was to become at the top level: I was happy to establish a working relationship with players by trading the shop floor talk that was commonplace in my working life. I was chatty with them, giving as good as I got verbally, and I loved it.

Very quickly I knew it was for me and wanted to give it a proper go, though I do remember having second thoughts when I did my first away game. It was in the Herts County reserve division, which you could go straight into after passing the exam, and a match at Borehamwood involving a home team called Elliott Star. The change in culture from refereeing to playing really hit me for the first time.

As a player, you have the banter and camaraderie of a dressing room. All of a sudden I was on my own in a small room, with not even linesmen – as they were still called then – in with me. The clubs supplied those, often substitutes or blokes who had come to watch and had a flag thrust into their reluctant hands. Listening to players enjoying themselves in adjacent dressing rooms brought it home to me how serious this now was. I confess to feeling lonely and nervous for a while: what if I get verbals and violence that I can't deal with? In the event, it passed off quietly.

In my first season, I combined refereeing – and running the line in the Premier Division of the Herts County League for a £12.50 fee – with trying to fit in games for Welwyn Garden City in the South Midlands League when they were short, particularly in midweek.

Although I had always been pretty well behaved as a player and never one to abuse an official – apart from Russell Foster on the line, that is – I now had to be very careful that I did not get into trouble. A sending-off would have meant a suspension from refereeing, too. I have to admit that there was a game, against Selby FC of St Albans, when I came out to a forward but decided to let him go round me rather than risk bringing him down.

It was probably just as well that a decision to quit playing and concentrate on refereeing was pretty much taken out of my own hands. At the end of my first season, I had done well enough to be promoted to level two, which meant taking charge of Herts County League top division matches. I just couldn't commit to playing any more. It was not too difficult a decision to pack in, however, what with the injuries, even if I was just 27.

Back then, that age was young for a referee. Not these days when they take it up in their teens and can be fast-tracked to a good career. That is all well and good but I know in my case that playing the game to a reasonable level helped me to deal with players and tricky situations, as did my job at Polypenco working on the factory floor. By now I was a charge hand, on about £300 a week, which helped as I would be getting less to referee than I had been earning as a semi-pro in the non-league game.

Still, a pay rise to £25 in the Herts County Premier was welcome and I took to that level comfortably enough – my appointments coming through Russell Foster, who was by now the league referees' secretary. There were iffy games and decisions when players and managers didn't see it your way but I was lucky there was nothing serious, even if some of that would come soon enough.

I had put in for my level 1 as soon as I received the two and was getting on well, including being given a Herts Sunday Cup final to referee at Letchworth Garden City FC. I would also in future years go on to do the Herts Junior Cup final and the Charity Cup final of 1992-93, won by St Albans City, who beat Boreham Wood 2-1 in the final.

After some favourable reviews in the six assessments a season I was subjected to, along with being top of the refereeing merit list for the Herts County for the second season running, I was duly promoted again. One of the assessors was Jim Poll – Graham's Dad – who gave me a mark of ten out of ten in one of my matches he had been assigned to. It meant I had been promoted to the top grade after just two seasons and was eligible to move up to the next standard – semi-professional non-league football.

I was given games running the line in the next step up, the Isthmian League, but the powers that be made me wait a season before I became a referee. I didn't really see too much of a difference in what was expected of me, just more professionalism in the way that clubs treat you. Mostly that meant a cup of tea in the boardroom before and after the game. Often there would be a great difference pre- and post-match. It just depended on whether you had given a decision for or against a team, whether they had won or lost, as to how warm or frosty they were towards you.

Quite early on, I was sent to officiate Hemel Hempstead Town v Whitehawk and a massive free-for-all developed after a head butt off the ball by a visiting player on a home one. I had no clue what had gone on and was floundering in trying to sort it out. I decided to talk to the Whitehawk number six, the biggest of their players. It made sense to me – it seemed like a good starting point.

'What did you do that for?' I asked him.

'Sorry ref. I don't know what came over me,' he replied.

Yes, I thought, bang. I've got you. I had taken a chance and found the guilty party. He had admitted it and so I sent him off.

Sometimes you need luck as a referee as well as a player and I had been able to quell the situation through luck. I'm not sure what the lesson for the player was, mind. Honesty may not have worked for him but justice had prevailed.

Mind you, it sparked a massive to-do in the dressing rooms after the game. The brother of the player who had been head-butted waded in and laid into the defender I'd sent off. The police were called and took statements. I gave them my version of events but was happy not to get involved, given some of the characters around the place. In fact, I seemed to be the only person who came out of it all right.

My progression continued and I knew how highly I was rated by Barry Simmons, the referees' secretary, who was very support-ive. I was saddened to hear of his death on Christmas Eve, 2009. I'm sure he had much to do with me being awarded the Isthmian League Cup final, then sponsored by Diadora, in 1992 at Dagen-ham, where Grays Athletic beat Enfield 3-1.

After three seasons in the Isthmian I was then deemed ready to make what was called a double jump, being promoted to the Panel Referees group, one below the Football League National List. It meant I could operate as a linesman in the Football League and referee at the highest level beneath it, the Conference, then known as the GM Vauxhall Conference.

It opened my eyes to what a serious business refereeing was becoming. It also introduced me in a small way to the politics and personalities, bitching and infighting that would come to dominate my world over the next 20 years. After years of being praised and promoted, now, in the 94-95 season, would come my first real taste of criticism.

Having been used to just those half dozen assessments a season, now I had a man watching and marking my performance at every game. It was now that my style began to change. Where once I had been friendly with players, even wanted them to like me, I guess, because I knew many of them and had played with or against them, now there had to be at more of a distance. And I began to question everything I had been doing. Was I too much of a players' referee? Was I doing the right things technically?

There was never any real coaching when I took up refereeing as there is in the modern game. You did it by instinct, fended for yourself. There were seminars once a season in the Herts County League and once a month in the Isthmian but they were more like social gatherings.

I picked up my technique from watching other referees and the advent of Sky television and the Premier League in 1992 helped me as I began to observe top referees in action. The accepted wisdom was for referees to run diagonally the length of the pitch with the play, either right to left or left to right, though you do have to come off the diagonal sometimes as the circumstances demand. I have always liked to run the diagonal to keep my assistant referee on my right and run towards them so that I can see their flag if they make a decision that needs my attention.

Whatever I was doing did not seem to impress many of the assessors I was getting, however. Very quickly I received a letter from Jim Ashworth, the head of the National List of referees – under whose auspices the Conference came – warning me that my performances were not deemed to be up to scratch. Please read your reports from the assessors, it added, and react to what they are telling you. I know I must have been somewhere near the bottom of the National List merit marks that first season.

One particular match stuck in my mind, between Farnborough and Bath City. I thought I was managing the game well enough, getting on with the players, and handshakes all round were exchanged at the end, with both clubs seeming happy. Even then, I reckoned that while I may not have been the most technically minded referee, I knew how to manage a game well with instinct and gut feeling.

My mark, though, from the assessor, Roy Capie – who was to have a big role in my career – was four out of ten. That was considered 'unsatisfactory' and his report slaughtered me. I should have given more yellow cards, should have sent off a player. I had missed too much, he reckoned.

It really knocked the stuffing out of me. How could players and managers be happy with me but the assessors weren't? Not that it was every assessor. There was a big variation in their marks and comments. That made it even more confusing.

Perhaps I might have done better up north. From all the talk among referees, there, it seemed, managing and controlling games between tougher physical sides was more valued than your technical qualities. Though it was a national competition, southern referees did not in those days get sent north, nor vice versa. My games were at places such as Stevenage and Dagenham and Redbridge.

I have to say that it all made me question whether I wanted to continue. You had no comeback on the report and I felt hurt by the injustice, as I saw it, of one man's opinion counting against me. It ruined my weekend. I felt knotted inside.

It came, too, against a backdrop of things getting difficult with my work. I was by now also refereeing games in the Football Combination, a competition for league reserve teams on midweek afternoons, and getting the time off work was proving tricky.

With a family to support, Michael was now ten and Jason eight, the pressure was on and I was torn between my job and what had become far more than a hobby. By now I had moved from Polypenco to a company called All Purpose Packaging, where I was earning around £500 a week, working from 6am to 6pm. I faced a tough decision if I wanted to continue refereeing.

It would have been easy to quit but I was not going to give it that easily. I decided to ride the storm of bad reviews and come out the other side. I gave up the job and concentrated on refereeing. I was getting £60 per game plus expenses for Conference and

Combination games, which even doing three games a week was less than half my salary and nowhere near enough to support us, and so I took on some taxi-driving to become my own boss.

I also had to give up managing Jason's under-nine team, Panshanger to ensure I had the time and energy to concentrate on the refereeing. I made sure, though – mindful of my own youth without a father figure – that I was there as often as I could be for him. He developed into a decent midfield player and got picked up by Barnet and I was there to watch as often as possible as he went through the age group teams. Michael was never interested in football, developing a passion for motorbikes.

Able to be more focused, I also decided to worry less and just get on with my game. I reasoned that this was all a test from the refereeing powers that be to see if I would sink or swim – and I was determined to swim. In fact, it might have been a compliment: they saw something in me, wanted to see what my temperament was like and whether I would bounce back. Being cruel to be kind is the old expression.

Certainly if you can't handle all the criticism from your peers, what chance have you got from fans or players or, at the highest level, press and TV pundits? I certainly feel, mind, that referees should be given some help in dealing with it as they climb the ladder at least in the form of seminars on coping strategies. There should be a better way than simply avoiding TV pundits or reading the newspapers.

Everyone makes mistakes, I reasoned, even the best refs. Two things separate the best from the rest: the fact that they don't make as many mistakes as others and, when they do, they park them and move on quickly. I wanted to be one of those.

I decided to take on board all the assessments I was getting but decided, underpinning all that, to stay true to myself and my style of refereeing that had got me this far. In my second season, I definitely worried less about assessors – though I never worried about one called Dougie Burns, who would always give me six out of ten no matter how well or badly I had done.

Once I would fret about whether I might get, say, the tough Dennis Lewis who would never give you a good mark or the sympathetic Dave Axcell or Dennis Hedges, who gave me a glowing report when I did my first reserve game between two Football League sides, Luton against Oxford United at Hitchin Town FC, mainly because I used my common sense in just giving a free kick against a goalkeeper for handball outside the penalty area when he had the ball already inside it and his momentum carried him out. Too many refs might have stuck to the letter of the law and shown a red card for a 'keeper handling the ball outside his area.

Anyway, now I began to relax and concentrate on my performance, no longer wondering if they were trying to cut my legs from under me, as I perceived it, simply because I liked to let games flow and often waved play on. Now had they been assessing my skills as an assistant referee, I might have accepted any criticism more readily.

After being promoted to the Panel, I had been quickly assigned to games in the Football League running the line and I remember starting my first season by doing Leyton Orient v Birmingham City, who had just been relegated into the third tier. To be honest, though, I was rubbish at the job and never really enjoyed it. I could hear everything that was being shouted, 'Stick your flag up your arse,' being among the kindest.

My problem, I confess, was that I didn't concentrate properly. The play would be up the other end and I would forget to get into position. Sometimes it would take a defender appealing for an offside to stop me daydreaming. I don't know how they do it as well as they do these days. I wouldn't want their job.

Being so bad, I don't know why I was assigned to the line at that level. Perhaps they wanted me to watch better referees in action and take note because they had better things in mind for me. Because they did seem to be appreciating me more. It all came together in a tough old game in that second season on the Panel.

Carshalton Athletic 3 Woking 1
FA Trophy first round proper
War Memorial Sports Ground, Colston Road
January 18th, 1996

There are big games for players and clubs. There are also big games for referees and this was a big game for me. It was tough. It was physical. And it would test all my skills as an official.

One thing not always considered when a referee issues cards is his desire to make the safety of the players paramount. In this one, I gave six yellows. While some might have said it was not the kind of game that merited six yellows, my reply would be that it was not that kind of game precisely because I issued six yellows. They were my tools in calming down some nasty situations.

I also issued two red cards, which was a rarity for me. They were both Woking players, the first for denying a goalscoring opportunity to an opponent, the second for serious foul play endangering a player's safety.

It was strange because the player committing the foul was Clive Walker, the former Chelsea winger, who was not regarded as a tough player during his full-time professional career. It just shows that while referees may be aware of reputations – they also talk and hear talk – they should always judge the incident not the player.

It also shows how heated and tough non-league games can be and how they can affect even the mildest of characters. Woking being down to nine men explained the result, a cup upset.

The assessor had come in before the game to let me know he was there and I was tense. Afterwards, he came in and told me that I had had an excellent game, to my great relief. It was Roy Capie, the man who had given me four out of ten the previous season. This time, his mark would be nine out of ten.

I remain convinced it was a turning-point game, one that would take me to the next stage of my career.

Now I had struck the balance properly between being a players' referee and implementing the edicts of my masters. I was playing their game, I guess you could say – by becoming tougher in my approach towards players, issuing more yellow cards where once a bollocking might have sufficed.

It must have been working because a few months later I received a letter from Jim Ashworth of the National List, this time not to chew me off but to invite me for an interview to be considered for promotion to the Football League List. And so, at the end of the 1995-96 season, I found myself sitting before the four wise men of refereeing at the Football Association's then headquarters in Lancaster Gate, West London.

They comprised the head of the Premier League officials, Philip Don, Jim Ashworth, Frank Hannah, the chairman of the FA referees' committee, and its secretary, Colin Downey. I was really nervous, uncomfortable in suit and tie.

Though I had taken note of referees on TV, I had never copied them and always been sure to be my own man. Thus did a question from Philip Don about my main influences as a referee and who I might have modelled myself on have me a bit flustered. I had to go along with it and came up with some bull about David Elleray, one of our foremost referees, and how he let the game flow, had achieved so much and became such a good ambassador for our profession at home and abroad. They seemed to like what I said but only later did I find out that Philip and David didn't really get on that well.

I was told that being summoned meant that they wanted you but that you could still cock it up in the interview. If you did, it would see you placed on the reserve list. I was also told that the shorter the interview, the more likely you had got the nod. After the Elleray guff, I was then asked something about the laws of the game, which I must have got right, and 15 minutes later, I was out of there.

A few days later, a letter arrived at my house informing me that I had been chosen to be a Football League referee for the following season. I was elated. It meant that just nine seasons after taking a game for the first time in a local Sunday League, I was one big step closer to the very pinnacle of my profession. Not that I was thinking as far ahead as the Premier League. I was delighted just to get this far.

The dream of a 15-year-old kid of being a player in the full-time professional game may have been dashed through his inability to see a bigger picture at that age, but as the 35th birthday of this big kid passed during this summer 20 years on, his dedication in his attempt to make amends had paid off. He was part of the pro game after all.

5

UP THE FOOTBALL LEAGUE WE GO

The game in England was on a high that 'Three Lions On My Shirt' summer of 1996 and so was I with my appointment to the Football League. I would be getting £185 a game plus 25p a mile in expenses – not enough to be a full-time living but I didn't mind. I was in the big time, as I saw it. I continued taxi driving, England flags on my car, and watched with the nation as England lost to Germany on penalties in the semi-final of Euro '96, trying to comfort my son Jason who was in tears as I had promised to get tickets for the final somehow if England made it.

The day after that defeat, I drove up to the Lilleshall Sports Centre in Shropshire to take my Football League fitness test feeling flat like the rest of the nation but my mood quickly improved. Having always been naturally fit, I passed the test comfortably. It comprised a series of 'bleep' tests, which involved first a walk to a cone 20 metres away and back, building up to six sprints of 60 metres there and back, all within a certain amount of time. The whole process took no more than 20 minutes.

In fact, it would prove down the years that I have always been among the fittest of referees. The following year, I would take the test under the watchful eye of the guru David Elleray at Harrow School, where he was a master, and found it easy. I actually did one sprint too many and, with him doing the work alongside, he was not best pleased to be shown up. I have often wondered down the years if that was one reason why he wouldn't like me when he became head of the FA's refereeing committee, the body who appointed the cup final referee.

Refereeing in the league was a tough regime but an enjoyable one. On a non-match day, I would get up about 6am and do a few taxi runs then after the rush hour drive over to the Watford Football Club training ground, then in Stanmore, and do a session there with the players, the club having agreed to me training with them.

They were a good bunch. They had just been relegated into Division Two – what was the old Third Division until the formation of the Premier League in 1992 – but Graham Taylor had come back as manager. His assistant was Kenny Jackett, with whom I had played a couple of games in the youth team, and the club was recreating its good old days of the 1980s under them. It would lead to promotion to the Premier League within three years and it was a buzzy place. Often they would let me play in five-a-side games and act as a goalkeeper for shooting practice.

I got to know Luther Blissett, who was a coach, and particularly the goalkeepers, Alex Chamberlain and Chris Day, and their coach Peter Bonetti, the old Chelsea and England 'keeper.

Some of the players even used me to taxi them around on their nights out, including Tommy Mooney and Robert Page. Steve Palmer, who would go on to be a refereeing delegate, was also there. They were lively, fun times despite early starts and some very late nights.

After training, I would be back to taxi driving till around 6pm. I would be in bed by 9pm, the alarm going off again at 5.30am the next morning. I have always been an early riser.

On match days, I could be sent anywhere from South Yorkshire down to Devon, and could even get midweek matches at Doncaster Rovers or Plymouth Argyle. I might not get back from Plymouth till two or three in the morning but would still have to be up for a cab run to Heathrow Airport at 6am. We had moved into a new council house in 1990 and began buying it in 1992. The mortgage wasn't going to pay itself. But at least now I was my own boss and could come and go as I pleased.

I did have a memorable start to my Football League career, I have to say, when I was assigned to Brighton and Hove Albion v Chester City at their old Goldstone Ground in the bottom division of the league, Division Three. The Brighton club secretary Derek Allen asked me to get there early as they were worried about fan demonstrations due to the Goldstone having been sold and them having to find a new home, which would happen the following year when they had to ground-share with Gillingham.

I set off at 9.30am but should have known better. An August Saturday? One of the most popular seaside resorts in the country? What should have been a two-hour drive maximum turned into twice that and I had to report myself for being a few minutes later than the proscribed arrival 90 minutes before kick-off.

Anyway, when I called the captains together for the coin toss, a streaker suddenly ran on to the pitch, picked up the ball and booted it out of the ground. He ran off to cheers, which seemed to take any sting out of the occasion, a 2-1 win for the home side also helping. I'm not sure if the bloke – and sadly it was a bloke – got nabbed but he certainly meant that I had a debut that I would never forget.

Otherwise, it was a gentle start to my Football League career, with three or four months of doing lower league games, though I recall one tough outing at the New Den in a Division Two fixture between Millwall and Blackpool that autumn of '96.

It was a night game and Blackpool got stuck in traffic, on their way to south-east London, forcing me to delay kick off until about 8.45pm.

When we did get going, Blackpool were winning 1-0 until the second half when I gave a penalty to Millwall. And then another, both scored by Anton Rogan, to bring the home side a 2-1 win.

The Blackpool manager Gary Megson went crazy. Looking back, to be honest they were soft penalties, both given for mildly questionable tackles, awarded by an inexperienced referee.

As I was walking off, I heard someone from among the Blackpool contingent shout 'You fucking cheat' at me. I was not having that, though it wasn't the industrial language that bothered me. I have always been ready to give and take that. Referees might be called all sorts of things, and might make mistakes, but they are honest mistakes. Cheats we are not. That really raised my hackles.

I asked Gary – whom I have always got on with since down the years – to come to my dressing room and said that I would be reporting him to the FA for foul and abusive language. At first he denied anyone from Blackpool had said it before saying that it was not him, but his physio, Mark Taylor, who had said the words. 'Okay,' I said, 'you will get the chance to appeal.'

Not long after Gary's appearance, Mark came to my dressing room insisting that it was him that had called me a cheat. 'Okay,' I said, that will go in my report. Then came a third visitor, the Blackpool captain David Linighan, to tell me that he was sorry for the scenes at the end of the game, and that Gary had not meant to say what he did. Thank you, I thought, I was right in the first place.

A few years later I would move up to Bolton and train at the club. By then, Mark was Sam Allardyce's physio and frequently reminded me that it cost him £600 to share the fine with Gary Megson. Gary would later became manager at the Reebok and also had plenty more to say on the subject, continuing to protest his innocence.

More controversy came with my first Football League top flight match over the New Year period. It started with a warm feeling of pride at the appointment and ended with frozen controversy. It also highlighted how much refereeing has changed in the last 15 years.

Swindon Town 1 Grimsby Town 0
Nationwide League First Division
County Ground
December 28th, 1996
(Match abandoned after 33 minutes)

I was professional, I was early on this bitterly cold December day, turning up to walk the pitch at 12.30 for the 3pm kick-off, having negotiated that tricky Magic Roundabout, made up of half a dozen mini-round-abouts near the ground.

All was well as I said hello to the few Swindon Town staff in the County Ground at that time and I retreated to the warmth of the officials' dressing room. Besides, I needed the toilet. My nerves were getting the better of me even though I was really looking forward to the occasion.

And there I remained with my assistants for the next couple of hours, interrupted only by the managers bringing their team sheets at 2pm. In those days there was no warm-up the way referees do now with a specific programme of exercises that almost matches the modern players for intensity. That would take a few more years yet.

Thus did it come as a surprise at six minutes to three when I walked out with my assistant referees – this being the year their job title was changed from linesmen to reflect greater responsibilities in supporting the referee. The pitch was freezing and I knew I had a problem. There were 10,000 people in the ground by now, though, and I could hardly call it off at this point.

My inexperience was showing. I should have made a check and inspected the pitch in those two hours before kick-off. But then, nobody had come to my dressing room asking me to make one. The managers had said nothing when they brought the team sheets.

Right from the start I was struggling to keep my feet on a rock hard surface. If that was what it was like for me, what about players struggling with a ball as well?

After 20 minutes or so, Grimsby's Graham Rodgers – who would go on to be their manager – committed a stamp on Swindon's Lee Collins and I had to send him off for violent conduct. After another ten minutes, Swindon took the lead with a shot by Kevin Watson.

Now Grimsby were in my ear to call off the game and it was indeed getting more and more dangerous as the sun was going down. So after another few minutes, I picked up the ball and abandoned the match.

The County Ground went ballistic. The Swindon manager Steve McMahon in particular was furious with me and gave me a volley of abuse. He was particularly upset as his side had just taken the lead. It was unfortunate timing, for me as well as Swindon, but it had to be done with the safety of the players paramount. Later I heard a Swindon player giving an interview about my decision and admitting the pitch was dangerous. Even McMahon calmed down eventually.

It took a while for some of the Swindon supporters to accept it, though. The police kept me in the dressing room till ten to six – more than two hours after I had called it off – because fans were still waiting for me outside.

People do lose their sense of reason in football in the heat of the moment but I could have handled the situation better, I have to admit. I should have gone to the police and the stadium safety people and explained why I was calling the game off. I could also have got the tannoy announcer to explain to supporters why I could not continue.

Then, it was down to referees simply to use their initiative and discretion. Nowadays, there are guidelines about pitch inspections that require local referees to inspect either the day before or the morning of the game or both. I had had no indication from Swindon that there was going to be a problem. These days, clubs are more aware of potential problems.

Grimsby remained unhappy about the sending-off that still counted, along with the costs they incurred for the return fixture. Normally a referee gets appointed to the return fixture. I didn't when it was played three weeks later and ended in a 3-3 draw. This time the safety issue was not about the pitch and more probably about mine.

I had learned a variety of lessons, from being more vigilant before the game to communicating better with representatives of the two clubs to avert discontent, both from them and spectators.

I was getting three games a month and making ends meet and at the end of the first season, I had finished in the top ten-rated league referees, which was rare for a rookie. Those ratings are based on a tally arrived at from the marks of the clubs involved and the assigned assessor, who give you a score out of ten. Often you would find the winning club would give you nine, the losing club three and the assessor six.

The talk that first season was that I might get promoted straight into the Premier League but old school thought prevailed that a new referee needed to do at least a couple of seasons lower down. Perhaps a bit of disappointment contributed to me not making the same impact next time around, having something of a mediocre second season in fact.

I had some tough games to officiate, notably an FA Cup first round tie between Farnborough and Dagenham and Redbridge. Though they were two non-league sides, Football League referees would still be appointed because it was the cup, though there was no assessor in those circumstances at that time. It was always going to be competitive. After all, this was the players' chance for glory, to seize a national stage with the third round, when all the big clubs come in, not far away.

In hindsight, I didn't handle things as well as I might have and it was just as well there was no assessor. I thought yellow cards might control emotions but issuing seven of them did not calm things, with two Conference clubs going at it hammer and tongs.

Then came an incident eight minutes from time where I sent off a Farnborough player for a second yellow card and while a Dagenham player was receiving treatment, one of their players squirted a water bottle in a home player's face. He had to go, the offence coming under the heading of violent conduct, even if there might be far worse things than that. It prompted a mass melee, the game out of control. After it calmed down and I managed to restore order, Dagenham scored a late goal to win 1-0. It all left a sour taste in my mouth.

That was nothing compared to a game at Fratton Park between Portsmouth and Sheffield United in the January, however.

The game was poodling along well enough, with the score 1-1 as half-time approached when the Sheffield United goalkeeper Simon Tracey came racing out of his area and brought down a Portsmouth player. I looked across to my linesman, Edward Martin, and saw him flagging. I went across and asked him if he thought it was a sending off, Tracey having denied a goalscoring opportunity. He confirmed it was.

I went and issued the red card, hearing a rumble of noise from the crowd near Edward. As I turned round, I saw him on the ground and the police and stewards grappling with a young bloke. When I got there, Edward was spark out, and would be unconscious for five minutes. It turned out that the lad had thumped him on the side of his face. Poor Edward had to be taken off on a stretcher and taken to hospital.

Meanwhile, I had a problem on my hands. What to do now? With my fourth official taking over the line, we got to half-time, at which point the police and ground safety officer came in to my dressing room to discuss it. We agreed we should carry on with the game, not wishing to provoke any more trouble, with thousands of angry fans milling about the streets of Fratton.

Thankfully the game passed off without any more incident and afterwards I went to see Edward in hospital, where he was groggy but had come round. It turned out that the lad was a 34-year-old Sheffield United supporter who lived in Eastbourne. Later in court, John Corker admitted the offence of actual bodily harm, saying that he was drunk, and was jailed for three months. He was also banned from football for a year, which seemed lenient to me.

The whole occasion seemed to typify what had a been a tricky second season in the league for me and promotion to the Premier League now seemed further away than it had done a year earlier. I found myself in Band B of the merit list, which placed you between tenth and 20th in the ranking of referees, having been in the top ten that comprised Band A the previous year as a rookie.

It was disappointing and I was annoyed with myself. While I had been happy just to make the Football League, now I really wanted to make it to the Premier but I was actually feeling unsettled, not only by some average performances but also by something that had cropped up in my personal life. Indeed, the season had brought up a whole host of issues for me, both professional and personal, that I needed to address.

6

FROM LOFTUS ROAD TO WEMBERLEE

My rise to the Football League had brought me some attention, with my name now appearing in newspapers, if only in connection with managers having a go at me, such as Steve McMahon at Swindon that time, or at the foot of match reports where the referee is named, usually with where he lives in brackets. I enjoyed seeing the formal title in the posh papers – Mr M. Halsey (Welwyn Garden City).

Someone who must have noticed was my father, Richard, who I had not seen for almost 30 years. Out of the blue, I had a message from my Uncle Len, who used to see my Dad around the East Acton area of West London now and then, saying that he wanted to see me again.

There was a curiosity about me and so I agreed to him coming to my house in Welwyn Garden City. I had always heard stories about him from my Mum and I wanted to know why he left us so young. I was very nervous and suspicious. He was a big, stocky man but we had similar looks. I think my brother Paul inherited his frame and I got his features.

He stayed for a couple of hours drinking tea with me and he tried to explain why there had been differences between him and Mum that could not be solved. For many years as I grew up, I had a sense of resentment about him not being there but as you get older, life becomes less black and white.

I could see the pressure that he must have been under – he

was only 19 when I was born, after all – and he was now a decent enough bloke. I didn't dare tell my Mum about the meeting as I felt disloyal. It also took me a long while to tell her about the occasional phone calls we have now, and the times down the years when I have visited him, mainly at Christmas.

It was strange going back to spend time in a family house near the Queens Park Rangers ground after all those formative experience at my Nan's and matches as a teenager at Loftus Road – just as it was going there in a professional capacity.

I had first officiated there as a Conference referee eligible to be a Premier League linesman for a Rangers match against Sheffield Wednesday. It was in my second season on the Panel, when I was promoted to do the line in the top flight.

I had been in awe going through the reception area and into the officials' dressing room, which was tiny, in keeping with an old-fashioned ground hemmed in by suburban streets. Funny how it all seemed so big going there as a kid.

This experience ended comically. My opposite number Dave Bryan thought he heard referee Steve Lodge blow the final whistle and ran on to the field. With the game going on and Steve concentrating on that, I was left yelling at Dave to get off the pitch. It was all a bit embarrassing for us as officials.

I was also a linesman for a massive game there in March 1996 when Manchester United came to town, with Robbie Hart the referee. 'We' were 1-0 up thanks to a Denis Irwin own goal before Eric Cantona grabbed an equaliser in added time to deny Rangers the three points. It was one of the results that spring that combined to relegate 'us' and down the years I have joked that I wished I had flagged Cantona offside, even though he never was.

The crowd went loopy at the amount of added time played by Robbie, who went on to become a refereeing assessor, and plenty of them were still milling around angrily outside the ground when we were ready to leave.

In fact, so many were there that we had to be smuggled out through a side entrance. How ironic that a QPR fan was in danger from some of his fellow supporters.

My first experience of actually being in the middle of the hallowed turf had come in my second season on the Football League list, with Rangers at home to Portsmouth in the First Division. A goal by John Spencer just before half-time would prove to be the winning goal and as the players dived on top of him in the six-yard box, little did anyone in the stadium know that I wanted to join in.

Now this season of 1998-99 I was assigned to an FA Cup third round tie between QPR and Huddersfield Town. With the game entering stoppage time, and Rangers a goal down, I found myself hoping that they would equalise, not just as a referee who wanted to get the replay, but also because they were my team. They didn't and Huddersfield won 1-0.

Once back in the dressing room, I realised that this could not go on. I had never declared an allegiance to a team and because my address was Welwyn Garden City, it was never questioned. I knew now in my heart that it was wrong for me to be reffing them, however.

In all honesty, I had never given a decision for Rangers that wasn't authentic. When I stepped out on to the field, I was just refereeing two teams. Or so I thought. My desire for Rangers to get a replay, on top of wanting momentarily to join in a goal celebration, told me something and did not sit well with my sense of professionalism.

Ahead of the next season, where it came to filling in the questionnaire for the Football League about your personal details, I wrote that I was a QPR supporter and should not be allocated any more of their fixtures. I have never been involved in one of their games since.

That third season was a much better one for me, a game

involving Darlington, on a midweek night at Torquay, illustrating a change.

In my second year, I had taken a game at the Abbey Stadium between Cambridge United and Darlington and had a stinker. The previous season, the assessor Kelvin Morton had given me a ten out of ten for one game but this time I got a hammering off him. I issued nine yellow cards but there was nothing wrong with that. The problem was that I gave a back pass against Darlington which never was and from it Cambridge scored what proved to be the winning goal. At the end, I was surrounded by angry Darlington players.

When I saw the video, it confirmed my error and I rang up the Darlo manager David Hodgson to apologise, out of a sense of duty and fair play. These were the days when you were allowed to do that in the interests of good communication, which would later disappear, sadly, certainly at the top level.

It meant that the following season, in that match between Torquay and Darlo at Plainmoor, when I issued a red card against one of his players, Hodgson came to me afterwards and conceded that I had made the right decision. A 2-2 draw to take on that long coach ride home probably helped his mood.

Praise could come from unexpected quarters. I did a game at Preston in which North End drew 2-2 with Millwall, after which I was walking across the car park back to my car. Three burly, shaven-headed lads began to approach me. As they got closer, with my heart racing, I could see they were Millwall fans, their huge forearms bearing big tattoos. I contemplated making a run for it but they were upon me too soon.

'All right ref?' one of them said. 'You had a good game today, as it goes.'

Then there was the time the following season when after another Millwall game, at home to Bristol Rovers, the away manager Ian Holloway said in his press conference that he did not wish to talk about the game but the outstanding performance of the referee, Mark Halsey. I don't think he was being sarcastic but it was surprising, and very fair-minded of him, since his side had lost 3-0.

I also received praise from an assessor, Derek Bray, for my handling of a fiery Humberside derby between Hull City and Scunthorpe United in 1999. Derek gave me an eight out of ten and I was relieved I had a good game. He had come to see me with a view to promoting me to the Premier League.

It was one of the contributory factors to me finishing in the top three of the merit list for Football League referees, which meant, to my great pride, that I was awarded a play-off final. I had been given two play-off semi-final legs that May, in the First Division between Bolton and Ipswich and Second Division between Preston and Gillingham, and not having made a mess of things, was then assigned to that Second Division final, which Manchester City had reached to play Gillingham.

It would be my first Wembley appearance – on the pitch, that is. I had been there as a spectator to see England play and I'd supported QPR in their FA Cup and League Cup final appearances of 1982 and 1985, there in my replica shirt and with my flags to witness them lose both games, to Tottenham and Oxford United respectively.

In the run-up to the game, I had a phone call from Philip Don, the head of referees at the Premier League, to say that I was going to be promoted for the following season. No interview was needed for this one.

I had been watched again taking a game between Stockport and Bury in early April and my assessor Joe Worrall, a good referee himself who knew the game and how to manage players, had recommended my appointment.

It was a real boost and I was chuffed. I went to Wembley with a spring in my step.

Gillingham 2, Manchester City 2
(After extra time. Man City win 3-1 on penalties)
Nationwide League Second Division play-off final
Wembley Stadium
Sunday, May 30th 1999

I had a quiet night in on the Saturday at the Hilton
Hotel near the grand old stadium, then a few years
away from being demolished to make way for a new
structure. It would contrast with a raucous occasion in
the same hotel that would get me into some bother 24
hours later.

With my two linesmen, Ian Blanchard and Dave
Babski, and fourth official John Kirby, I walked the few
hundred yards to Wembley around three hours before
kick off. It wouldn't be allowed now, what with the
potential for running into members of the public –
though that would be the cause of the bother later –
but this was 1999 and things were more relaxed then. It
was quiet enough and an untroubled walk.

The first thing that struck me was how small the
officials' dressing room was. You expected it at QPR
but not at Wembley. There was not really enough space
for the referee, two assistants, a fourth official and a
masseur with a treatment table. That had to be set up in
the shower area – which had just one shower.

I suppose it was built for just three all those years
ago. I imagined the trio of officials sitting in here
waiting to take charge of the 1966 World Cup final. I
thought of Tofiq Bahramov, the Azerbaijani linesman
who would rule that the Geoff Hurst shot had crossed
the line, sitting there with his fateful flag.

Suddenly the significance of the occasion really

hit me and I felt very nervous as we went out for our warm-up, which was by now a part of pre-match routine, and to soak up an amazing atmosphere. It intensified when we walked up that slope and emerged out of the tunnel for the game proper to a full house. The walk across the pitch to stand in front of the Royal Box was still there then, and I felt very proud. I was edgy but sharp, ready for the game. The hairs on the back of my neck were standing up. It is the same for referees as players.

I felt that the game went well for me. There were no really controversial incidents, despite me issuing five yellow cards, which was about par for the course for an intense final, and after Carl Asaba and Bob Taylor scored for Gillingham in the last ten minutes, it looked all over. I signalled to my fourth, John Kirby, that there were five minutes of added time. Manchester City, a huge club who had hit on hard times, would be staying down.

I could see the Gillingham manager Tony Pulis going nuts on the sideline – setting the tone there for the rest of his career – when that board for five minutes was held up. It said more about his agitation than the reality of the game. One of his players had gone over to their fans after scoring, which took up a good chunk of time, with all that area around the pitch that accommodated a greyhound track to negotiate, and there were also those yellow cards to take into account.

What with injuries and substitutions as well, it was a fair amount. In fact, when I came to look back at the video later, it could have been seven, I thought. In those days, five minutes was seen as being a lot but commonplace now. As the referee, you have to be scrupulous about the amount of added time as people can even bet on the amount added.

They certainly proved to be five big, turning-point minutes in the history of Manchester City as the many of their supporters who have down the years insisted on thanking me have always pointed out. Just before the added time began, Kevin Horlock had pulled a goal back for City. Now in the extra minutes, Paul Dickov grabbed a dramatic equaliser to take the game to extra time.

That failed to produce a winner and so we went to penalties. Gillingham proceeded to make a hash of theirs, missing their first two, and with City 3-1 up, they had to score their fourth. The City 'keeper Nicky Weaver saved it, though and suddenly I was trying to avoid a stampede of City players rushing towards their goalkeeper in jubilation.

Soon I was rushing too – up the tunnel pursued by a furious Tony Pulis but he didn't catch me. His opposite number Joe Royle was naturally delighted but as a referee you have to discount both reactions. You can't please everyone. I certainly wouldn't that night.

Back at the Hilton later, I decided to wind down and went down to the bar for a drink with the Football League's north west refereeing coach, Dave Allison, who I got on well with and would do down the years after. It was pandemonium, full of City fans partying. Well, it was 1999, as Prince sang. They were in full voice and I was soon recognised by a group of them as I had a drink with Dave.

I was hugged and cheered and one fan stuffed a load of money in the breast pocket of my shirt, which I quickly handed back. It was quite enjoyable and funny – and open to misinterpretation.

Yes, I did have fun that night. I was 37 and had done well, I felt, on my first Wembley appearance. Referees have to retain their dignity, I accept, but they are also human beings who need to let their hair down now and then.

I did stand on a stool and join in the singing – a rendition of 'There's only one Queens Park Rangers' – but very soon got down realising that this might make me vulnerable. But I was drinking mineral water. It all felt innocent to me.

Then a story about it appeared in the *Manchester Evening News* in the next couple of days, probably leaked by a City fan, and suddenly I was in big trouble. Perhaps prompted by a complaint by Gillingham, Jim Ashworth, head of the National List, instigated an investigation. I began to hear from my officials and Dave Allison that they had been contacted and asked some probing questions. Fretting, I became convinced Jim wanted me suspended.

I received a phone call from Philip Don to say that any potential promotion would have to be put on hold. I was hearing some worrying things, despite feeling that I had done nothing wrong. My Premier League refereeing career, I thought, could be over before it had even begun.

7

PREMIER PROBLEMS

They were ten anxious days before Philip Don rang me again. Any allegations of impropriety following that Gillingham v Manchester City play-off game were unfounded, the investigation had concluded. I was going to be offered a position with the Select Group of Premier League referees after all.

It was a huge relief, though I would come to suspect that the incident in the Hilton would count against me with Jim Ashworth at the Football League for a long time. I sailed through the summer fitness test and felt I fitted in well at the week's pre-season gathering of the group at Lilleshall. Having been an assistant in the Premier League, I knew most of the referees already but I was still a nervous new boy, wondering and worrying what people thought of me, even if I did reckon I deserved to be there.

After doing pre-season training with Barnet Football Club, then managed by a good man in John Still – I could no longer train with Watford as they had been promoted to the Premier League and Philip decided it would not be appropriate any more – I was ready and raring to go for my first appointment, which came on the second Saturday of the 1999-2000 season.

Wimbledon 1 Coventry City 1
FA Carling Premiership
Selhurst Park
Saturday 14th August, 1999

It was a blazing hot day as I drove down from Welwyn
Garden City to Croydon's Hilton Hotel – another one,
ironically, a few months on – to meet up with my fellow
officials, negotiating the South London traffic and roads
with difficulty in the days before the satellite navigation
that has eased my life as a referee in finding grounds for
me. In fact, in those days, I don't think I ever went the
same way twice to Selhurst.

Among my colleagues that day as my fourth official
was Graham Poll, the country's best and best known
referee. I would come to have a turbulent relationship
with him down the years, both of us suspicious of each
other – but him without foundation, in my view – and
on that day the seeds of it were probably sown.

I think Philip Don had sent him to keep an eye on
me and ride shotgun to a rookie. We were both from
Hertfordshire and he probably thought we would get
along, Graham using his experience to be supportive of
me. I would have preferred someone of less profile like
Mike Reed or Peter Jones, though I was in no position
to choose these things.

I had to get over any sense of awe about Graham
and also intimidation, for Graham could be that kind
of figure with his big presence. I was always nervous
and superstitious before a game. I liked to arrive in the
dressing room at the same time, change the same way
every time in taking clothes off in the same order, but
that day I was even more tense on my top flight debut.
Graham's imposing presence seemed to add to the
pressure.

Being a fourth official is a strange discipline and one
that I came to experience plenty. You have to. Some
fourth officials you don't want as they are indifferent to

you and the job. Others will jump in the trenches and fight for you and with you, and dig you out of the mire by helping you. These days with the headsets that were introduced into the Premier League for officials after the 2006 World Cup, there is the potential to help the man in the middle in their ear with red cards and penalty decisions. Graham Poll was not one for the trenches. I wasn't convinced he wanted me to do well that day.

It was a tricky game. Wimbledon were not quite the Crazy Gang of the mad days of Vinnie Jones a decade earlier but they were still a handful, with hard men like Ben Thatcher and John Hartson in their side. In the event, I only had to issue two yellow cards.

Carl Cort gave Wimbledon the lead midway through the second half but the game was drawn 1-1 thanks to my award of a last-minute penalty for Coventry, which Gary McAllister converted. I got no grief for it, though might have expected some from Wimbledon. Easy, this Premiership.

My assessor was Roy Capic – the man from that Carshalton v Woking game – who seemed to relish getting his teeth into a new referee that he could write plenty about. He gave me a decent mark – a Len Goodman 'seven' that the *Strictly Come Dancing* judge delivers as 'Sev-en' – but I later heard that it could have been an eight. One or two of my fellow refs would tell me they had heard that Roy was going to go higher until a conversation between him and Graham Poll.

It was an early indication to me that Graham did not like the thought of competition at the top of the merit list marks. I felt sure he would be going back to Philip Don and talking about me. And not bigging me up. It left a nagging concern in the back of my mind on what should have been a joyous day for me.

Strange, really. Graham had been assigned to me as my mentor. That day, and a few other things I saw and heard, led me to stop phoning him after a few months.

Philip had told me that I might get ten games in my first season in the Premier League – then called the Premiership for a few seasons – and would mostly be doing Football League matches. I got more than I expected, though, and was actually awarded 13 to go with the 25 other matches I took charge of. Philip was good like that. If you did well, he would give you games even if you were a rookie.

I enjoyed that first season and thought I refereed well. In those days, the Premier League was not quite the intense, pressurised environment it is now, though the scrutiny was still trained on you and obviously more than I had ever been used to. I was also a comparatively young referee – at 38, and just like a young player, I was fresh and full of enthusiasm.

More than any criticism from fans or media, it could be the barbed remarks of an assessor that would bring you down. I recall doing one game, Tottenham v Southampton, which finished an amazing 7-2 to Spurs, and came back into the dressing room elated at what had been a marvellous game. We referees, after all, do love football and enjoy watching good matches. Facilitating them is a bonus of a thrill. At that point in my career I didn't have to remind myself that I was a fan of the game, after all, and would probably have been paying to watch if I wasn't out in the middle.

Very soon after the game, though, I was brought down to earth by the assessor, Martin Bodenham, who was always very picky and would go on to become a county cricket umpire. He just told me how many free kicks and yellow cards I had missed. It was deflating. My assistant, the senior Dave Horlick, could not hold his tongue. 'What planet are you on?' he asked of Martin.

My own view of these things is that, fair enough, point out things that a referee has missed by all means, but give him some carrot with the stick. Start with the things that went well, go through the things that didn't, then end with a constructive, encouraging verdict. Don't leave a referee to drive home 200 miles stewing on his errors.

It was a tough time to have my baptism at the top, with so many modifications of the laws and so many new instructions coming in around that time. There had been plenty to adapt to already, with the backpass being stopped and the tackle from behind outlawed. It could be tough differentiating between a careless and reckless tackle, one of which warranted just a free kick and the other a yellow card, which could also be awarded for technical offences such as infringing the ten yards at free kicks, wasting time or dissent.

From the reckless tackle, there is a gap to a red card for serious foul play endangering a player's safety, a distinction that pundits and media do not always make. Violent conduct, which generally pertains to off-the-ball matters, and denying a goalscoring opportunity, are other straight red card offences. I had had to change my outlook on the game, having been a player in the 70s and 80s when a tackle was a tackle.

I made plenty of mistakes. In just my fourth Premiership game, at Pride Park between Derby County and Bradford City – remember them at the top level? – and won 1-0 by City, I sent off two players in the first half, Esteban Fuertes for the home side and Andy Myers for Bradford. I was probably too hasty.

In fact, I issued eight red cards that season and while most were undoubtedly valid, one or two were probably a result of me being over-eager. Instead of the calmness that would come with age and experience, I was still tearing around like a blue-arsed fly as I had in some non-league and Football League games. I had again grown too conscious of pleasing an assessor and ticking all the boxes, which was not really me.

After that Derby game, it took me another month to get another Premiership game and for long periods I would be up and down the divisions, going anywhere, driving between 20,000 and 25,000 miles a season at 30p a mile at that time. I recall doing Middlesbrough, Plymouth and Brighton on three different Saturdays. This was quite apart from all the taxi-driving I was still doing during the week, which was probably as many miles again.

I recall one long trip on Boxing Day that season to do a fiery derby between Lincoln City and Scunthorpe United at Sincil Bank when, for a change, I had some company on the journey. I knew the Lincoln goalkeeper Chris Day from when he was a Watford player and I trained at their training ground. I picked him up in Stevenage where he lived and told him to behave himself because I didn't want to have an awkward journey home. In the end I did send off a player and book five, though not him, in a 1-1 draw.

Just as there are for clubs, for referees there are leagues within the Premier League. I would not get to go to the top tier games at Liverpool or Manchester United just yet. Mostly I would get middle or lower ranked clubs.

As if to be reminded that I hadn't made it right to the top, I ended up doing Darlington v Hartlepool in a Third Division play-off. I didn't mind. I enjoyed it. It was a good atmosphere and a cracking, competitive game, won 1-0 by Darlo.

Like that Lincoln game, it was an early indication of what would develop into a pattern for me. I am sure I was assigned to the game as the powers-that-be thought my management of potentially tough and feisty games was sympathetic and I was good at defusing explosive moments.

That may have been why I started the following season being allocated Wolves v Sheffield Wednesday in Division One. It was an intense affair – one live on Sky TV – between two big clubs who would be keen to start what they surely believed would be a promotion campaign with a win.

For Sheffield Wednesday, the start would be anything but the way they would have wanted it. Just 13 seconds were on the clock when the Wednesday goalkeeper Kevin Pressman rushed out of his area and handled the ball. My assistant Tony Green was flagging like a good 'un and I knew I had a decision to make. I am not a referee who enjoys sending players off but I knew I had no choice and showed the red card, even though I was almost apologetic.

Such could be the vagaries of appointments that the following weeks saw me officiating in the top flight as Bradford City beat Chelsea 2-0, then doing Cambridge United v Bristol City in the Second Division. After that, it was back to the Premiership, and Leeds United v Ipswich Town, which took on some significance, though I did not find out until afterwards.

I have always enjoyed going to Leeds, as I like the passion of the fans and the atmosphere inside Elland Road that they generate, and I had a decent game as Ipswich won 2-1, during which I issued four yellow cards. How could I tell I had a decent game? Up in a lounge afterwards, in the days when I went into lounges post-game, I met John Baker, then head of referees for the FA. He had been watching me that day, he said, with a view to me being put forward for the UEFA international list. He told me I had done well.

Soon I heard from Joe Guest, the FA referees' officer, to say that my name would be going forward for nomination to UEFA for the following season. Philip Don was pushing me, I was sure, and I was grateful to him. I would be doing games in Europe. It was a proud moment.

It was also a big sign of my progress, which included as well that season my first visits to Stamford Bridge, where I took charge of Chelsea's 3-1 win over Newcastle, along with Old Trafford and

Anfield among the 16 Premiership games I refereed.

In November, I had done Manchester United at Sunderland, where they lost 2-1, and in the process sent off Dwight Yorke for serious foul play as well as turning down a United penalty claim. It prompted Sir Alex Ferguson, who had been knighted the previous year, to tell the press that I was too inexperienced a referee to be handling that calibre of game. He never said anything to me at the time, though. I didn't get too upset about it. It was all part of the game and I knew enough by this time about managers deflecting attention away from their side's performance or a defeat by commenting on the referee.

Later I would get to know Sir Alex very well but I still did not speak to him when I was sent to do Manchester United v Charlton at Old Trafford the following April. He had plenty of players who were capable of getting in my ear at that time. Gary Neville springs to mind.

I was surprised by how small the officials' dressing room was – not for the first time at a big stadium; it showed historically how officials were regarded – but was certainly awe-struck at the top of that long, downhill tunnel in the corner of the Stretford End out on to the pitch. It was also quieter than I expected during the game. Corporate hospitality was now big, as Roy Keane would a few years later point out with his dig at Old Trafford's prawn sandwich brigade in the boxes and corporate hospitality.

As my game passed off peacefully with United winning 2-1, I was just grateful to avoid any moments like poor old Andy D'Urso had to endure the previous season when he had Keane, Jaap Stam, a young David Beckham and other various snarling United faces forcing him to backpedal. It was his first season in the Select Group and his first visit to Old Trafford too.

As colleagues in the Select Group, we were all outraged watching players bully him and by the level of dissent after he had awarded a penalty to Middlesbrough. There was a lot of talk that he should have stood his ground and allowed himself to be pushed over, which would have sent out a strong message to misbehaving players and forced the FA to act, but Andy managed the situation as he saw best in the heat of battle.

Later, he himself admitted he should have stood still but I have been in those situations myself and sometimes you don't even know you are backing away. Some good came of it, I think, as people looking at the game from the outside were genuinely shocked. It didn't last long. Contesting every decision is a way of life in football, sadly, and it would not be eradicated by one incident.

I personally had more sympathy for Andy than I did for Paul Alcock, who was subjected to a push by Paolo Di Canio three years earlier when playing for Sheffield Wednesday against Arsenal. After sending off the Italian, quite rightly for some hot-headed behaviour, Paul was pushed and though it was clearly serious, he had no need to fall like a sack of spuds as he did after taking five or six steps backwards. To be honest, it was a bit comical and privately as referees we had a bit of a laugh about it. It was not funny but it was, if you get my meaning.

Anyway, Anfield for the last game of the season, for Liverpool's 3-0 win over Newcastle, was also a pleasure and it was a first visit, not even having been as an assistant as in my earlier guise running the line. Then, as an assistant based in the south, you were not sent north as they are now.

I defy anyone who walks up those steps in that narrow tunnel and out on to the pitch not to touch that sign saying 'This Is Anfield'. I certainly did. To emerge to the Kop singing *You'll Never Walk Alone* made the hairs on the back of my neck stand up and I felt ten feet tall. It helped that I had a very supportive assessor in Peter Willis, the referee who showed the red card to Manchester United's Kevin Moran at Wembley against Everton in 1985 for the first sending off in an FA Cup final.

Otherwise, while it was a satisfying professional season, with

Philip Don reassuring me that I was doing well in the monthly one-to-one meetings we had, it was a painful time personally.

By the start of 2001, my marriage was breaking down. It was sad, but Jackie and I had grown apart. All the travelling and what was basically a selfish lifestyle of dedication to refereeing had not helped, but we were different people now from the school-leavers who started going out together.

In mid-January, I was assigned to Bolton Wanderers against Tranmere Rovers in Division One and up in one of the lounges before the game, I met one of the Bolton hostesses, Michelle Farthing. There was an instant chemistry between us. We exchanged phone numbers and when I was allocated an FA Cup tie back at the Reebok Stadium not long after between Bolton and Blackburn Rovers, we arranged to meet up for a drink afterwards.

We did, but I didn't referee the game, tweaking a hamstring in the warm-up. Then when the game ended in a draw and I was appointed to the replay at Blackburn in the March, we met up again and soon we were embarking on a relationship.

Logistically the whole thing caused a lot of problems, with me commuting between Welwyn, where I was now staying with my old friend Russell Foster, and Bolton for four months. My colleagues joked that I spent half my time sleeping in my car at an M6 service station. Quite literally I was a man in the middle, in my private as well as professional life.

Jackie and I had just had too many ups and downs and we would argue over the boys quite a lot. They were teenagers with issues of their own, Michael then 17 and Jason 15. Jason in particular was proving difficult and his time with Barnet FC had come to an end. He was hanging around with a crowd that was not good for him. Naturally they took their mother's side when they found out about my relationship with Michelle.

In fact, at one point so angry were they that they threw bricks through the windows of my Ford Mondeo, which was parked outside Russell's place. It was what convinced me that it would be best if I left properly and in the April I moved up North – though not for good at that stage – with my emotions still in turmoil.

I have mended fences with Jason since, and he has gone on to do well, working in football after I helped him with some introductions as he scouted for various clubs and took exams to become an agent. He even has two young daughters, Lily and Poppy, making me a Grandad. Sadly Michael, though, will still not speak to me and we have had no communication, unfortunately, for more than ten years. I guess there are echoes of myself and my own father not speaking for such a long time but with my father, I did not know where he was until he contacted me. Maybe one day...

It was, therefore, something of a relief to get away that summer of 2001 and with my UEFA appointment confirmed the previous January and now rubber-stamped by FIFA, I was invited to officiate at the Toulon international Under 21 tournament in France. It was an enjoyable three-week experience – apart from my arrival when I was left at the airport for two hours before someone met me. It was interesting meeting referees from around Europe and taking charge of a semi-final before running the line for the final between Portugal and Colombia.

Here I was, having made it from parks football to the international list in just over ten years. Very few referees have done that.

I was also assigned that summer to the World Student Games tournament in Beijing. China was a fascinating experience and a chance to see a country – including, amazingly, the Great Wall – that was on the brink of huge modernisation and change. With the hotels not as Westernised as they are now, I was concerned about being unable to eat the food, though. At one point, I rang Michelle to ask her to send me out two big boxes of chocolate bars – only one of which made it through.

These were good and bad days, of sadness one moment and

optimism the next. And the turbulence of personal change was about to be matched by a huge professional shift. For a decision had been made that would not only change my life but refereeing in England for ever.

8

FROM PERSONAL TO PROFESSIONAL

The call had come while I was away in France at the Toulon tournament. Would I be interested in going full-time, Philip Don asked, with the Premier League having decided it was time to have professional referees committed fully to the game from the 2001-2002 season? The salary would be a basic £35,000 a year with £450 as a match fee on top, a package replacing the £1,200 per Premier League match. The mileage rate would be 40p for the first 10,000 miles then 30p.

Would I be interested? I jumped at it. After giving up the day job, I could also now pack in the demanding cab driving. More than the money, however, it was a chance to devote myself to football. I had mucked about at school and not achieved much, blowing an opportunity to have a full-time career in the pro game with Tottenham. Now I felt I was being given a second chance. What was to think about? Doing something I loved and was good at and being paid a good wage for it? Bring it on.

The first full-time professional Select Group featured 24 referees, including some big figures in the world of refereeing such as Graham Poll, Jeff Winter and Paul Durkin. David Elleray was also among us, though not full-time as he retained his job as a master at Harrow School. It became a bone of contention with Philip Don as David did not attend our new important fortnightly get-togethers at the Staverton Park Hotel in Northamptonshire and thus had a different fitness regime to the rest of us.

91

Of that initial group, four of us – the other three being Mike Dean, Chris Foy and Phil Dowd – would go on to give more than ten years' service each. In addition, Mike Riley would later become general manager of the Select Group.

After the previous season of preparation for full-time professional refereeing, when I did 16 Premiership games, in this campaign I would do 20 of my total of 37 in the top flight. My red card count of seven, down from ten, would show that perhaps I was relaxing into the job more and not reacting to situations so hastily. That previous season, I was keen to be seen doing the right thing as a new boy and not let players take advantage of me.

Early on, I ticked off another big ground when I did Arsenal v Charlton Athletic, the visitors surprisingly winning 4-2, and was in awe of the marble halls that made up the reception area at the old Highbury. It was a game at another London ground, though, that most sticks in my memory that season as I got it wrong in a big game.

It was a League Cup – then the Worthington Cup – semi-final first leg at White Hart Lane between Tottenham and Chelsea on a cold January night but in a white-hot atmosphere.

I felt well-equipped, though. Just as players go into games with confidence, so can referees and I had handled a tough Leeds v Arsenal game the previous weekend with no major incidents despite bad blood existing between the sides from a meeting earlier in the season.

Tottenham were leading 3-0 early in the second half when I gave a free kick against Chelsea's Jimmy Floyd Hasselbaink for a foul on the Spurs goalkeeper Neil Sullivan. A melee broke out as Hasselbaink came running towards me to protest, a Spurs player got between him and me. I then saw a black arm raised and a fist punch a Spurs man in the face. To me, it looked like Jimmy had thrown the punch and I sent him off.

There was, of course, mayhem on the pitch but it was only later when I viewed the footage from another angle that I saw I had got the wrong man. In fact, TV initially got the wrong man as well before showing replays. Directly behind Jimmy, Mario Melchiot had delivered the blow, which I lost in the general confusion. Although my assessor, the former FA Referees' Officer Colin Downey, supported my decision, I could only admit my mistake and ring up the FA, who upheld Chelsea's appeal for a wrong dismissal, which meant a three-match ban for Mario rather than Jimmy. Injury was added to insult for Chelsea as Spurs won 5-1 to reach the final.

Otherwise, I felt I had a really good season, reflected in the games I was getting. The Premiership season developed into a three-way race between Arsenal, Liverpool and Manchester United and I was assigned to them all in the run-in, handling well West Ham 3, Manchester United 5, when David Beckham had a fantastic game to make it a pleasure to be involved in; Liverpool 1, Chelsea 0 and Arsenal 2, Tottenham 1.

I was also assigned to what could have been the title decider between Arsenal and Everton on the final day of the league season in the May, though by the Saturday, Arsenal had become champions with a midweek victory at Old Trafford over runners-up Manchester United.

It was a carnival day of celebration instead and I was even happier than usual to let the game flow, there being no need to issue any yellow cards. After Arsenal's 4-3 win, it was a privilege to be on the same pitch as Tony Adams and co lifted the Premiership trophy. The game marked the retirement of both Tony, though he did not play that day, and Lee Dixon.

It was the second part of Arsenal's double that year and I had also been present the previous week for the first part, though with somewhat less relish, I have to admit. Perhaps my appointment to Highbury at season's end was consolation, in fact, for not being awarded the accolade that all referees aspire to.

Arsenal 2 Chelsea 0
FA Cup final
Millennium Stadium, Cardiff
Saturday, May 4th, 2002

The FA Cup was already losing its lustre by 2002, with much press and public dismay at Manchester United being allowed by the Football Association to opt out of the competition the previous season due to a new format of the World Club Championship. For a referee, though, taking charge of the final remained a high point and career goal.

My performances that season should have given me a real chance of being selected to take the final, I believed – which would be borne out by statistics at the end of the season. The merit list, which we were sent by post, showed me as finishing second, behind only Graham Poll, who had already done the final, in 2000, between Chelsea and Aston Villa. My average mark per game was 96.2 out of 100.

Instead, the appointment went to Mike Riley and I was to be his fourth official. Mike finished sixth in the merit list.

The call had come from Joe Guest at the FA to tell me I would be fourth official. 'What, I'm not refereeing it?' I replied. It was actually meant in jest but I am not sure Joe took it that way. Perhaps he saw me as being cocky, but I wasn't, just confident in my ability. Perhaps my voice betrayed the disappointment behind the joke because in all honesty I did feel like a player who might have done well all season but was then put on the substitute's bench for the big game.

After I got over my initial disappointment, however,

94

I was determined not to sulk but instead enjoy the occasion. Mike was okay, a quiet man, and I got on well with him in those days. I did not want to spoil it for him and would give him my full support.

There are some fourth officials who resent the job, see it as demeaning just to hold up a board to show substitutions or how many minutes of added time there will be. I liked to think I was part of the team and as such would help my referee as much as I could.

I would be in his earpiece if I had seen something he hadn't, like an elbow or a red card challenge, to aid his decisions. I would also try to encourage him and praise him when he had made the right decision. I hoped my colleagues knew they could rely on me and I wouldn't let them down. Part of the role was also to be the human sponge, the one who took the grief from the managers and coaches in the technical areas.

In fact, once I got my head round it and set aside my personal disappointment, I enjoyed the experience.

We went down on the Friday night, put up by the FA at the Holiday Inn on the edge of Cardiff, and Michelle came with me. By now we were together, though I was still feeling guilty and torn, thinking I should try to make more effort to save my marriage after all those years together. Jackie was clearly upset too. She had phoned Philip Don about our troubles and he called me in for an informal meeting with him at the Premier League to find out what it was all about. I told him that I was determined not to let the professional and personal clash and he was fine with that assurance.

The final itself was a great occasion. I signed programmes and savoured the day. At the end of the game, won 2-0 by Arsenal with goals by Ray Parlour and Freddie Ljungberg, I received a commemorative medal and Patrick Vieira gave me his shirt signed, which I would give to my Gooner brother Paul on his 40th birthday.

I did get caught up in events, though, to the point that I only logged three yellow cards to Mike's five. I knew I would have got it right if I had been in the middle, though, and one day I would make it there, I felt sure. I was still only 40 and had plenty of time.

It did make me wonder more about the politics and personalities within refereeing, though.

That first season of full-time professionalism saw us meeting as a group with Philip Don and his assistant Keith Hackett every fortnight for a two-day summit at Staverton Park as part of our new professional contracts. We would turn up on the Wednesday afternoon, when some would play golf, others using the spa, then have dinner.

On the Thursday there would be an intense training session before more meetings to discuss points of law, analyse any issues that had been highlighted the previous weekend, and watch videos of our decisions and performances. On the Friday, after another demanding training session, we would disperse to whichever match we had been allocated at the weekend.

I always thought that doing a major fitness session on Thursdays and Fridays was a mistake and could lead to injuries and made my point to the Select Group sports scientist Matt Weston, which led to some friction with Philip Don. In another couple of years, the get-togethers would be changed according to the group's wishes to a Tuesday and Wednesday so that we didn't do such a major physical test so close to a game.

The old Thursday afternoon sessions became known as the video nasties and they got monotonous and even embarrassing at times. People dreaded it and I always used to come away from my game on a weekend worrying that I had made a bad decision that would make the video. To my mind, it sometimes became personal, with the same faces up on the screen quite often while others escaped.

It could be demoralising for some and I made my fair share of appearances, I have to admit. You did feel you had to defend your corner, especially if Graham Poll was sitting in the front row and taking the piss out of you as the clips were being played.

Graham was a big noise at that time and with other figures like Paul Durkin and Jeff Winter around, there could be plenty of conflict. He came to dominate the conversations with Philip at times in front of the rest of the group, which I thought was designed to assert his own status and undermine our general manager. After dinner in the evenings, Graham's group would go off into their own corner and gossip and giggle before adjourning to his room with bottles of wine. His disciples included such as Durkin, Graham Barber, Rob Styles and Mike Dean and they became known as the Red Wine Club.

I was never part of it, preferring the company of men like Phil Dowd, Andy D'Urso and my room-mate Peter Walton. There was no doubt that an unhealthy rift showed signs of developing that first season that would lead to problems in years to come.

That summer of 2002 was another strange off season for me. On a personal level, I decided to make one last attempt to heal my marriage and left Michelle again to go back to Welwyn Garden City. She went on holiday to Greece while I headed south to talk things over with Jackie.

Within two days, however, I realised I had made a terrible mistake and rang Mike Reed, my Select Group coach, and Dave Allison, my old coach from my Football League days, as mates to ask them if they would talk to Michelle for me to tell her I wanted to go back to her. I was worried about getting an earful from her

– with some justification as she told them that she wanted nothing more to do with me. I decided to pluck up courage myself and just fly to Paphos. Fortunately when I knocked on her door, she was glad to see me after all and we never looked back after that.

That summer, I also travelled to Japan to do the World Disabled Championships, which was quite an experience and quite a challenge. There were certainly some rough games that needed a firm hand and plenty of yellow cards were issued. Unfortunately for me, though fortunate for them, England made the final in the same Yokohama stadium used for the World Cup final that year and I was thus disqualified from taking the game. I hoped one day that I might get a chance to do a World Cup.

My career certainly should have been on the up. I was one of the fittest referees around, passing with ease our new test – the Cooper Test, designed for the American military and which required you to run 2,700 metres in under 12 minutes. Taking charge of 24 Premiership games in the 2002-03 season would also suggest I was doing well but I was concerned that I wasn't getting more of the big games.

But then I wasn't the only one who felt that Graham Poll seemed almost to dictate to the decision makers which games he wanted to do. Glenn Turner, one of his regular assistant referees – and one I also loved having because he was so good – would later tell me that Graham would go through his diary with him on trips away for European games together to tell him to note the big games back home that they would be doing together. We are not supposed to know our games until they are assigned on the Monday before.

I wasn't sure how he got to choose but in fairness to Keith Hackett, he would probably say that Graham had to get the biggest games as he was being groomed for a European Championship or a World Cup and needed them for his development. The same happened with Howard Webb in later years.

When I did get a major event like Liverpool v Arsenal, something strange happened. I got a call from Keith a few days before the game to report a curious conversation between Philip Don and an Arsenal club official who had phoned in to complain. Arsenal had been reliably informed that I had something against Ashley Cole and was going to send him off at Anfield, the club told Philip.

Now Ashley down the years would become a spiky character for referees on the field but I told Keith it was ridiculous and asked where Arsenal had heard it from. All they were saying, he relayed to me, was that it had come via a refereeing source. In the end, I was kept on the match. I never did know who had phoned Arsenal and goodness knows what their motive was.

Otherwise, I think I was seen as a safe pair of hands, a man you could send to a potentially tricky match. I had become more and more reluctant to issue red cards unless absolutely necessary, preferring to manage the game and players with words and personality, but I had no choice at Newcastle that December in dismissing Everton's Joseph Yobo for denying a goalscoring opportunity.

It was the game in which Alan Shearer scored an astonishing volley from 30 yards in their 2-1 win and I was right behind him. As he turned to celebrate, I just said to him 'that's a fantastic goal' and shook his hand. I just admired the shot and it had nothing to do with bias.

I have to admit I did speak a lot to players during games. Sometimes one would be running with the ball towards goal and I would say 'Hit it, hit it.' If he did and scored, I would smile at him and say: 'I told you. You can listen to me when you want then.' They often smiled too, though some did not like it and I kept quiet around them. I believed, though, that you had to enjoy the game and a player in full flow.

The Everton manager David Moyes had been unhappy with

me for sending off Yobo and I phoned him on the Monday to explain why. He appreciated the call in the cold light of day and it was worthwhile. In those days you could do such a thing without reprimand.

My ability to keep calm in a crisis meant that I was seen as a natural stand-in when Mike Riley fell ill before a Monday night live Sky game between Aston Villa and Birmingham City that season. It was a game that was primed for trouble after a volatile first encounter between the two Second City clubs during which the Villa goalkeeper Peter Enckelman had allowed a ball to go over his foot and into the goal.

This time he was confronted by a Villa fan who ran on to the pitch to taunt him about it as the match took a nasty turn. When Robbie Savage rashly challenged Dion Dublin, I just had to caution him – and then send off Dion for a head butt in retaliation. Later, I also had to send off Villa's Joey Gudjonsson for a second yellow card for a bad tackle though it should really have been a straight red.

It was mayhem, what with pitch invasions and all the cards but I didn't come close to abandoning it. I wouldn't have done that even if a player had got thumped. I would if I had, mind.

The atmosphere remained intimidating after the game as we officials were kept in the dressing room until 11pm, after which we were given a police escort back to the Crowne Plaza hotel where we had left our cars.

I was on a hiding to nothing but there is not much a referee can do when the mood is so menacing except try to manage the game in a cool way. At least the Birmingham manager Steve Bruce felt I had done well as he wrote to me to congratulate me on my handling of the game. But then again his side had won 2-0 to do a double over their main rivals. I rang to thank him.

I also got on the right side of Sir Alex Ferguson later that season when assigned to Arsenal v Manchester United in the April, an appointment that made one or two fellow referees jealous. It was a match that would go a long way towards deciding the title and United's draw helped them towards another championship but more important to them, the 2-2 draw denied Arsenal the three points.

Given what was at stake it was a good, clean game with only two yellow cards – rare on such a big night – until Arsenal's Sol Campbell elbowed Ole Gunnar Solskjaer, which I had a clear view of. My assistant Nigel Miller called me over and when he said he had seen it, it confirmed to me that I needed to issue a red card. I knew it would mean that Sol would miss that season's FA Cup final but I had no option but to do my duty.

As I left, Sir Alex – my relationship with him still in its early stages – applauded me and shook my hand but naturally Arsenal did not see things the same way. Arsene Wenger's assistant Pat Rice, who always seemed to detest referees, came to my dressing room to complain that it had not been a deliberate elbow and I told him they could appeal if they believed that. Arsenal did and lost.

Stone me if my first game of the next season didn't send me to Highbury for Arsenal's opening home match against Everton. In the tunnel before the game, Sol refused to speak to me after what had happened four months earlier. Fair enough, but as the game went on, I told him it would be in his best interests to communicate with me and he agreed, apologising for ignoring me earlier.

Five minutes later, just 25 minutes into the game, Sol denied an Everton player a goalscoring opportunity and I just had to send him off. I was mortified at having to do it. Nothing was said. He knew he had to go. The next time I reffed him at Newcastle, he blanked me again but gradually he mellowed down the years. He was the only player I ever sent off twice.

By then I had remarried, my divorce from Jackie having come through in the February of 2003 and my marriage to Michelle

101

taking place in the May. The wedding was at St Matthew's Church in Little Lever and before our honeymoon in the Dominican Republic, something funny happened on the way to the reception in Chorley – the wedding car broke down on the M61 and we were forced to wait on the hard shoulder for a replacement. Meanwhile all the guests drove by waving at us. They seemed to think we had stopped to have some photos done. On the M61?

Now I felt settled and was doing well in my career, with a reputation growing as a good controller of a game able to pour oil on troubled waters.

And so I was given some very tasty derby games that 2003-04 season. I did both of the North London confrontations between Arsenal and Tottenham, which is very rare, and got away with just the eight cards over the two games, though Arsenal were none too pleased at me denying them a double with a late penalty award at White Hart Lane.

They could hardly contest it, mind. It came when Jens Lehmann clambered over Robbie Keane – and you had to keep an eye on the Arsenal goalkeeper as he was always liable to do something daft – and I issued yellow cards to both after Keane retaliated with a push. He then stepped up to equalise from the spot for a 2-2 draw. In the end, though, Arsenal did not have to worry that season as their 'Invincibles' side went the whole season without losing and won the title by 11 points.

I also did the Manchester derby at Old Trafford and got a rousing reception from the City fans, who never forgot that Wembley play-off against Gillingham, somewhat to my embarrassment at times. On holiday in Spain, I would be minding my own business, for example, and a couple of City fans would send over a beer for me, even though I drank only wine. To this day in Manchester itself, I rarely go further than 100 yards without a City fan reminding me of those five added minutes.

I could do nothing for them that day, though. United were far too good for them and won 3-1. There was an obligatory booking for Joey Barton.

In April, I was back at Old Trafford for United's game against Leicester City, a game that was goalless as half-time approached. I suddenly found myself needing the toilet very badly and thus instructed my fourth official that there would be no added time. I knew I could always add it on at the end of the game anyway.

I could see that this did not go down very well with Sir Alex Ferguson and he did what he normally does when riled at a referee – makes a dash along the touchline to catch the ref at the top of that long tunnel in the corner of the stadium and give him an earful before he can reach the dressing room.

In my distressed state, I was quick enough off the pitch, but even so he was there ahead of me. I was in no mood for a conversation, however.

'What's that all about?' he asked.

I instantly recalled that episode when Sir Alex had been caught driving on the hard shoulder of a motorway to avoid traffic but got off because he said he had been caught short due to a stomach upset and was rushing to the United training ground to use the toilet.

'Listen,' I replied. 'I need a shit so don't bother kicking off. That excuse worked for you so don't start on me.'

It stopped him in his tracks and he just laughed. And he had the last one, as a second half goal by Gary Neville gave United a 1-0 win.

I wish others sometimes had been able to show a sense of humour, the England full-back Danny Mills, then playing for Middlesbrough, for example. At the Middlesbrough v Everton game, I happened to mention to someone from the home club before the game that Danny could be a right prick at times, and it was true, given some of his tackling and his verbals afterwards.

Anyway, during the game he missed a chance, and I think I said

'Unlucky son' or something similar – and not in a sarcastic way. His reply was 'Don't talk to me. You called me a prick.' My conversation must have got back to him. 'Well you are a prick,' I said.

I did not forget the incident. On the last day of the season I was sent to Portsmouth v Middlesbrough, a meaningless mid-table match. Boro, who had won the Carling Cup in the February, did not look up for the game and were a goal down inside five minutes to Yakubu. They would go on to lose 5-1.

At one point Yakubu went past Mills and into the box, only to tumble under a minimum of contact when he might have stayed on his feet. I immediately awarded a penalty – a decision with which my assessor later agreed – and soon had Mills in my face screaming that it was not a penalty.

'You're probably right,' I said. 'But that will teach you not to piss me off.'

'Right,' he replied. 'I'll fucking see you outside. I'll have you.'

'You want a fight?' I asked.

'Too right I do,' he said.

'Okay,' says I, 'I'll wait for you outside afterwards.'

After I had changed at the end of the game, I went outside to the car park and where was he? Already on the team bus, clearly unwilling to wait around for me.

Those in charge of appointments early the following season must have had a sense of humour because third game in, they sent me to Manchester City v Charlton. And Danny Mills had just signed for City.

In that August week leading up to the game, I rang Lorraine Firth in the City commercial department about some tickets and she asked me if I was looking forward to coming to Eastlands. I was, I said, having always got on with people there, including having a good relationship with the City secretary Bernard Halford, but I had a bit of a problem with Danny Mills and told her about the previous season.

'Don't you worry,' said Lorraine, who has herself fought breast cancer. 'Leave him to me.'

When I arrived on the Saturday, I walked past Danny in the tunnel. 'I've been told to be nice to you because you are one of the club's favourite referees,' he said, somewhat grudgingly.

Five minutes into the game, I gave a free kick against him and where once I would have received a volley of abuse, there was nothing. I asked him if he was feeling okay.

'Yes,' he said. 'I am being nice to you.'

'There are miracles then,' I replied.

By the end of a game that was easy to handle, he was in a good mood as City won 4-0. And as he departed, he said: 'It's true then. You are a City fan.' I smiled and shook hands. After an end to the previous season that left a sour taste, this one had begun with more promise.

As that 2004-05 season drew to a close, two major events that would herald great change in refereeing and the English game were on the horizon. There would be the departure as head of our organisation by Philip Don. Then there was the arrival in the Premier League of a maverick character who would have a major impact on my life and the sporting life of the nation, a man who styled himself 'The Special One.'

9

ME AND JOSÉ

There were inevitably going to be teething troubles with full-time professional referees and by the spring of 2004, Philip Don had become a casualty of some pressing problems and issues. In fact, it turned quite nasty as he became a victim of the game's politics and backbiting from within the Select Group he ran. He would even think I was at the heart of that, only to apologise to me later once he had discovered who really was the prime mover in his downfall.

Philip had been a brilliant referee in his own right, being awarded the FA Cup final of 1992, the Champions League final in Athens between AC Milan and Barcelona in 1994 and officiating at that year's World Cup. He also did the League Cup final in 1995, after which he retired at the age of just 43 due to pressure of work from his duties as a headteacher. He had the respect of players and managers and he was in many ways a natural selection to be general manager of the first professional Select Group.

I got on well with him by and large, and there was a mutual respect though we did have our disagreements. I was unhappy with him early on, for example, when he seemed to accept the word of Rob Styles, one of Graham Poll's proteges, that I should not have been refereeing a West Ham v Manchester United match because I still looked injured.

Styles, my fourth official that day, knew I was coming back from twisted knee ligaments sustained during training that I was now doing at Bolton Wanderers. The episode led to me having words with him.

Philip was an honest, decent and upright man, a firm believer in upholding the laws of the game and it often meant instructions to referees to clamp down hard on anything from diving – or simulation, to give its technical term – to tackling to dissent. He was very black and white when sometimes there were shades of grey in managing games, I felt. He wanted to see yellow and red cards rather than giving players the benefit of the doubt and letting play go on. Referees had to be allowed to use their initiative and instinct, too, in my opinion.

It was where he and I often disagreed and where I agreed with Graham Poll on something. The difference was that Graham was frequently in Philip's ear about it and it made for some uncomfortable sessions at Staverton with a battle of wills going on.

If it made for a tense relationship internally, so it did externally, with some of the Premier League club managers getting upset with all the cards and player suspensions. I know that there were talks behind the scenes for some while. Philip, as I understand it, was fighting for the independence of referees against what he saw as the desire of the Premier League and its clubs to exert more control over games being refereed a certain way.

He was a principled man but was fighting a losing battle with the clubs – the stakeholders – as they would become known, who were becoming more and more influential. The Premier League, after all, contributed 80 per cent of the costs of running the PGMOL, the full-time Select Group being the most expensive area of that, with the Football League contributing 15 per cent and the FA five per cent.

I know that Philip also had his battles with the FA and Football League over the Select Group's pre-eminence. The two bodies were keen to preserve their own control over refereeing, particularly in appointing the FA Cup and League Cup final officials. In the end, he was called into the Premier League offices one day and told to leave the job by the end of the week. His pay-off took a little while longer to negotiate.

It was portrayed that certain influential and unhappy managers in the north west had conspired to remove Philip, notably Sir Alex, David Moyes of Everton and Sam Allardyce at Bolton. And because I was based in the north west – spoke to Sam every day at the Bolton training ground – and knew the managers well, Philip came to believe that I was behind it.

Nothing could have been further from the truth. I suspect that certain people had been in his ear about me. Indeed, I had warned Philip that he often listened to the wrong people within our group, believing them to be his allies, and also confided things to them.

I couldn't help asking whether he listened too much to Graham Poll's analysis of other referees and assistants, highlighting Graham's position as top dog. There may have been differences between Philip and Graham but in his role as general manager, Philip had to listen to him as our top referee.

A few months after his departure, he phoned me up. He had, he said, indeed thought it was me behind him being ousted but he had since found out privately from some people – other referees, certain Premier League officials and some managers – that I was not. He knew who had really stabbed him in the back, he added. He apologised to me and said he wished he had listened to me. I admired him for having the courage to do that. He was straight and I had a lot of time and respect for him. He was badly let down by certain referees when we should have been united as a group.

Philip went to live in Spain and I got the feeling from the last time that I spoke with him that he remained hurt by how he had been treated, though he was content with his life and glad to be out of all the bitching.

He even told me that during his time, he once had meetings with UEFA refereeing bigwigs who asked about England's best referees. At that time, he said, he told them that I was the best, ahead of our top three ranked in Europe's Elite Group, the Tring duo, Grahams Poll and Barber, along with Mike Riley.

That surprised me – and lifted me during some dark times later in my career when I would worry about some bad treatment I was subjected to. Sadly, it was not Philip, but figures within the FA, who were the main influences on UEFA, however.

What I admired about Philip was that he was always open to discussion. You could have frank talks with him and he would not hold a grudge. There would be times later in my career when Mike Riley became PGMOL general manager that I felt that if you voiced a strong opinion on something, you would be taken off the fixtures. Then I found myself pining for Philip and his excellent leadership.

I was happy enough with Philip's successor, I have to say though, with his assistant Keith Hackett taking over. Keith was a big supporter of mine and would almost become a mentor and father figure to me. I soon saw that after I made a serious mistake in a big game early in the 2004-05 season.

Fulham 0 Arsenal 3
Barclays Premier League
Craven Cottage
Saturday, September 11th, 2004

No excuses. I had a complete off day, one that saw a first for me as I gave a post-match TV interview. It would also be the last one I would give – until my final day in the job, that is.

I suppose I could cite the fact that I felt a bit tired before the game, maybe due to the regimen at Staverton that our new head Keith Hackett would come to accept was too physically demanding in the second half of a week, but in all honesty I simply messed up.

Just over half an hour had gone when Ashley Cole brought down Andy Cole and I gave a penalty to Fulham. I was then surrounded by Arsenal players, who were insistent that Ashley had played the ball. The vehemence of their reaction suggested that I might have got this wrong. One or two of the Fulham players looked a bit surprised by my decision, too.

I bought some thinking time – over both the penalty and whether to send off Ashley – by deciding to consult my assistant, Dave Bryan. It was in the days before earpieces and Dave had a good view. He told me that Ashley had in fact played the ball so at that, I changed my decision. I called the captains over to inform them, and gave a drop ball, dropping it to the Arsenal goalkeeper Jens Lehmann.

Soon after, I turned down an Arsenal penalty appeal when Thierry Henry was brought down by Moritz Volz. Replays would later show it should have been a spot kick. A make-up call? One to even the score? Most definitely not but we are only human with an inbuilt sense of justice. I would hope that disallowing a header by Collins John just before half-time for a push shows that I was trying to make correct decisions and not just ones to please people.

I certainly didn't seem to please anyone. As I walked off at half-time, jeered by the Fulham fans and with the two managers, Chris Coleman and Arsene Wenger, both upset, I knew there would be controversy. And so, at the end of the game, which Arsenal won 3-0 with second-half goals by Freddie Ljungberg, an own goal by Zat Knight, and Jose Antonio Reyes, I agreed to a TV interview.

The floor manager came to the dressing room and asked if I would be willing to explain the decisions I had taken. It was at a time when referees were being urged to be accountable the way players and managers were and to speak up after games. In those days, we were allowed to if we felt it would help and it concerned points of law. Why not, I thought. What's the worst that could happen?

'The players' reactions from both sides put a little bit of doubt in my mind,' I said. 'I thought, "Have I got this decision correct."' I was asked what would have happened if Arsenal had not complained. I don't know, I said; maybe I would have stuck with my decision. I felt it best to get the decision right, though, and admit my mistake. Little did I know, however, that all hell was about to break loose.

For my honesty and for not sticking with my original decision, I was hammered in the aftermath of the game. On *Match of the Day* – these were the days when I still watched it regularly, or could stay awake to – I was accused of giving in to player power. The next day, the less forgiving newspapers put it more bluntly: I was letting the lunatics run the asylum.

I felt devastated. People think that referees just pack their bags and go home but they don't. I didn't eat or sleep properly for days. We worry. We care. And we do feel the criticism. Sometimes, you don't want to show your face in public, just want to stay indoors.

When I went in for my training at Bolton on the Monday, Sam Allardyce said to me that I should not have changed my mind, but stuck with my original decision, right or wrong. He made the point that if I had given the penalty, people would have talked about it for the weekend. This way, it became a debating point for a week. I took it on board – but I did hope that people would appreciate me getting the decision right and being willing to endure criticism for that principle.

Naturally I got a bad report from the assessor, Ken Ridden, on account of both penalty incidents, and Keith Hackett told the press that I was wrong to give an interview as it was not about a point of law. I should never have been influenced by player reaction, he said. I accepted his criticism, made also to me in a phone call on the Sunday, of my naïvety with the media.

From that day on, I never again changed my mind over a decision. As for referees giving interviews, I understand the clamour for them to explain themselves and like to think I am a very open character but my experience told me that I was on a hiding to nothing, with anything I said likely to be misconstrued, pored over and fodder for easy headlines.

At least in private Keith was very supportive, telling me I had made a mistake but accepting my good intentions. And I was not punished as I might have been by less confident leaders, but told to get over it and get back in the saddle. There was a weekend of being stood down, but it was genuinely to take me out of the spotlight for a week rather than suspension and I felt Keith showed trust in me.

The next week, I was sent to do Middlesbrough v Chelsea and I think I did pretty well, to the extent that the Chelsea assistant manager Steve Clarke made a point of telling me after his side had won 1-0 that he felt I had done myself credit after being under so much pressure.

That day was my first contact in England with the new Chelsea manager, some young buck called José Mourinho, though it was only a passing, polite shaking of hands and a few words of 'well played'.

As a lover of football, I welcomed his arrival in the country, based on my first impressions of him. Watching his early interviews – as he declared himself the 'Special One' after winning the

Champions League with Porto – I thought he would be good to spice up the game in this country, to challenge Sir Alex, Arsene Wenger and Rafa Benitez, who had just taken over at Liverpool from a true gent in Gerard Houllier. I could see through the cockiness to the charisma.

I had met Mourinho once previously when I was fourth official to Graham Poll at a Champions League game in Porto when they played Marseille – a game when I am sure Didier Drogba's powerful performance for the French side convinced José to sign him for Chelsea.

I can't say I took that much notice of José that night, though, as he was not yet well known around the game. I just tried to keep him calm on the sidelines as I would do with any manager when fourth official. I recall nodding when he said to me in his excellent English: 'Marseille number nine – good player, very strong.'

Actually, my abiding memory of the trip was more to do with Graham, who drank a bit too much after the game in my opinion and was a bit too talkative, shall we say, about a number of our colleagues. I know his assistant Glenn Turner felt the same.

Taking charge of my next Chelsea game came in the FA Cup the following January and I certainly heard more from José that day. Chelsea were on a long unbeaten run, looking like being champions under him and fighting on other fronts, in the Carling Cup and Champions League, when they went to St James' Park to face Newcastle United.

Patrick Kluivert's goal after just four minutes proved decisive, Newcastle winning 1-0, leaving José to complain about a handball he thought I should have given for a Chelsea penalty. He could hardly argue, however, about a late sending-off for his goalkeeper Carlo Cudicini for denying a goalscoring opportunity. I didn't take his post-match criticism personally. I realised this was a fierce competitor who didn't take kindly to defeat. He had not been getting much practice at that around that time, after all.

It was my first red card that season and I would only issue one other, in a match between Charlton and West Bromwich Albion, in the March. It was probably a sign both of things being more relaxed under Keith Hackett, after the more stringent regime of Philip Don had ended, and me feeling less duty-bound to issue cards.

There would be no problems with José that season, not surprisingly given what a good mood he must have been in. I did Chelsea twice more, in 3-1 wins at Norwich and Southampton, as he led them to their first title in 50 years, and with a record Premier League haul of 95 points. I remember watching on TV and seeing him throw his medal into the crowd after the last home game and thinking with a smile about how much he enjoyed all the attention.

My first Chelsea game at Stamford Bridge under José came in the August of the following season, 2005-06, against West Brom and won 4-0 by the home side. This was the season I got to know him reasonably well, though our friendship would only really blossom later.

People will ask me how I became so friendly with a man who was often seen as the scourge of referees given some disparaging comments, most notably in his assertion that Anders Frisk had contravened UEFA rules by inviting the Barcelona manager Frank Rijkaard into his dressing room at half-time of a Champions League tie at Stamford Bridge in 2005 for discussions.

It was something that UEFA decided, after taking evidence, had never happened but damage was done. Chelsea fans began issuing death threats to Anders and sadly he decided he had had enough and retired. It led to a touchline ban for José. I know he has the reputation of being mischievous, and I did feel sorry for Anders, but I did wonder if José had been misinformed about Rijkaard trying to influence the referee and blurted it out in the heat of the moment.

And despite what many may have said about José being an enemy of referees, most of the referees I know liked him and enjoyed him being in the Premier League. Years later, when head coach at Real Madrid, he would say in a press conference, that there was only one referee he liked – 'my friend Mark Halsey' – but he was better disposed to English referees than others. Whenever Mark Clattenburg or Howard Webb was taking a European game for his teams, I would text José in advance and he would make a point of having a chat with them during their stay. Just being friendly – nothing untoward.

You have to speak as you find and from my perspective, while José and I had our disagreements, they were always respectful, never resentful. For some reason, we just hit it off and he began to call me 'top ref'. I think he had respect for me because I was a players' referee, one who would give players a chance and not get the yellow out straight away but give them the benefit of the doubt. In fact he has described me as the 23rd player on the pitch. My assessors and refereeing figures often didn't see things the same way as I did, although at this time I was glad Keith Hackett did.

Mind you, Newcastle weren't so well disposed towards me – and with good reason, to be fair to them – when I failed to award a penalty against John Terry for bringing down Lee Bowyer in a match at Stamford Bridge in the November. I thought John had just nicked the ball but it would later be proved I was wrong. It was 0-0 at the time and Chelsea went on to win 3-0. In fact Lee Bowyer would have a bad season with me. I had to send him off at Liverpool on Boxing Day for a bad tackle.

There are always going to be mistakes over a season and naturally they stand out amid the many you get right. I hope I have always been one who will admit to them, as they are made in good faith. There was another that season when I sent off Zurab Khizanishvili of Blackburn at Liverpool for denial of a goalscoring opportunity, which it was later shown not to be and Rovers' then manager Mark Hughes quite rightly questioned my decision, which was overturned by the FA.

Otherwise that season came a curious week that showed the ups and downs of the job. In early November, I was assigned by UEFA to a midweek international under-21 European Championship play-off game between Germany and the Czech Republic in Leverkusen. At the Premier League, meanwhile, they omitted to give me a game the Saturday before, which I needed to stay sharp.

The Conference came to my aid, and gave me Kidderminster Harriers v Exeter City and I enjoyed going back to my roots. It was nice to hear the Exeter director of football Steve Perryman, the old Tottenham captain, saying after the game that he wished they could have a Premier League ref every week. Kidderminster on the Saturday, Germany a few days later. The varied life of a referee that I was loving.

In what was a mixed season, I also had to sit out a month injured after being caught at the back of my calf accidentally by a Stoke player in their game against Leeds over Christmas. That meant losing five games at £320 a match, to which the rate had been changed, down from £450. It was because the basic salary had gone up from £35,000 to £50,000.

To add insult to injury, soon after coming back I got a bad assessment from Kelvin Morton at the Arsenal v West Ham game I took when he said I didn't look fit. I may have been taking it gingerly but I was always among the fittest of referees and some empathy would have been nice.

Curiously, I also found myself doing quite a lot of Doncaster Rovers games around that time when not assigned to the Premier League. Their chairman John Ryan had been involved in some disagreements with the Football League over refereeing and personally asked for me a few times, I gathered, after being impressed with me when I was a young referee doing an FA Cup tie at Southend in which he was involved. I think the Football League sent me there to appease him.

One Rovers game, against Huddersfield Town, saw me send off three players for the only time in my career. They were all merited red cards and nobody complained. In fact, everyone seemed to think I had had a good game.

Not long after, in another match in South Yorkshire, between Sheffield United and Reading – a match deemed to be needing a Select Group official as happens each weekend with a few games outside the Premier League that have an especially significant competitive edge to them – I remember giving a penalty against United in a 1-1 draw and the home manager Neil Warnock coming into my dressing room afterwards.

Knowing how fiery he could be, I told him to leave but he said he had only come to tell me what a good game I had had and that his goalkeeper Paddy Kenny had agreed it was a penalty. That benign moment would prove to be a rarity when it came to Neil.

When it came to Chelsea, José and me, I hope my impartiality once I crossed the white line was shown in the March of that season when they went to West Brom as they sought to retain their title and Albion sought to avoid relegation, both of which outcomes would come to pass. Chelsea took a lead through Didier Drogba but soon after I sent off Arjen Robben for a two-footed tackle, which led to John Terry disagreeing vehemently with me.

After that, Drogba got up to some of his tricks and went down dramatically with barely a touch – and yes, referees are aware of players and reputations. You get to know them and of course you see them on television and swap information and opinions with fellow referees. As soon as you see the team sheet, you are like a manager weighing up the opposition and working out how to deal with certain tricky players should the occasion demand.

I was one who liked a simple word with them and I didn't perceive all challenges where there was contact and the ball was missed as fouls. Sometimes players go down too easily and are trying to con you, which means they may not get the foul next time as you don't trust them. And sometimes it is a simple collision with nobody to blame.

Anyway, things kicked off on the touchline between Mourinho and the Albion manager Bryan Robson after the Drogba drama. My fourth official Howard Webb would later be criticised for not asking me to send both to the stands but I thought he managed the situation well and the last thing I wanted was to send the managers off.

To be fair, after the game – won 2-1 by Chelsea – José admitted that both the sending off and ignoring Drogba's theatrics had been correct decisions. It was at odds with his reputation as someone who simply criticised referees for getting things wrong and never praising them.

He certainly earned his own fair share of praise that season as Chelsea went on from there to make it back-to-back titles that spring of 2006. It seemed that the stage was set for a long and beautiful relationship between him, Chelsea, their owner Roman Abramovich and English football.

As for me and Michelle, there was a happy event for us that April, on the 10th in fact, when our daughter Lucy was born. She was the joyful product of a difficult process of IVF that had begun painfully, for me at least.

I'd had a vasectomy after the birth of my two sons and when Michelle decided after our marriage back in 2003 that she wanted a child of our own, I decided to have a reversal. Without getting too technical and gory, the first operation was not a success but the second later in the year managed to extract sperm from where it was stored and which could be frozen.

On the drive home, I asked Michelle to drive slowly over the bumps in the road, which she did not, much amused by my discomfort. When we got home, I could barely get out of the car and walk to the front door. During two years of treatment that cost £13,000, we went through all the worrying and wondering if this would work but finally Michelle fell pregnant in the late summer of 2005. Lucy's birth really was a special occasion for us both.

In fact, it was the start of a rewarding new phase of my life, certainly from a personal point of view. Professionally, though, an ending was in the offing.

10

HOME AND AWAY

During the summer of 2006, home thoughts turned to abroad. There was a World Cup going on but I didn't really want to watch. It was a strange time when I thought that it might have been me officiating in Germany had things been different over the previous few years but I knew now that it was too late. I turned 45 in the week of the final, the age at which international referees were forced to retire.

Even though Lucy required plenty of attention as a new-born, I could hardly avoid the tournament, though. We spent the time in Spain in the villa we had bought and everybody knows what a football-daft country that is.

Then there was the day my phoned buzzed constantly with texts from people within football about a bizarre event in a group game between Croatia and Australia.

I have to be honest and say that when Graham Poll issued three yellow cards to one player in that match to blot his career copybook, I was at first amused and felt that he had got his come-uppance. I may just have conveyed the impression earlier that I was not his biggest fan, after all. While he was England's then best known and most successful referee, whom I respected as being a top-class practitioner of our profession, I had little liking or respect for him as a person and the way he conducted himself.

All those texts following his oversight in not sending off Josip Simunic of Croatia after issuing the second yellow card to him, for which Graham was sent home, confirmed that I was not the only one who may have thought he was a great referee but not a great colleague. For some of us, it seemed to be a rough justice for some of the things that had gone on behind the scenes down the years.

As I thought about it, though, I began to realise that this was not good for refereeing, and certainly not English referees. I may have had my run-ins with Graham, but I wouldn't wish that to happen to any referee. In the end, I even felt sorry for him.

Why my dislike of him? The reasons were many and varied and his cock of the walk attitude around Staverton Park was just one them. It actually started with a phone call that confirmed my suspicions about Graham born on my Premier League refereeing debut. The call came from a colleague, Alan Wilcy, and was to congratulate me on being elected to the UEFA panel of international referees in 2001. Alan had also been nominated at that time but not recruited as UEFA belatedly realised he was over 40 and new recruits had to be under that age. Steve Bennett made it along with me.

'Congratulations,' Alan said to me. 'But I don't think you will get very far.'

'How come?' I asked, surprised.

'Graham sees you as a threat to him getting big games,' Alan replied.

From that time on, I was wary of Graham and it would prove with good reason. That Champions League night in Porto, when I first encountered José Mourinho, I had seen for myself how he could talk badly of his colleagues and it made me wonder if he talked the same way about me behind my back.

What made it so artful to me that night in Porto was that he had got wind that Mike Riley could be going to Euro 2004 six months later and over a drink or three afterwards, Graham was not exactly complimentary about Mike to the match observers, who were on the referees' committee. In fact, he was telling them Mike was not good enough.

He may have had a point about that, mind. David Elleray, now chairman of the FA referees' committee, was said to be no great fan of Graham's, preferring Mike. Perhaps, like me, Graham was not from the professional classes, unlike Mike, who was an accountant. Anyway, Mike did not have the greatest of times at Euro 2004, which was why Graham got the nod for the World Cup of 2006.

Where my wariness crossed into distaste for Graham came following a bizarre, even astonishing, incident on our Select Group bonding and fitness get-together at the British Army facilities in Aldershot in the summer of 2005.

One night, the Army hosted a function for us at the Sergeant's Mess and Graham had too much to drink, by his own admission later. That's fair enough, nothing wrong with letting your hair down now and then at the right times. What followed was certainly not acceptable, however.

Graham was first rude to the sergeant then, outside, jumped on a car bonnet. I watched that from the bus that was to take us home and on to which he was then bundled by our colleagues, Uriah Rennie, Phil Dowd and Chris Foy, Graham having a particular go at Phil as they did so.

When we got back to our hotel, the Holiday Inn, Graham was sick in the reception area and up the stairs into his room. He quite rightly apologised the next morning but that was far from the end of the matter. The story made the papers and was reported to the Premier League. Graham was subsequently suspended for two weeks but managed to get permission to referee a game in Jamaica during that time.

Then, at an early gathering of the Select Group in the August at Staverton Park, Graham got up in front of us all and expressed his disappointment that the story had got into the press and been reported to the league via an anonymous email that he believed had been sent by one of his colleagues in the room.

I thought it was a bit rich that he was the one who had created this issue and now was trying to divert attention from that and blame somebody else for it. It was the old trick of having a go at the whistleblower – if there was one, that is. He also complained that it showed a lack of unity in the group. I also wondered about that unity given he had created his clique in the Red Wine Club.

Anyway, Peter Heard – then the chairman of Colchester United, an FA board member and, most importantly from our point of view, chairman of the PGMOL board – was also in the room and announced that he would be speaking to four of us who Graham believed might have sent the email. One by one names were called out and they left the room until just myself, Phil Dowd, Chris Foy and Alan Wiley were left. We were all a bit baffled, wondering what this was all about.

Peter then told us that he would leave us alone in the room until one of us was ready to confess. We sat there at first stunned, then amused. Chris and Alan were police officers and would not have done this. Phil insisted he had not done it, as did I. Email was new to me then. Didn't even know how to use it. All these years later, I will swear on the lives of my family that I did not send any email to anybody about Graham Poll.

After a while of this laughable kangaroo court, Peter came back into the room and asked if any of us was ready to admit to it. None of us was because none of us had done it. The matter was dropped but left a terrible legacy of mistrust. How could a man who had got drunk, insulted people and thrown up in a hotel, want somebody else disciplined for it?

I would later find out that Graham had believed I was responsible for that email. I was told so by his regular assistant referee Glenn Turner, to whom he spoke about everything. Glenn told me that the four suspects were gathered together because, 'they are not in our club'. Graham, according to Glenn, believed that people were either with him or against him. I am not sure how that squared with his own attitudes towards other officials. Neither do I know how he was so powerful that he could engineer that whole charade at Staverton and get the PGMOL to do that to us.

My belief that it was all designed to deflect the flak from himself was compounded by the fact that two of the Select Group's then coaches, Dave Allison and Keren Barratt, had witnessed the whole scene for themselves. Surely Graham must have known that they would report him to our head, Keith Hackett?

Some time later, Peter Heard – who would be very supportive of me during my illness – said to my great friend in our group Peter Walton that he regretted the episode. The whole affair had been an error of judgment, he told Peter, and he accepted I was not the culprit, if there ever had been one from among us, which I doubt.

From that day on, any benefit of the doubt I gave Graham disappeared. Alan Wiley's words proved true and coupled with Philip Don telling me that he informed a UEFA panel that he considered me for a time the best English referee – and I would not be surprised if Graham found out that piece of information – I began to wonder why I did not get on as well as I might have, certainly in Europe.

After my first experience as Graham's fourth official in Porto that time, I was sent with him once more, and a magnificent experience it was in the Nou Camp for a Champions League match between Barcelona and Juventus. Afterwards, Graham said to me: 'Don't worry. I'll give you a good report this time,' it being a referee's job to comment on his colleagues in his report back to the FA. 'This time?' I thought. 'What does that say about last time?'

The whole shame about this was that Graham had no need to be so Machiavellian about things, in the way he was always manoeuvring in the background, ringing up people in power to get in their ear. That was never my style. It was just too tiring. I just – probably naïvely – believed that if I refereed to the best of my abilities, I would be good enough to get to the top. Graham was certainly good enough to get to the top on ability alone and without the need to act as he did.

He even fell out with Glenn Turner, who was one of the most loyal and honest assistants you could have. Glenn was Graham's assistant at that World Cup match of the three yellow cards and while Graham publicly accepted responsibility for his mistake, he also let it be known that he thought he should have had more help from Glenn and his other assistant, Phil Sharp, who were the best in the business in the English game. Glenn was certainly unhappy about that and it wasn't fair on him.

Mostly in Europe I was assigned to the UEFA Cup, the odd international and under-21 games. Don't get me wrong, I enjoyed the travelling and the different cultures but I don't feel I achieved what I might have done over my six seasons.

When I joined the international list back in 2001 at the age of 40, there were ten English referees officiating in Europe. We started out at level three, with various smaller nations having to start at lower levels. Then it would ascend to two, one, Elite Development Group and ultimately Elite Group. You could only have three of any one nation in each group. Our Elite trio in my time were Poll, Riley and Graham Barber.

To my disappointment, I reached only level two before my enforced retirement at 45. In all, I made 38 appearances in that time. These days with officials behind the goals, there would have been a lot more over such a time. The FA naturally had a lot of sway over appointments and I might have done better had David Elleray not been so influential and Colin Downey remained as referees' officer as he was a fan of mine. His successor, Joe Guest, was not. Perhaps I was seen as too lenient a ref for Europe. I also think it was about who was backing you in positions of influence.

And how they were influenced themselves.

No matter the game or the venue, though, I always wore the FA blazer with its three lions on the breast pocket with great pride and savoured all the experiences, good and bad.

My first experience of European football actually came before I got on the international list and it was quite an eye-opener. It came at the end of my first season on the Football League list back in 1998 when you could be assigned to UEFA Cup games as a fourth official.

Colin Downey sent me as 'fourth' to Dermot Gallagher to Vladikavkaz in southern Russia near the border with Georgia. It was a flight to Moscow, then another two-and-a-half-hour internal flight. That plane was a rustbucket, which had steam in the cabin – at least I hoped it was steam – and the captain was collecting money at the top of the steps to pay for the fuel. The toilet at the back of the plane was behind a curtain. We were relieved to make it to our destination, I can tell you.

In those days, clubs themselves looked after you – delegates nowadays are appointed by the national federations – and we were met at the airport by bodyguards and a representative who became known as 'Go-Getter'. Anything you wanted, he would go and get it. 'You want girls?' he asked us. 'I go get girls if you want.' Dermot was even offered a Mercedes. The bloke was serious and it was a bit unnerving. It did make you wonder what went on with other officials in and from other countries.

On the way back to the airport the day after the game, Go-Getter decided we should stop for a meal and a drink on the way to the airport. I say a drink, he insisted that we have a shot of vodka with every mouthful of food. That included the driver. Eventually he took us to the airport, where we were driven straight onto the runway to the steps of the plane. When we got on, four people were turfed out of their seats at the front to accommodate us.

Mind you, that episode was not as scary as the time I was fourth

126

official to Uriah Rennie for a game between two bad Scrabble hands in Torpedo Kutaisi of Georgia and Crvena Zvezda of Serbia in a Champions League qualifying tie in 2001. It was a three-hour drive from Tbilisi and a horrendously bumpy one at that, boiling hot in a van and with such a dangerous driver that the delegate reported him to UEFA.

Then, over dinner, we started hearing the crashing and banging of shells and gunshots in the distance and began to wonder what was going on. 'Nothing to worry about,' we were told. 'Just rebels in the hillsides. It's normal.' Neighbouring Hatfield may have been a bit rough, but to a lad from Welwyn Garden City this was far from normal.

Often there were trouble spots on the pitch too and in doing Standard Liege v Parma in a UEFA Cup group match in 2004, it felt like war had broken out. It was certainly my toughest European game, between two sides who patently did not like each other.

There were niggly moments and bad tackles all through, with players going down like skittles, and I was forced to issue nine yellow cards, including one for a substitute who ran on to the pitch to celebrate a goal and another for a player still arguing in the tunnel at half-time. I needed all the help I could get from my fourth official, Chris Foy.

I feared the worst from my assessor, a German by the name of Aron Schmidhuber, who had a tough reputation. In the event, he gave me a good mark of 8.5, which just went to show that UEFA were looking for firmness.

It was certainly a good job I didn't do that night what I once did in Sweden, during a UEFA Cup tie between Halmstads and Sampdoria. As I reached for my yellow card in my pocket to discipline a player, I realised I had left it in the dressing room. I quickly made the gesture of holding up the card and putting my hand back in my pocket. I think I got away with it. My assessor didn't notice, at least.

If cold winter nights like those could be a downside to the job – though they always had their attractions – the upside was getting to travel to interesting places. I did a game between Lens and Wolfsburg, for example, and toured the Allied war graves of Northern France, which was a very moving experience.

You also got to some warm places, which for someone like me who loves the sun was a bonus. Nicosia in Cyprus, nice and sunny with the game between Anorthosis and Palermo on an artificial surface, was one of those. And it was after a game at Villareal, against Hammarby of Sweden, that I decided to buy a place in Spain.

Then there was the Intertoto Cup, a summer competition for smaller European clubs that may have seemed unappealing to many, but it had its appeal for me. Perugia in Umbria, for a match against AC Allianssi of Finland in a July, was a case in point. It also had the advantage of featuring English player Jay Bothroyd playing for Perugia and I used him to help me control the players.

And of course there was the hospitality and the gifts.

Early in my European career, I was sent to Slovakia for a UEFA Cup tie between FK Matador Puchov and Bordeaux in the town of Zilina, a few hours' drive from Bratislava.

There, I was told that the owner of the club owned a massive crystal factory and they asked me if I would like a tour. I said I would, for the experience and to fill time before the match, and there was some marvellous stuff that I admired. I was told to take my pick, which I did after clearing it with the match delegate.

Later, there was a knock on my hotel room door and a man was standing there with an armful of crystal glasses, bowls and decanters. When I thanked him, he said it came with one condition – no yellow or red cards for their side during the game.

Naturally I smiled and shook my head. I was not going to be influenced. He smiled, shrugged his shoulders and handed it over anyway. As it happened it was an easy match to control and I didn't have to give out a card – to either side. How I got all that crystal home on the plane I will never know.

Everywhere you went you would be given mementoes by the home club, with 'goodie' bags often being left in your hotel room. They would usually contain kits, coats, tracksuits and polo and replica shirts. There would also be notepads and watches – one a Viceroy from Real Madrid – and pens. With Bayern Munich it would be a Mont Blanc. There would also be wine and Champagne. In addition, I recall Bayer Leverkusen giving us a voucher for 100 Euros to be spent in their club shop.

I was never, I have to say, directly offered a bribe and would most certainly have informed the game's authorities immediately if I had been. Everything I was given was approved by match delegates. It has happened, though. In the Bundesliga, Robert Hoyzer was jailed for more than two years for fixing German league games while back in the 90s, Kurt Rothlisberger, a top Swiss referee, was banned for life by UEFA for offering to get other referees to fix European games.

FIFA also found many 'bent' matches after an investigation into betting rings but I can only say that I was never approached about getting involved in anything like that. Neither did I ever suspect a game I was refereeing was dodgy, with players either giving away penalties deliberately or goalkeepers throwing the ball into the net.

Mind you, there were times when you did wonder what went on in the game in some countries.

In 2006, the Libyan FA asked our FA for three officials to take the big Tripoli derby between Al Ittihad and Al Ahly because, at that time, no home officials could be appointed because of the fear they might later be the subject of reprisals, depending on the result. I was sent with two assistants, Dave Bryan and Roger East.

When we arrived, we had our bags and passports taken from

us and were assigned bodyguards, who followed us for the next three days. We were treated very well but there was always an element of being on edge.

Luckily the game finished 1-1 to satisfy everyone, though a goal in the last few minutes – by a goalkeeper with a header from a corner – did set the place off. Flares were fired all over the place and missiles were thrown but I was too far away to get hit, fortunately. The goalkeeper celebrated by running like a dervish round the running track but Roger East suggested, quite rightly, it might be as well not to book him.

Afterwards, we were thanked by the President of the FA, Muhammad Gaddafi – son of the Colonel. The police were also grateful. They reckoned if it hadn't been a draw, there could have been a riot in the city.

When it came to internationals, I was only ever assigned to two, just one an 'A' category. That took me by surprise when a call came from Joe Guest at the FA as I was training in the gym at Bolton. He asked me to stand in for Steve Bennett, who was ill. After three years of being on the UEFA list, I was only too delighted to and soon found myself on a Eurostar to Brussels.

Belgium 0 France 2
Friendly international
King Baudouin Stadium, Brussels
February 18th 2004

A delight of a match between two teams full of talent and who wanted to play football.

It may just have been a friendly but it was a wonderful occasion in front of 43,000 people and I have to admit to being just a bit in awe of the French team in particular, who were building, as holders, towards that summer's European Championships in which they would play England in Portugal.

There was just the one yellow card, for William Gallas, but he seemed to bear no grudges and gave me his shirt signed afterwards. As did Patrick Vieira. I wish I had also managed to get Zinedine Zidane's.

He was the leading light on a night when the French were not quite at full strength, with Thierry Henry absent. Zidane, in fact, was the best player I ever got to witness close up. His touch was immaculate and he just seemed to have so much time on the ball, which he moved around beautifully.

The French were comfortable winners with goals in each half from Sidney Govou and Louis Saha and the game was over before I knew it. Some games can drag. I was surprised when the 90 minutes were up and I reluctantly blew the final whistle.

My only other international – indeed my last game in Europe – was Portugal v Azerabaijan in October 2006 and it was not a great note to go out on, sadly. Portugal won the game easily enough by 3-0 and I had a decent game – apart from one incident.

Cristiano Ronaldo hit a shot from 35 yards that hit the underside of the bar and bounced down over the line but my assistant, Kevin Pike, was not in a position to see it. Fair enough, the responsibility fell to me and I got a 'below-average' mark as a result for not giving the goal. Any referee will tell you that kind of incident is why we wanted technology in the game. Whenever I have seen Cristiano since, he always reminds me of that day.

Still, I managed to get his shirt afterwards, and signed by him, having told him it was my last game. Later I would get one signed by him at Real Madrid, which meant I had a full set of Manchester United, Portugal and Real. I also have signed Everton and Manchester United shirts from Wayne Rooney. I'm told collections like that would be valuable but I don't want to sell. Unless hard times should arrive, that is.

On top of all the gifts from European games, I have down the years managed to collect a fair bit of memorabilia both personal and for charity or fundraising when asked. Favourite items I own – all of which I keep at a safe location – include a signed Pele shirt from the film *Escape to Victory*, a Real Madrid shirt from David Beckham and numerous items signed by José Mourinho.

I also have plenty of watches, such as a Raymond Weil that Roy Keane gave me for refereeing his testimonial. Gary Neville gave me an iPad for taking charge of his, which I have never known how to use properly. Lucy likes it.

They are all happy mementoes of my career travelling to football grounds at home and abroad but we all have regrets in our careers and one of mine is that I did not do bigger and better games in Europe, and didn't go to a major championship.

But then I was operating in the Graham Poll era when he was pre-eminent and made sure off the field that he remained so on it. It is a bit like a player who finds someone exceptional in his position in his own era and can't get past them to the England team. Though I'm not sure how it would be if that player was in the manager's ear all the time – along with various officials at the FA, the chief executive and head of the international committee.

I do think I was good enough, yes, to officiate Champions League games and big internationals and tournaments. I was always extremely professional. As a referee abroad, you are head of a team of two assistants and a fourth official. I was always happy to let my team enjoy themselves within reason but always insisted on them being prompt for everything.

Sadly, not being a yes man or possibly from the right background, I don't think my cause was ever pushed by the right people at the FA and I was never promoted to the Elite Group.

As well as Graham's international retirement after the World

Cup of 2006 along with mine a few months later, Graham Barber, Steve Bennett and Mike Riley also departed the scene.

It meant there was a void for an English referee to fill and after Andy D'Urso fell by the wayside, Howard Webb was in the right place at the right time. He was a very good young ref who became a good friend and I like him a lot. He has deserved his success for an ability that was good enough to get him the World Cup final of 2010, and he handled the match between Spain and Holland well when it was such a physical game. He also accumulated more than 100 Champions League games, which was quite an achievement.

I am not jealous of him, just pleased for him. He has shown you can be a nice guy as well as a top referee. The two are not exclusive despite what some people may have portrayed.

And while I am tinged with sadness that I didn't have a better European career, I remain grateful that I had one at all. At least I was doing well domestically and that season of my international retirement, 2006-07, I felt I was on top of my game.

There did come an episode early in that season that made me very angry. At the time, I had a column in the Bolton Wanderers programme. It was my local club and I trained there and knew all the staff well. In fact, I declared my interest with the Premier League and so was quite properly not assigned to their games. Except once, when my bosses prevailed upon me to be a fourth official at Anfield for one of their games against Liverpool because there was a shortage of officials that weekend.

Reluctantly I agreed and have to confess that when Bolton scored, I was out of my seat between the two dug-outs to cheer before realising where and who I was. I had to pretend that I was leaping up to calm down Sam Allardyce and his then assistant Phil Brown. QPR would always be my team but I did have a soft spot for Wanderers.

Anyway, what got my goat came at another of their games involving Liverpool this particular season. In the column, I praised

Steven Gerrard and said how good it was to see such a great player at the Reebok. Then at the end, I wished the best of luck to Bolton's management team, Big Sam Allardyce and Little Sammy Lee. It was just a routine way of signing off the column.

But Liverpool took offence and I was reported to the Premier League. I was promptly removed from top-flight games for four weeks with the loss of income that incurred. What made it so galling was that I had been writing the column for a while and all my notes were read by Keith Hackett and my coach Dave Allison before being passed for publication. And these had been passed.

Keith was fine with me but it was probably taken out of his hands by the Premier League, who were under pressure from Liverpool. Graham Noakes, the league's Company Secretary, said there would be an investigation and I had to write to him with my side of the story. I did so, and four weeks later I was told that the investigation, if ever there was one, was over and I could return to the Premier League. It was all very frustrating not being able to speak out publicly. As a referee you had to take these things, something that would come to annoy me more in later seasons.

Otherwise it was the standard mix of triumphs and disasters – getting decisions right the majority of the time and not being noticed and getting the odd one wrong and the dogs of war being unleashed on you.

In managing a melee in the Spurs v Middlesbrough game, for example, I sent off one from each side, Didier Zokora and George Boateng, but Boro appealed and Boateng got off. Ah well, you do your job on the day and you move on.

There was also another encounter with Neil Warnock in an unpleasant spat that showed the other side of a man who had praised me for getting a decision right the previous season in the match between Sheffield United and Reading at Bramall Lane.

This one was between the same two sides, this time at Reading's Madejski Stadium and this time in the Premier League, both sides having just been promoted. The game was going smoothly until Warnock made a substitution and brought on Keith Gillespie. Before the game had even restarted, Gillespie elbowed Stephen Hunt and my assistant, James Linington, flagged. Out came my red card but even then Gillespie was not finished and had another go at Hunt.

On the sidelines, I then saw Warnock and the Reading assistant manager Wally Downes having a go at each other and I had to get in there and sort them out. Wally would later claim that Neil had made a gesture with his foot, studs raised, for one of his players to 'do' Hunt but Neil, who claimed Wally pushed him, would say he was referring to an earlier challenge by Reading's Steve Sidwell. I had no choice but to send them both to the stand.

Later, Wally came to the dressing room almost in tears. He was most apologetic about his reaction but said that Warnock's behaviour had been unacceptable. I told him it would be reported to the FA and joked that he was going get a ban for a push when he might as well as have had a proper go at Neil. Wally had to laugh. At least I had my own sense of humour back after that Liverpool incident.

That season, I was assigned to Chelsea matches seven times and it was always a pleasure to renew acquaintance with José. By now I would be asked for a pre-game cup of tea in his office, a spartan little box room with a desk, chair and fridge just off the home dressing room. There for ten minutes before going about our business, we would discuss games, players and refereeing. And sometimes Graham Poll. José had the same dislike and mistrust of the man as me.

Not once in those seven games did they lose but then such was José's record with Chelsea – which included 65 unbeaten games in a row at home – that quite a few referees around that time didn't see them defeated.

The last two Chelsea games I did were draws with Newcastle,

0-0 – when José complained again about me not giving a penalty – and 1-1 with Everton in the last game of the season, which was notable for an exchange I had with David Moyes. James Vaughan had given Everton the lead but Drogba equalised, Moyes insisting that Paulo Ferreira had fouled Mikel Arteta in the build-up. He even brought a laptop to my dressing room afterwards to show me and I could only agree and apologise.

After two seasons of winning it, the title had slipped away from José and Chelsea this time around with too many drawn games as Manchester United became champions again. Horror of horrors, for Roman Abramovich at least, Chelsea had finished second under José.

There were rumblings around Stamford Bridge that the owner was getting annoyed with José, both over his public statements sometimes about his contract and certain players he didn't want that Abramovich did, such as Andriy Shevchenko, and with the team supposedly not playing the exciting football that the Russian had in his mind as Barcelona were now starting to dominate European football.

In fact, though it was not fully apparent that last day of the season, we were witnessing the beginning of the end of a glittering chapter in his career. For me though – perhaps even thanks to Graham Poll, in a perverse way – there would turn out to be new openings rather than a closure, as if compensation for my unfulfilled European career.

11

OUT OF THE SHADOWS

When it came, the appointment was a surprise, even if I was a Select Group referee. Despite feeling fit and effective in my refereeing, I had grown to believe that I was out of favour with some of my superiors, certainly at the FA. I was definitely not going to complain, however, about being awarded the 2007 FA Community Shield at Wembley between the two clubs who were by now the biggest in the English game, Sir Alex Ferguson's champions Manchester United and José Mourinho's FA Cup winners Chelsea. The European door had closed; a new domestic portal was opening.

The reason for that was a changing of the guard both on and off the pitch in refereeing. By now at the FA, their Referees' Officer Joe Guest had departed to be replaced by Neale Barry with his new job title of Head of Senior Referee Development. Neale had been on the Select Group with me. He was not yet touched by the politics in the administration of the game – though that would change – and then much more his own man, unlikely to be as swayed by the opinions of David Elleray, chairman of the referees' committee.

I am sure Keith Hackett was also fighting my corner, although he would not have been directly involved in the decision to give me the Community Shield, as the FA were always keen to retain their authority over their games rather than let the PGMOL have too much sway. The FA were losing power to the Premier League in so many areas that they fought to hold on to what was left.

And of course, Graham Poll was no longer around. He had had one more domestic season after that 2006 World Cup howler and then retired, ending with the Championship play-off final at Wembley when Derby beat West Bromwich Albion 1-0 to reach the Premier League.

For my own Wembley occasion, I bought expensive bottles of wine for Sir Alex and José, a Sardinian red called Marchese di Villamarina that would cost about £80 in a restaurant. I also bought bottles for my three fellow officials – fourth official Chris Foy and assistants Darren Cann and Martin Yerby – which I got the staff to leave in their rooms at the Hendon Hall Hotel in North London, having arrived there first on the night before the game.

It had now become the traditional hotel for Wembley refs, and although it is a little faded these days, you still feel part of history there as it was where the England squad stayed during the 1966 World Cup. I handed over the bottles for Sir Alex and José to them in the tunnel outside the dressing rooms on the day and they seemed grateful.

It was a good game, drawn 1-1 and won on penalties by Chelsea, though I had to issue four yellow cards. One was for Wayne Rooney, who chased me down the pitch.

'Mark, that was never a yellow,' he said, an expletive in there as well. 'Now I've got one on my record going into the season.'

'Don't worry,' I replied. 'Cards don't count in the Community Shield.'

'Oh right,' he said, calming down. 'In that case it was a yellow. Thanks Mark.'

Sometimes, players really do not know the laws of the game or even the rules of competitions.

Afterwards José came up to me, gave me a hug and said: 'Well done, top ref.' It was a poignant moment for it was the last time I would referee his side. In six more weeks, he would be sacked by Chelsea despite his remarkable record of six trophies in just three years. It sounded crazy to an outsider like me, one who liked the guy and had become friendly with him, but given the friction between him and the owner Roman Abramovich, in those situations there is only one winner – the man with the money.

In the October, José rang me up and invited me and Michelle out to Vilamoura in Portugal for a break. Before his sacking, fraternising with a manager would have led to me getting the sack, not unreasonably, but now I was free to be a proper friend. And a generous one he was too as he paid for our hotel costs, after we had paid for our flights.

After the Community Shield, Keith Hackett sent me an email congratulating me for getting the season off to a good start. It was exactly the sort of support and simple touch you wanted from your boss.

By now Keith had made his own mark on the Select Group, having re-arranged the coaching system for referees. He had been one of five coaches when the Group turned full-time professional before becoming Philip Don's assistant. He then put in place three regional coaches, Ron Groves, Dave Allison – my coach – and Keren Barratt. In another change now, Keren had become his assistant. Dave had moved on to become head of the National List, the Football League referees in effect, in succession to Jim Ashworth.

What I liked about Keith was his honesty and straightforwardness. In my first season as a Football League referee he had come to assess me at Chesterfield v Leyton Orient and told me afterwards that I was the best thing he had seen in a long while. It gave me a lot of confidence.

Then, the following season, he came to another game of mine, Lincoln City v Leyton Orient, where he felt I had not performed well and told me so. 'What's going on?' he said. 'If you ref like last season you will go far but not reffing like this.' I appreciated that

139

truth too, designed to keep me improving.

As a good communicator, Keith knew how to manage and talk to you. He treated you like a man. Like Philip he had been to the very top himself – Keith rarely missed a chance to talk about refereeing at the World Cup in Mexico in 1986 – and understood the pressures.

He was also very approachable. During his time, we would have several disagreements but if you went to him with a grievance, or he came to you with a complaint about you, it always felt that it would be forgotten the next day once the air had been cleared, even if it had been quite a ding-dong. I always felt like he was an ally and a mentor and though in public there were times he had to be critical, in private he was always supportive.

As a consequence, my confidence rose and that season I really felt I was back in the game, being given good matches and being appreciated. My style was back in fashion – play on the Mark Halsey way. Let the game flow.

One such was the game that became the Premier League's highest scoring match – Portsmouth 7 Reading 4. It was a great game, and I think I only gave 12 free kicks, but afterwards I had a killjoy assessor in John Martin telling me I had missed an act of violent conduct. One player, he said, had punched another. When they went through the DVD, though, they could not find it and I was not reprimanded.

My reputation remained for being able to handle games with powderkeg potential. Morecambe v Accrington was another derby to be defused – smashing game with players just getting on with it and not looking to con you – as was Fulham v Chelsea.

Sheffield Wednesday v Sheffield United was easier to handle on the field than off it as I got through what is always a torrid affair without showing one card. The players were certainly more polite than the family of Sheffield United fans at the main entrance when I arrived, the woman greeting me with: 'Not you.

We get fuck all out of you.' 'Ooh look, it's the Clampetts,' I replied in reference to the old TV series *The Beverly Hillbillies*, before asking a steward if he would mind moving them on.

There was certainly plenty of powderkeg potential to the game I was given just before Christmas that season: Liverpool against Manchester United, both sides competing at the top of the table.

It didn't start well, with me forgetting my whistle as we came out, meaning that I had to borrow my fourth official Phil Dowd's to call the captains together for the coin toss. He went off to get mine, meanwhile, and when I went to give him the coin prior to kick off, which was my routine with the fourth official, he handed over my whistle.

Whilst near the touchline, I had a word with Cristiano Ronaldo, who was in the middle of controversies over simulation at the time. 'Don't you be diving today because you'll get nothing out of me,' I said. He smiled and within a few minutes of kick off he was going down too easily under challenge and I didn't give a free kick.

Cristiano complained, and I could have given it since there was contact, but I showed I was not going to be conned and after that there was no attempt to deceive me. He got what he deserved in the way of fouls and I got decisions right.

This is what people who criticise refs for individual decisions often don't take into account. This was game management. An early decision – right or wrong, depending on circumstances, if the offence is none too serious – can set the tone for a game and make it enjoyable and free of controversy to the benefit of everyone, be it referee, players, managers, supporters and TV audiences.

I must have had a good game as the next day I received an email from the chief executive of the Premier League, Richard Scudamore, congratulating me on my handling of the game, which Manchester United won 1-0.

And so it was in good heart that I took off for a crafty January few days in the sun at my place in Spain with a few of the lads for what would become an annual event. Pete Walton, Lee Mason, Alan Wiley and I hardly expected the near international incident that we were to run into out there, though.

The idea was to relax, sunbathe and play a bit of golf for those who liked it, with just a bit of warm-weather training thrown in. That was until we noticed a poster advertising a game between Accrington Stanley and the local Torrevieja team, who played in a regional league of the Spanish Third Division, roughly the equivalent of the Conference. Stanley were out of the FA Cup and must have decided on some warm-weather training of their own.

We jumped into a car and headed off there, a few locals recognising us as we went up into the main stand. Then came a booming voice from the back of the stand ordering us to come and join him. It was the Accrington chairman, Eric Whalley, who knew Lee well from Lancashire football going back years and was happy to regale us all with tales of games he had refereed.

It soon became clear in the game that local refereeing standards were not what the Accrington manager John Coleman and his team were used to in the Football League. Two-footed tackles by the home side were going unpunished and the Stanley players were beginning to fear for their safety. John and his assistant Jimmy Bell were getting angry with the home coaches and we began to sense trouble. Eric Whalley's cheerful mood was changing.

Jimmy Bell decided to send himself on as a substitute to try and calm things down but he was soon scythed down. Eric Whalley had to be restrained from leaving his seat and John Coleman now decided to put himself on. He too was soon caught, this time by an arm that would have been a red card back home.

Now Eric rose and pushed past us, reaching the side of the pitch. He was just about to enter the fray when I managed to get to him and pull him away.

The game had descended into a farce due to weak refereeing.

Thankfully it was soon over, however, and a diplomatic incident was averted.

We had a drink in the clubhouse, the locals – including lots of expats – telling us this was how it was out here most weeks. English officials were the best, they insisted. After a couple of drinks, Eric had calmed down enough to say that the ref had made Lee Mason look like Jack Taylor, England's World Cup final referee of 1974. 'I'll never call you lot names again,' he promised. We laughed. Eric's vow probably lasted a week when we got back home.

I was in even better heart in February when I was chosen to referee the League Cup final, then sponsored by Carling. It was another example of how things were changing behind the scenes in refereeing, with new personnel deciding on the appointment.

Now that Jim Ashworth had gone from the Football League and Dave Allison taken over, I sensed I would be a candidate and although David Elleray at the FA may not have approved, Keith Hackett was pushing my claims. Peter Heard, the Football's League representative on the FA board, was also a supporter of mine. I was delighted then, but not surprised any more given that my assessment marks were good, to be chosen to referee the first League Cup final to be back at the rebuilt Wembley.

Later, Dave Allison would tell me that he had a phone call from his predecessor Jim Ashworth, who had never rated me, about my appointment. 'I would have put my house on you giving it to Mark Halsey as soon as I went,' Dave told me that Jim had said to him. Dave told me that he replied: 'He got it on merit.'

Chelsea 1 Tottenham Hotspur 2
(After extra time)
Carling Cup Final
Wembley Stadium
Sunday, 24th February 2008

After not getting a Wembley game since that Manchester City play-off final eight years previously, it was now two in a season and very exciting – for our partners too as they were treated to a weekend in a hotel with us as well. The only problem was that it was costing me a fortune in gifts of wine for my officials. That day Martin Yerby was again one of my assistants, the other being Andy Garratt with my old mate Pete Walton the fourth official.

It was a cracking game. Chelsea, now being managed by Avram Grant, took a first-half lead through Didier Drogba but Spurs equalised in the 68th minute with a penalty I awarded for handball on the say-so of Martin Yerby. He had John Terry in his ear for his trouble and I had to sort that situation out but it was the correct call. Dimitar Berbatov converted the penalty.

Then, in extra time, Jonathan Woodgate headed a winner and Spurs held on for a 2-1 win. Both teams seemed pleased enough with my performance. I got signed shirts off both.

The yellow card count of seven – six of them in extra time as players tired – was above my average but not outrageous for a final between two fierce London rivals. Luckily I did not have to show a red card. As a referee, that is the last thing you want in a final.

I recall during the pre-match warm-up telling myself to savour this one, to enjoy every moment, but once again the occasion had flown by.

As we were travelling back in our transport to meet up with our families at the Hendon Hall Hotel, my phone rang. It was José Mourinho. 'Chelsea did for me and now Tottenham have done for Chelsea,' he said. I couldn't help smiling.

After the Community Shield, this was the second time in the season that Chelsea had finished second best and there would be two more occasions. They finished runners-up to Manchester United in both the Premier and Champions Leagues.

A few weeks later I was back staying at the Hendon Hall Hotel, this time ahead of a match between Arsenal and Middlesbrough at the Emirates. It was an example of how you frequently do not see the game in the same way as players and managers – which is as it should be since they are deeply involved and you are objective.

On the morning of the game, I had a pleasant conversation along those lines over breakfast with the Middlesbrough manager Gareth Southgate, chance putting us in the same hotel – though it would never happen these days with referees and teams kept well apart in the run-up to the game.

Then in the match, I sent off Boro's Egyptian striker Mido for a high kick that caught an Arsenal player in the head. Having seen it clearly, from my angle – and that is the crucial point for a referee – it was serious foul play endangering an opponent but Boro appealed, claiming that Mido had not seen the opponent coming. It was an understandable argument, but he should have known not to have his feet that high. My argument was always that the safety of the players is paramount and the FA agreed, rejecting the appeal.

Mind you, my safety didn't always seem paramount to my bosses. On a Tuesday night doing Carlisle United v Nottingham Forest, I tweaked a hamstring and had to come off at half-time. When I phoned Keren Barratt the next day to tell him that I was a doubt to do Fulham v Sunderland on the Saturday, he told me – pleadingly but firmly – to get myself fit because they were short of top-flight referees and they needed me.

I went into Bolton Wanderers and had treatment and passed

a fitness test on Friday morning thanks to their medical team but was worried about letting myself down on the Saturday. As a referee, you wonder if your assessor is going to give you a bad mark so instead of doing people a favour, you might be damaging your own reputation.

It happens with players as well – the older and wiser they get, they don't play through injury, not only to avoid further damage but so as not to let down themselves and the team. Young bucks want to play through it but sometimes have to be saved from themselves.

I did go on, and thankfully I had a good assessor in Dennis Hedges who said he would look after me. I had known Dennis since my Conference days and trusted him. He would note it all right if you made a mistake, and would tell you so, but he would also support you. If the Premier League had a dozen Dennis Hedges, it would be a better place to referee. You are not looking for favours, just fairness, and Dennis always gave me that.

In all that season I refereed 44 games, 24 of them in the Premier League and two major Wembley occasions as a bonus on top. I felt I was back in the spotlight – or the firing line. But I even felt comfortably able to cope with all that entailed at this high point of my career with my bosses giving me confidence with their backing. I was refereeing well and getting good games.

Michelle and I went to Spain for our summer break feeling well. Lucy was now a toddling two. There was also another few days' break that got me into a spot of trouble before the next season began.

12

THE MAKEOVER BLUES

Michelle was adamant. She needed a break, what with Lucy being such a bundle of energy, even if she was also a bundle of joy, and wanted some time on her own. Take her down to your Mum's in Welwyn Garden City for a few days, she ordered. She can be a very persuasive Lancashire lass, can Michelle. I did what I was told.

When I returned, it was with a mixture of confusion and concern. As I drove into our street, I could see vans parked and what seemed like hundreds of people milling around. In fact, I couldn't get near the house as police had closed the area around it. Then I saw the reason: something was going on at our house. What the hell was happening? I did worry there had been some kind of incident.

It turned out that Michelle had contacted one of these TV programmes that do up your house, *60 Minute Makeover*. I was useless at decorating and she had got fed up waiting for me to do anything. I had TV cameras on me as I turned up, looking appropriately shocked.

They took us in the house and filmed our reaction, which was to look fittingly pleased and grateful. Mostly I was, but when they had gone I could see what a mess they had made of some of it, none of which was shown on TV, of course. They put a big plasma screen on the wall of the living room, for example, but had not wired it up. It was just for show. There were areas not picked up by the cameras where there was no wallpaper.

Elsewhere they had put on nice expensive wallpaper, I have to say, but it had to come down as we had to get a bloke in to cut into the wall to put in trunking to take the wires for the TV. I was thankful for some of the work but it did end up costing me money. I was not entirely happy, shall we say.

Keith Hackett was not best pleased either. I must have told one or two of my fellow referees and it must have got back to him as it would not go out on TV for a while yet. He told me that I was in breach of my contract because I had made a media appearance without getting permission. How could I get permission? I didn't know a thing about it. It also had nothing to do with refereeing and I was hardly bringing the game into any disrepute, I argued.

Michelle was furious and rang Keith to tell him how petty this all was. He later told me that he wished his wife stood up for him the way mine did for me. It made no difference. I was disciplined and had to stand down from the Premier League for a week.

The show finally aired the following spring, making it a double dose of embarrassment as my fellow referees took the mickey out of me relentlessly first at the start of the 2008-09 season as well as when it went out.

By now, Keith had moved our base to Warwick University from Staverton, though we continued to use the Barnsdale Hall Hotel in Rutland for some get-togethers. It was at Barnsdale, I recall, that we had once been sent on a long bike ride that had us all shattered. Except for Lee Mason, that is. He paid a lorry driver £20 to take him back to the hotel, him and his bike on the back. When we came back knackered, he was waiting for us with a beer in his hand.

It was not a great start that season, though I felt I was clearly in the right over a controversial decision in a high-profile game. Well, when the England captain is involved, it is bound to excite debate and opinions.

Manchester City 1 Chelsea 3
Barclays Premier League
City of Manchester Stadium
Saturday, 13th September 2008

Chelsea were cruising when it happened. Although City took the lead through Robinho on his debut, having that summer turned down Chelsea, they were soon conceding goals.

Ricardo Carvalho equalised before half-time and Frank Lampard put Chelsea – now managed by Luiz Felipe Scolari – ahead early in the second half. The game was all but over when Nicolas Anelka scored a third.

All but over, that was, bar a red card for John Terry with 13 minutes to go.

Another City Brazilian in Jo had escaped Terry just inside the Chelsea half and was setting himself for a run on goal when the England centre-back brought him down with what amounted to a rugby tackle. I deemed it a sending off. We were not playing with an oval ball, after all.

All hell would break loose after the game. Chelsea would be missing their leader with a suspension for the next week's game against Manchester United. England were just a few weeks away from two important World Cup qualifiers and the national team needed him in the groove, not sitting out a suspension.

John came to my dressing room and we had a decent conversation about the incident. He wondered why I had sent him off when Jo was such a long way from goal and everyone reckoned Carvalho would have got round to tackle.

I agreed with him. But, I told him, I had not sent him off for denial of a goalscoring opportunity but for serious foul play. He then conceded that it had been a deliberate foul, though intent was no longer part of the law, having been removed from its wording in the mid-1990s, and he could not be punished just for intent. I could see why. Referees couldn't be expected to guess at motives. John seemed to understand, said he had no complaints.

On the spot, my assessor Roy Pearson said he backed me. Later that night, however, he phoned me to say that he would be giving me a mark of 59, which was classed as below standard, because he thought I had made an error. Normally my mark was between 75 and 80.

What can have happened? Did Chelsea or the FA ring up Keith Hackett to query my decision? Whatever it was, I felt I had made the right call but knew that Chelsea would be appealing. And I just knew that they would win and the red card would be overturned.

It was another nail in the coffin for the referee's authority, though we have got used to them down the years. Not even Sir Alex Ferguson's support for me subsequently in a press conference when he was asked to comment on the affair would count for anything, though I know he had a vested interest in Terry being banned.

I knew that conversations went on in the background, that the PGMOL general manager would get calls from clubs, or from the FA on behalf of clubs, seeking to get decisions amended or elements of refereeing changed. I remember, for example, Keith once telling me that Rafa Benitez had complained about where we stood as referees for Liverpool free kicks as it interfered with one of their routines and we were told to change our positions.

I also knew what would come next for me. I spoke to my two regular assistant referees Andy Garratt and Trevor Massey to prepare them for a little stint in the Football League. Sure enough, when the next set of appointments came out, we were down for Chester v Shrewsbury – though Keith insisted I was down for it no matter what. The week after it would be Sheffield United v Watford.

The refereeing authorities always say that officials are not being relegated to the lower divisions because of controversial decisions but trust me it does happen – sometimes to the ire of the Football League, because they don't want a referee who has just made a mistake. How else are they to stay active, though? It is partly punishment and partly – the Select Group rulers would say anyway – to spare a ref from the limelight should any more controversy arise. I believe it is often done also to appease Premier League managers.

I asked Keith Hackett to issue a statement saying I had not been demoted because of the John Terry incident but he would not and so some of the papers said that I had been punished for mistakenly sending off the England captain, even though I had plenty of support in other areas of the press and on TV.

If I am honest, it did make me think for a while in subsequent games whether to issue a red or yellow card. You're only human after all and wonder if it is worth the grief, especially with big players who are going to attract publicity for you. I was always a referee who did not send off lightly anyway.

Sometimes, it is easier not to give a decision rather than give one. That way, it gets glossed over rather than analysed. And people who say you don't give decisions in the penalty area that you would elsewhere on the pitch are right. No one is going to comment so much about one outside of the defending third of the pitch. You give that same free kick in the penalty area and then everyone's talking about it. You just don't give the cheap ones in the box that you do outside of it. That is the pragmatism of refereeing sometimes.

You just have to have those arguments with yourself, get over it and get it right as often as you can. And I had to accept that Keith was my manager, he was right, and get on to the next game. As he held no grudges, I was soon back at a big stadium, doing Manchester United 4 West Bromwich Albion 0. Mind you, I still got grief from another England player, Wayne Rooney berating me for disallowing a headed goal for a push.

The next time I went to Old Trafford, though, to take charge of their game against Everton a few months later, Wayne came up to me in a corridor before the game and asked if I had seen that disallowed goal against WBA again. I said I had and that it should have been a goal because there was no push. He thanked me for the apology and promptly told me I was his favourite referee – though I wondered if he said that to all of us. I appreciated him saying it and cheekily asked if I could therefore have a signed shirt from him after the game. He agreed.

It was in the days when it was still allowed to ask for signed shirts, something that Keith Hackett's successor Mike Riley would put a stop to in new PGMOL directives, along with anything else that might have been a bit human, though it did continue on the quiet. You were supposed to snitch if you saw a colleague getting one but when fourth official I never would and I don't think any of my colleagues would have reported me.

Unfortunately, with United 1-0 up in the last five minutes, Wayne chased down Tim Cahill and fouled him. I was keeping up and saying under my breath 'Wayne, don't you dare,' but I knew it was coming and I would have to give him a yellow card. 'Don't worry,' said Wayne when I did. 'I deserved it and you can still have your shirt.'

I was enjoying the football and the games I was getting, such as the Newcastle 1 Liverpool 5 game over Christmas when Michael Owen scored a hat-trick. It featured a rare booking for the mild-mannered Shay Given who kicked the ball into the crowd after I had given a corner when he thought it should have been a foul. It was the season Newcastle went down and he was good and angry. The next time I saw him, after he had been sold to Aston Villa, he even apologised for the incident but I understood his frustrations as a professional, even if I had to do my duty.

My enjoyment was brutally interrupted in the period between Christmas and New Year, however.

Michelle had been feeling unwell for three months, suffering from a dull ache under her left rib, bruising in her legs, frequent sweating and a constant tiredness that saw her lose patience quickly with Lucy, which was unlike her as we treasured the daughter we had been through that arduous IVF process to have.

The doctor told Michelle she had a pulled muscle and to take painkillers but it got worse. She lost nearly three stones in weight and developed a lump in her stomach and a pain across her pubic bone. Two mouthfuls of food and she was full. She went back to the doctor who was taken aback by her condition and sent her for a blood test. Then, on New Year's Eve, he rang to tell her that she had chronic myeloid leukaemia.

She phoned me as I was driving home from training at Bolton. I had no clue what it was but knew it was serious and was in a daze. I decided to drive to the doctor to see him and find out about it. He told me that it was a form of blood cancer but that I would discover more when she went to hospital.

We were shocked and worried. I was due to do Hartlepool v Stoke in the FA Cup on the Saturday and wanted Michelle and Lucy with me. Our friend Steve Bennett, came over from his hotel near Sunderland, where he was refereeing, on the Friday night and after Michelle had gone back to our room as she was so tired, he broke down in tears at how ill she looked. We all shed tears, in fact.

Michelle had waited so long for a child and now she was worried she was not going to see Lucy grow up.

I must confess I was thinking about Michelle throughout the game but I got through it without too many incidents, Hartlepool pulling off an upset by winning 2-0. I was getting abuse at one point from some idiot in the crowd and I thought to myself, 'If only you knew what my family is going through.'

The rest of that season was a struggle. Michelle was put on a drug called Glyvec to control her condition but her blood test results were not that healthy for some time and the side effects took it out of her, in the form of tiredness, diarrhoea, back pain and aching in her shins. She had a lot of up and down days and some days could not even get out of bed. There was talk that she might need a bone marrow transplant and we had that hanging over us.

We were also under a lot of stress with the Italian restaurant, Sottovento, in Farnworth, that we had bought as silent partners two years earlier only to be put in a position of having to buy out the person we had invested with as the place was failing and then having to sack a manager we had hired.

For a while, with Michelle so ill, I took over the running of the restaurant, along with shopping and the school run with Lucy. I myself began to feel the strain, even though Michelle's mum was always helpful. I was starting to feel ill myself. The rest of the season became a bit of a blur, what with Michelle's problems and my developing symptoms of sore throat, ear infections and lethargy getting us down.

Despite my physical issues, I still think I refereed well enough for the rest of that season and I was determined to keep going having got myself back on some big games.

Keith and Kelly Wright, his PA at the PGMOL, were great, asking if I preferred matches nearer home to spend as much time as possible with Michelle but I wanted to carry on as normal. I was busy helping her as much as I could during the week but the weekend games offered respite that would enable me to go back refreshed for another week at home. I also didn't want to be given special treatment as there was a lot of backbiting going on at times within our group, especially over appointments.

My appointments included being assigned once more to the games where it might all kick off, including another trip to Sheffield for United v Wednesday. At Birmingham v Wolves, I sent off the home side's Lee Carsley for a nasty tackle but to his credit he waited for me after the game to apologise and also made a public apology to his opponent as well.

I was also given Leeds v Millwall – always a game that had my name on it – in the Championship play-off second leg and it was as traditionally tough a game as might be imagined between two clubs whose passion reflected their fans. My first yellow came after just three minutes and by the ten-minute mark, I had issued another couple. There would be nine in all.

In the end, after their 1-0 win in their home leg, Millwall went through with a 1-1 draw even if they were not happy with a penalty I awarded Leeds for a shirt tug. Personally, I thought it was a great spot.

I would have liked to have done the play-off final but that went to Mike Dean as a consolation prize. He was going to get the FA Cup final but did not because Liverpool reached Wembley and Mike lived on the Wirral.

Still, I was not going to worry. There was still time to get both the big Wembley occasions of Championship play-off final and FA Cup final. And I did seem to be getting closer to the latter, having done a quarter-final this season, between Everton and Middlesbrough, won 2-1 by the home side.

Besides, I had plenty of more important things to worry about in my personal life. And soon that worry would increase to a fully blown terror.

13

THE DARKEST HOURS...

They were 48 long, agonising hours following that Everton v Arsenal game, a match which represented the start of the 2009-10 season, though I was more worried that it spelled the end for me. And not just the end of my professional refereeing career.

I tried to make it a normal Sunday, just a chill-out day, with a walk in the park and a meal at our restaurant, not only for little Lucy's sake but also mine and Michelle's. I also didn't want to worry my Mum. I phoned her just to say that it was nothing more than having my tonsils removed the next day. I paced, I fretted. I wanted Monday to come. But then again, I didn't.

When it did arrive, I took Lucy to playschool, Michelle's Mum and Dad picking her up afterwards while we went to the Beaumont hospital early in the afternoon for my scheduled 4.15pm operation. The surgeon, Mr Christopher Lobo, came to my room to reassure me, to repeat that they would be removing the tonsil, and to tell me that the next time I saw him would be the following Friday for the results. As it turned out, I would see him just a couple of hours later.

After they had given me the pre-med, the next thing I remember was coming to. It was around 7.30pm after a one-hour operation, I was later told. The first thing I saw when I opened my eyes was Michelle crying. Anxiously, blearily, I asked her what the problem was.

While I was in the recovery room, she said, Mr Lobo had come back up to the room to give her a progress report on the surgery. The tumour was indeed sinister, he said, and he would come back to explain more about what that meant when I was back in the room myself. Michelle had phoned a friend, a paramedic, to ask what sinister meant. 'Brace yourself,' Jo had told her. 'It won't be good news.'

A nurse had told Michelle that they would bring me back up when she felt more together but she was unable to stop crying when I reappeared. The surgeon stood at the bottom of my bed and told us that it was a bigger tumour than they had anticipated. He had performed more of a biopsy on the tumour rather than a full removal, he said. It was a cancer, all right, but the tumour would need to be analysed to determine exactly what kind before they decided on the next move. He would see us again later in the week once he had the results.

Now we knew what sinister meant. A medical dictionary defines it as 'ominous, presaging trouble'.

'Am I going to die?' I asked him.

'Not if I can help it,' he replied.

They kept me in overnight and I was almost hysterical at times, I have to admit, veering between gratitude that they had found this and now it was being sorted out and wondering if I was going to make it through. What was I going to tell my Mum? Michelle rang my best friend Fred Barber, the goalkeeping coach at Bolton Wanderers, to tell him what had happened and she burst into tears again as she did. It was that kind of night.

There followed three days of more uncertainty while the tumour was sent away for analysis and the hospital worked out my treatment. I could do little but lay on the sofa feeling miserably ill as Michelle took care of Lucy and ran our restaurant. I was often beside myself with fear as I contemplated what might happen next. First her with her leukaemia, now me. All within the space of nine months. We wondered what we had done to deserve this.

On the Friday, Mr Lobo explained the situation graphically. They had removed one tonsil and part of the tumour but it was too dangerous a procedure to remove more. Tests had shown it was a B cell lymphoma, whatever that meant. I would not only need the radiotherapy but also chemotherapy. He wanted me to see Dr Mark Gray at the Royal Bolton Hospital, who was Michelle's doctor, but she thought we should go private at The Christie specialist cancer hospital in Manchester and checked with the Premier League's health insurers to see if I was eligible. Thankfully I was.

Michelle rang The Christie, told them my situation and was put through to Doreen Fox, personal assistant to Professor Tim Illidge, whose job title described him as Professor of Targeted Therapy and Oncology. In fact, he was an expert in lymphoma. I would later find out that he was one of the best in the world. He certainly became that to me.

Doreen said that she would ring him. He was abroad on holiday in Portugal and could not see me for another five days but gave me an appointment. I was told that first I would need an MRI scan so that the results were ready for Professor Illidge when he returned. It involved drinking a liquid that contained a dye that would show up on a screen as my body passed through a long, thin tube. It was not pleasant, but at least I didn't feel claustrophobic.

Michelle had booked a week away in Spain for that week and, reassured that I had an appointment, she flew off. Not before having obtained the disc with all my medical records from the Beaumont and taken it to The Christie.

By the time my consultation with Tim Illidge came around on the Wednesday, I was feeling really ill again. I wasn't eating because I just couldn't swallow properly. I thought it was just the scarring from the operation.

As an avid football fan, Tim knew who I was. In fact, he had listened to the Everton v Arsenal game on the radio in Portugal – because he was an Everton supporter. And he wasn't best pleased with that opening day 6-1 defeat, he said. I told him it wasn't my fault, not to blame the ref, and he smiled. He did then say that he thought I was a very good referee and that Everton had not turned up, what with the Lescott affair affecting them. After that we got on famously.

My scan was telling him, he said, that I needed more immediate treatment than had been thought. The tumour had grown again. In fact, it was now the size of a golf ball. He did not know why, nor what was driving it, but I would need chemotherapy as quickly as possible. He wanted me back at 9.30am the next morning. There was no time to waste. If it went on for much longer without being treated, the tumour could choke me to death.

'So when will I be able to referee again?' I asked him, probably not having quite grasped the seriousness of the situation. But then refereeing was my life. The thought of being back as quickly as possible was keeping me going. His reply was honest, if not encouraging.

'Not this season and maybe not again,' he said. 'Perhaps park football but never at elite level.'

My whole world caved in but by now I was not in control of anything. All I could do was what I was told. I phoned Michelle to tell her what was happening. She felt guilty about being out in Spain but there was nothing she could do either.

Professor Tim Illidge: *A provisional diagnosis of an aggressive B cell lymphoma had been made and the tumour was growing back quickly and occupying most of the throat, making it hard for Mark to swallow. I decided on what is known as the R-CHOP combination of chemotherapy drugs – Rituximab, an antibody which binds to a target on the B cell cancers, Cyclophosphamide, Adriamycin and Vincristine, to combat the cancer,* *and Prednisoline, which are 5mg tablets to be taken for five days after the chemotherapy, 20 tablets a day to a total of 100mg. I had to impress on Mark the gravity of the situation. There was no way he was going to be back refereeing that season. The Adriamycin, which is a red cytotoxic liquid, can be damaging to the heart, for example.*

I turned up at 9am that Wednesday morning, my friend Steve Bates driving me. He was due to be leaving me there before returning in the evening. We had been told that the process of chemotherapy was going to take eight hours.

As I walked upstairs on to the chemo unit through the doors, the first thing that hit me was the smell of the drugs that were being administered to people. I will never forget that aroma, sickening and pungent, and the only thing I can imagine that comes close is the smell of a badly run old people's home. It will always live with me; returns readily to my nostrils whenever I start to think about it.

I pressed on down the long corridor with the private rooms off it until I got to mine, where they settled me into bed. Now chemo is never pleasant at the best of times, with its injecting of heavy duty drugs into the vein in your wrist through a funnel called a canula that is taped on, but you endure it because you have to. You somehow find the strength in these situations to get through it because what is the alternative? It didn't bear thinking about. In fact, I had one of the worst possible reactions, I was told.

After setting me up with a drip into my wrist, the nurse left for other duties but told me that there was a buzzer if I needed help. As the drugs began to enter my body, it seemed like I was being electrocuted and I felt more and more sick. I went to get the buzzer and realised it had been left on the other side of the room. I tried to shout for help but nobody could hear me. I crawled across the room and made it to the buzzer and soon help arrived.

I very soon found myself back on the bed with an oxygen

160

mask over my mouth and those heart suction pads applied to my chest. I went into fits. I was terrified, conscious but in some kind of traumatic dream.

Professor Tim Illidge: *Mark's reaction to his first day of chemo, and the chemo itself, was very unusual and certainly very dramatic. Some people can be very sensitive to smells, particularly when they are anxious and have a tumour in the throat, but no others among more than 1,000 patients have mentioned the smell he describes to me before. Mark then experienced an unusually severe reaction to the antibody Rituximab and went into full blown rigors, shaking violently. I had only ever seen one such reaction so severe before, amongst hundreds treated with the drug. Most people are fine, with around 20 to 30 per cent suffering a mild 'flu-like reaction, but this could have been life-threatening. The ECG monitor showed a high heart rate of 165 and his temperature reached 40 degrees. We administered intravenous steroids and anti-histamine. There was a moment when we thought of transferring him to intensive care but it passed and thankfully Mark pulled through with the supportive medications given.*

I calmed down and the crisis abated but they kept me in overnight, ringing Michelle's Mum and Dad to tell them to pass a message on to their daughter in Spain. Steve came back to pick me up the following day and my Mum and brother Paul came up from Welwyn to help me out.

I was glad when Michelle flew back. I could do nothing for myself and was wrecked. I just lay on the sofa being physically sick, flicking through TV channels. All I could eat for now were protein drinks, which tasted disgusting, and some mashed up Weetabix. My weight had dropped from 84 to 72 kilos – a loss of more than two stones. My urine would quickly turn red as a result of one of the chemicals they were putting into my body. That was scary until I was told what it was.

Soon we had to tell Lucy what was going on, because they

had told me that within two weeks my hair would start to fall out. Without frightening her, she needed to know why so that it would not come as a shock to her. It was tough for a three-year-old just at nursery school. First her mother gets cancer, then her father. She was resilient though, as kids are, but naturally she became very clingy to us.

Sure enough on day 14, I woke up to locks of fine hair on the pillow. By the next day, it had all come out. I took a shower and it just washed away in clumps. And not just from my head. I was bald all over, just a stubble left on the top of my head. When we went to pick up Lucy from nursery school, I was wearing a cap and sat in the car. Michelle later told me that when she picked Lucy up at the school gates, she told her that most of my hair had gone but it was still Daddy and she was to say I looked gorgeous.

When Lucy got in the car, she asked me to take the hat off.

'I'm sorry, Mummy, I can't say it,' she said by way of reaction. 'He doesn't look gorgeous, he looks horrible.'

Kids eh? You have to love their honesty. The next day, I had the stubble on my head shaved off and later we would take Lucy to one of my chemo sessions so she would know what was going on and feel that she was playing a part and we were all in this together as a family. She just took the session in her stride. She just liked playing with the control for the bed that raised it up and down.

Before that, though, Tim Illidge wanted to see me. Although the first session had decreased the size of the tumour, he was concerned by the pathology results from the lab. He wanted me to have another biopsy, at the Alexandra Hospital in Cheadle, with a surgeon he trusted, Mr Andrew Birzaglis, to clarify the underlying type of lymphoma and whether the same virus that causes glandular fever was 'driving' the tumour.

I was terrified of yet more surgery but it had to be done. Funny what sticks in your mind – like pulling into the car park at the Alexandra and receiving a text from Wayne Rooney to say he was praying for me. And then waiting to go for the op and having an arrow drawn on one side of my neck so that they got the right area. I certainly felt like a target. Again I got through it, again because I just had to – what choice did I have?

Professor Tim Illidge: *The second biopsy revealed that Mark had been suffering from the Epstein Barr Virus, which causes glandular fever, and it was integrated into the tumour. He was using a lot of his immune system trying to fight the virus, which was perhaps why he had a bad reaction to the first chemotherapy and why he was so wiped out. Ahead of the second chemotherapy, we gave him GCSF – Granulocyte colony-stimulating factor, an injection designed to boost the blood count and thus make him more able to cope with having the chemotherapy every 14 days.*

The second chemo was scheduled for three weeks after the first and this time I did not have as bad a reaction nor any of the same convulsions. Along with a drug injected into my stomach to boost my blood count, this time they put the liquids through the canula more slowly. I stayed in hospital overnight, though, as I was frightened not to be in a safe place if something happened like the first time.

Tim seemed to be more encouraged after that second session and told me that the cancer had been feeding off the glandular fever virus. They had, after all, been using the right combination of drugs for the chemo.

I had four more sessions to endure and Tim said I could change from having them every three weeks to fortnightly. I was all for it. Anything to speed up this process and get back to refereeing.

I settled into a routine but still felt exceptionally ill and frequently sick, struggling to focus on anything. I remember watching that amazing Manchester derby on TV when Michael Owen scored late to give United a 4-3 win over City but could hardly get excited. That was very unusual for such a football fan as me not to get a thrill from a game like that.

When I came home on the Thursday after the chemo, Michelle made sure that the heating was on nice and high in the house and then I would have a bath before a corned beef sandwich and a cup of tea. That would be the only thing I would eat until a bit of fish at our restaurant on a Sunday night when I next felt able to keep anything down.

I would not be able to surface until a Saturday 48 hours after coming home and then we would go for a short walk together, the three of us. I would start to feel better for a while and tried to take Tim's advice. He had said that he read a medical paper saying that if you could do some cardio-vascular work during treatment, you enhanced your chances of survival. I would go to the Bolton Wanderers' training ground on Mondays, Wednesdays and Fridays for short sessions on a treadmill or a bike. It was all I could manage but it got me out of the house.

As time went on and I felt a bit stronger between the chemo sessions, Keith Hackett let me come down to train with the Select Group, my fellow referee from Bolton Lee Mason picking me up and driving me down. Michelle and Lucy also came with me for a two-day session at Barnsdale, where they could use the pool while I trained.

Professor Tim Illidge: *Changing the chemotherapy from every three weeks to fortnightly came because of pressure from Mark. He wanted to get back as quickly as possible. There had been a national trial to see if a greater intensity helped to speed recovery and Mark was ready and willing to have the treatment every two weeks. Mentally and physically, sports people need to do exercise to help them both with their treatment and their recovery. Later, I would be astonished by Mark's exercise regime. His heart rate got to 180. He pushed himself like a madman to keep fit and was so motivated to get back to his job and prove a lot of folk, including myself, wrong.*

Despite the exercise, on the Mondays before the next treatment I would go into a downward spiral knowing what was coming up in the middle of the week. I would feel physically sick and be – Michelle told me – aggressive and short-tempered. I would fall into a cocoon of just lying on the sofa, not eating or sleeping properly. I had no energy to play with Lucy and felt guilty about that. There were a lot of days when I cried.

What often kept me going was the amount of goodwill I received from people as football rallied round. The Everton secretary Dave Harrison invited me to be a guest for one of their home games, all arranged by my friend and the Goodison kit man Jimmy Martin. I even managed to get to the odd Bolton match and I was in the tunnel at their game with Chelsea when John Terry, Ashley Cole and Joe Cole all came over and put an arm round me, wishing me well.

I also made it to Stockport County v Exeter City, to watch Mike Jones referee. It was his first season on the Select Group and I had volunteered to mentor him and tried to keep the commitment. I was pleased when he later described me as 'open and constructive'.

The Stockport manager at the time was Gary Ablett, the former Liverpool and Everton defender and in hindsight it was a poignant meeting with him. Some time after I got a call from Jimmy Martin at Everton asking me if I would ring Gary, who also had been diagnosed with a lymphoma. Gary had just got a job as Ipswich coach at the time. I got him in to see Tim Illidge but sadly he did not come through the treatment and died in 2012 at the premature age of 46, two years younger than me when I was diagnosed.

It was nice that people were sometimes making a fuss of me and for my morale's sake, I didn't want to be forgotten, which was why I agreed to BBC North West and Sky Sports coming to interview me at home. I looked rough but I also thought I might be able to offer encouragement to others going through this so they did not feel that they had to hide away when they didn't look and feel so good.

I was also very fortunate that as well as the texts and phone calls from people within the game, I received much goodwill from the general public, both in Britain and around the world, with TV having made referees recognisable.

One day, the postman brought a whole sack of letters, saying that they had been saving them up at the sorting office. 'My God,' he said. 'You're as popular as Father Christmas.' Some just had addresses saying: 'Mark Halsey, somewhere near Bolton.' Someone even sent Lucy a little teddy bear, 'so she is not feeling left out'. It was a heartwarming example of the kindness of strangers.

As for the rare idiot who made a comment to me one day, I just tried to shrug it off. I was paying in a petrol station when he said, 'Hurry up baldie.' I just turned and stared at him before walking off. I just had to remember all the good people.

I didn't always feel grateful, though, I have to admit. When I went to watch Bolton v Blackburn for a Sunday game live on Sky, I thought I would be okay to drive myself the ten miles or so to the Reebok but I was just not well, my immune system was shot and I felt freezing. The Sky TV cameras panned in on me and when I saw myself later, it hit home how ill I looked. I left just after half-time and collapsed once I got home.

Michelle called Tim the next day and he wanted me in at The Christie as I felt so ill with sickness and diarrhoea. They kept me in for a couple of days, which I detested. I felt even more ill as I just could not take that smell of chemo from around the place and could not wait to get home.

But it could all have been worse so much worse. All the while as I lay on the sofa at home watching the TV news, I was seeing soldiers being killed or maimed in Afghanistan. I was suffering enough, but was surviving. My family was suffering enough but what about theirs...

My chemo finished on November 25th but there was still 15 days of radiotherapy to be endured. I went in between the chemo and radio for fittings of a mask for my face to protect it from the radioactive beams that would be directed at my throat. It took three or four attempts to get it fitted right. We put up a Christmas tree to help me feel better, and also because most of December was going to be taken up with the radiotherapy.

I went back to the Christie for a CT Scan – similar to the MRI but not full body – on December 1st to determine the state of the tumour. I was not in the best of moods as I waited for the results. The treatment had got me down and I was depressed by it all. It didn't help that Michelle and I had had to cancel a trip to New York that I had booked as a birthday present for her.

Then Tim appeared. He was smiling.

Prof Tim Illidge: *Mark was charming but anxious until around the time of the last of his six chemotherapy treatments. He became irritable and angry that he had had to come into the hospital for a couple of days after the final cycle such was his disappointment and frustration. But I came to the conservatory, where he was sitting, with the results of the scan. The disease had cleared and I took great pleasure in telling him that he was in remission. Seeing people achieve remission – that's my joy. For me, it was like scoring a goal.*

I'm sure I remember Tim saying things like: 'I can't believe it... The scan is showing clear... The cancer is gone... It's great news.' I am not ashamed to say I wept tears of relief and happiness.

Grateful as I was, I just could not shake off feeling so ill, however, and at times I was still up at nights with diarrhoea. And I had 15 daily sessions of radiotherapy still to be endured. Tim said they were for 'consolidation', to mop up cancerous cells around where the tumour had been, but if I didn't feel up to it, it could be postponed for a short time. I wanted it over with, having calculated that I could be finally free of all the treatment by

December 24th, just in time for Christmas. It would mean that I was also on schedule to try and referee again in the New Year...

I had to take about 30 tablets a day, steroids and all sorts, for five days in advance of the radiotherapy, and the whole regimen played havoc with my insides. I wanted to drive myself each day so that I was no longer a burden to Michelle, who was still having to cope with the restaurant that had become a millstone to us.

But on day one of the 15, I was suffering from terrible gastro-enteritis. I had to get out of the car and dash back into the house three times before we could even set off for The Christie. I guess that's why they call it the runs. It was embarrassing dashing into the hospital when we did get there but luckily but I made it through without accidents.

The radio beams lasted two minutes each on neck and jaw, each side of my face, and from putting on the mask and taking it off, the procedure took no more than ten minutes. But while it may not have sounded like much, the whole experience drained me daily.

In fact, I began to feel as bad, if not worse, than with the chemotherapy. My throat was especially sore and it was like having thorns down there. It was strange, really. I knew the treatment had worked and that all of a sudden I was clear but I still felt like hell. I found it hard to derive any pleasure from anything. I just had to have faith in Tim's wonderful news that I was in remission.

As celebration that I had come through, we decided to have family for Christmas, around half a dozen of Michelle's as well as my Mum, who was shocked at my bald and pale appearance when she arrived. I did not feel well, though, and could not eat, which was hard when everyone was around the dinner table. The lining of my throat was just red raw. By 7pm, I was feeling so ill that I just had to ask them to leave, which they graciously did, so that I could have peace and quiet in the house and I soon took myself off to bed.

Still, no matter how bad I was feeling, however weak and sick, I had plenty now to cling on to. Tim had told me that I would start to feel better very soon and I believed him. I had trusted him all through my treatment and I saw no reason to stop now. He was, is, a great man as well as a great professional and I owed my life to him, for which I would be forever grateful.

At one point, it looked as if I may not even have seen another Christmas so it was a bonus just to be alive. And now, as a New Year beckoned, I wanted to get back to doing what I did best with the life that was being given back to me. To heck with any advice. I had had enough of feeling like this.

14

...AND THE DAWN

I was leaning on a goalpost at Barnsdale Hall on that trip there during my chemotherapy watching my Select Group colleagues go through their paces when Steve Bennett came up to me for a chat during a break in the proceedings.

'What you have gone through is an inspiration to us all,' he said to me. 'But just bear in mind that if you come back, and we all hope you do, they'll make it harder for you.'

I wasn't quite sure what he meant at the time but I would quite quickly come to know early in the new year of 2010.

I had plenty of reasons for wanting to reconnect with my fellow referees. One, quite simply, was for morale purposes, just for the company of being around kindred spirits who I liked and got on with. Another was the fear of losing my career, a fear that came both from within myself and from without, with a new, key figure in the PGMOL putting me under pressure.

At the get-togethers I did attend, I pushed myself and managed to complete a running programme under the watchful eye of our sports scientist, Simon Brevitt, even though I was way behind the others. I kept remembering what Tim Illidge said about keeping active improving your chances of survival. I would collapse at the end of the session, but a few of the others picked me up.

In the afternoon, they would put the massage table in the seminar room so that I could have a lie down as the technical meetings were going on but I would often fall asleep during the sessions. Then again, I probably did when I was healthy sometimes. Armed with the good news from Tim before Christmas that I was in remission from the cancer, I began to feel better in the January. The feeling of having thorns in the back of my throat gradually eased and I started eating better. I had no sense of taste, but I could enjoy the texture of food again, at least.

I used to have a sweet tooth for chocolate, but that went, and I found bread, cheese and potatoes hard to swallow. Because there was now a big cavity in the back of my throat on the right side where the tumour had been, sometimes food would slip into it and I had to regurgitate it. It could be embarrassing in company and sometimes food would even come back out of my nostrils. The only good thing was that it all kept my weight down.

Now that I was feeling better, I really began to think that I could make it back to referee this season. Tim had certainly made a mistake in telling me I wouldn't, because I like to prove people wrong. I went to Tim to see what he thought about the idea. He smiled and agreed that I could have a go.

And as well as my own self-motivation, I was spurred on by people phoning or texting me to say that I was missed and they would like to see me back – people like José Mourinho, Sir Alex, Sam Allardyce, Owen Coyle, David Moyes and Gary Megson. In addition, my old coach Dave Allison, now head of the Football League referees, came to see me during my chemo and reinforced my goal of wanting to come back.

There was also a big element of wanting to try to be an inspiration to those suffering from cancer to show them that they could beat it and get back. At that time, Lance Armstrong was a big inspiration to me with the way he had come back to cycling and won the Tour de France after his cancer and I wore the yellow Livestrong wristband to remind me of what he had done. I do remember wondering how he managed it all when I was struggling so much physically and to my great disappointment I would later find out just how, when his performance-enhancing drug use was exposed.

I was also feeling a bit under pressure to return. The PGMOL, led by Keith Hackett, had been fantastically supportive of me, as had the board of directors – Peter Heard, the chairman, Richard Scudamore, chief executive of the Premier League, and Mike Foster, the Premier League secretary. Keith's assistant Keren Barratt had also been to see me during my chemotherapy.

The organisation had kept me on full pay and I could not want for anything from them. I needed it. I had a mortgage that I had increased due to losses in the restaurant but no critical illness cover – unluckily. After Michelle had become ill, we decided to take some out but when we got round to it and filled in the form, my diagnosis came the very week that we did.

Things were changing at the PGMOL, though. Keith Hackett had reached 65 and the PGMOL said that his contract would not be renewed so he stepped aside and became a Premier League ambassador. Mike Riley took over fully that January and it immediately became clear to me that he was going to put me through hoops before I would be allowed back into the Select Group.

I didn't think they could sack me. There were only two grounds for that, which comprised failing the fitness test and poor performances. Well, I had passed the test the previous summer and had had only one performance, which was satisfactory.

And age was no longer a factor. I may have reached the old retirement age of 48 but two years previously, back in 2008, Pete Walton had successfully challenged the PGMOL under European legislation about age discrimination and they could no longer enforce that. My own view was that with us being fitter than ever these days, to lose good experienced men at 48 would anyway have been daft.

On top of all that, I thought they would see what a terrible

PR move it would be to terminate the contract of a man who was recovering from cancer. We were on rolling one-year deals, from August to August. In fact, I had hoped that new man Mike Riley would simply tell me not to worry too much about this season and that my place for the following season would be assured provided I passed a fitness test in the summer.

But I got no such feedback from Mike. In fact, the impression within our group was that he wanted the older referees – myself, Steve Bennett, Alan Wiley and Pete Walton – out of the way so that he could bring in new people. In a few months time, that would be confirmed for us by a worrying personal meeting with him...

At this time, it combined to leave me feeling that while I wanted to give it a go for the remainder of that season, I also had to. My motivation was always to prove to myself that I could do it but now it seemed I had to prove it to my bosses.

I went to see Mike in mid-January to tell him that I was thinking of taking the fitness test I needed to pass anew ahead of coming back but he immediately said no. He wanted me, he said, to have a second opinion before I even attempted it, and would need some physical tests in London. I told him that I had had the all-clear from one of the best in the world in Tim Illidge, but Mike was adamant.

What also upset me was that Mike told me he had made up his mind about this in the middle of December. He had omitted to tell me that, however. I was to go to the Royal Marsden in London, another great cancer hospital, for a consultation, he said. I could have already done it by the middle of January.

When I went back to Tim to tell him about all this, he told me not to worry. He would write to the Marsden on my behalf, he said, and would tell whoever was dealing with me that I was doing well and in the clear.

I went down to London and had an interview and tests at the

Marsden, with another fine man in Professor Kevin Harrington, and also some cardio-vascular tests with the England doctor Ian Beasley and physio Gary Lewin at a private clinic. As I entered the hospital, I recall being stopped by a workman in the street who was a football fan and who had recognised me. 'Great to see you fighting this illness,' he said, which cheered me up

A favourable report duly came back to the PGMOL. I would be allowed to continue, they said. They could hardly say anything else but I got the impression that Mike was none too happy about it and my relationship with him had not got off to a great start, though in hindsight I felt he would have preferred me to have just gone away.

It was strange because I thought he would have seen all this as a good thing for the PGMOL. It should have been good public relations for them given all the grief we as referees get. This was the human side of us. But Mike would not see things like that as a totally different character to his predecessor Keith Hackett. Keith was open and supportive, Mike more closed. It just wasn't his style. He was also probably very nervous in his new job.

Possibly he was worried that this went beyond any good news story and could come down to legal issues. I don't think they were concerned about me messing up in a match so much, but would explain this treatment by saying that they had a duty of care to me. More likely, they didn't want to be liable if things went wrong. If I dropped down dead during a game, maybe they thought my family would sue them. I offered to sign a disclaimer but that cut no ice.

The whole regime was different now. I remember requesting to share a room at Warwick with Pete Walton but was told by Keren Barratt that they would decide who shared rooms and if I didn't like it, I knew where the door was. Nobody in the group liked that. When we quietly tried to change their arrangements with the front desk, they changed the rooms back again.

In addition, the PGMOL's sports scientist Simon Brevitt was

stopped from giving me a fitness programme, and also told he was no longer allowed to speak to me, I guess because that might mean they were responsible for any problems. So instead, I went to Bolton Wanderers' doctor and physio and they gave me a training schedule. Owen Coyle, then manager, would often run with me and I spent long, hard times in the gym with two of the injured Wanderers' players, Joey O'Brien and Sean Davis, who kept me going with their great sense of humour.

I also went away to our place in Spain for a week and ran out there. It was part work, part pleasure. The referees I had been closest to during my illness and who were ringing me regularly came out with me as I wanted to say thank you for their support. One night, I bought Lee Mason, Alan Wiley and Pete Walton a Champagne dinner on an emotional night – with them all having a cry and setting me off – that was just missing my other great friend Mark Clattenburg, who could not make the trip.

I decided to have a go at the fitness test at an athletics track in Warwick at the end of January. It involved six 40 metre sprints within 6.2 seconds each, with 90 seconds of recovery time between each, and then 20 runs over 150 metres inside 30 seconds with 35 seconds of rest between each. It was a punishing test, one that would later intensify with just 30 seconds of rest between each being introduced by Mike Riley, probably to try and make life tougher for us more experienced ones.

I got through the sprints all right but, even with Mark Clattenburg running with me and encouraging me, I was never going to complete the longer runs. I managed three or four before collapsing. I was wrecked. Kelly Wright, who was now PA to Mike Riley, came to watch along with Simon Brevitt and they both consoled me, as did Mark, who put his arm round me but when I was back in the dressing room alone, I just burst into tears.

I couldn't even ring Michelle, so distraught was I, and Kelly did it on my behalf to explain what had happened. I couldn't face the other refs, either. I just got in my car, numb, and drove home. My mobile was ringing all the time with colleagues wanting to help me out but there was only one person I could really talk to.

I rang Tim Illidge but barely remember the conversation that he told me lasted 20 minutes. He also said that I was completely distraught and told him there was no reason to go on living. Only in the next few days would his words, both consoling and encouraging, sink in: I had taken the test too early and needed to keep a sense of perspective.

Right then, though, I felt I was finished, that I would never be able to pass this test again. What was I going to do? I had a life back but my career was over, it seemed. I should have felt grateful to be alive, at least, but at that moment I just didn't.

I had been a full-time professional since the start of the Select Group, a top ref since 1996. I had cancer. My wife had cancer. I was coming up to my 49th birthday. Who would employ me? Where was the money going to come from to pay the mortgage and the bills and support Michelle and Lucy? The severance package from the PGMOL at that time was just £1,000 for each year of service, which would mean £9,000. It all felt very frightening.

I wasn't expecting a free ride back but I thought this was a shabby way to treat someone recovering from cancer. I would have thought they would have wanted to facilitate my return as caring employers, rather than put me through hoops. The strange thing was that later, at the end of the season, Mike Riley would give me a bonus of £5,000. I was grateful and thanked Mike, who told me I had earned it.

It must have been compensation for missing out on all the match fees for the season and I guess it was easier for him as someone not good at communication to make a financial gesture rather than any human, emotionally supportive, ones.

Michelle booked us a half-term holiday in Lanzarote in the February and I thought I would use the time to think about my future. In the event, I decided to use the time to get myself fitter. I really was going to show them, I had decided, if that was how they wanted to play it. I was not having this. I spoke to the fitness coach at Bolton, Jimmy Barrow, and got a programme off him for some warm weather training.

I was up at 6.30am every morning, creeping out of our hotel room so as not to wake Michelle and Lucy but to be back early so we could still have the day together. I felt like Rocky in the film as I went about it all, running the roads before too much traffic was about.

Working to Jimmy's regime, I started with a series of eight 50 metre runs inside two minutes then took two minutes' break. After that, I would be blowing hard but would force myself through a weights session in the gym.

Then it would be breakfast in the hotel dining room with Michelle and Lucy and it was nice to be recognised by some English people, who said it was good to see me getting healthy again. By now my hair was growing back, if a bit haphazardly.

All the while I had mixed feelings. I had a goal, a need to prove to myself and others that I could do this. But I also felt I shouldn't have needed to. All I had wanted was for Mike Riley and his assistant Keren Barratt to tell me to work myself back to fitness gradually, that if I took the test in the summer and passed, a new contract would be there for me. But I believed I needed to come back this season to show them I was worthy of a new contract.

I still felt nowhere near fit enough to come back when I returned to England but I went to Simon Brevitt in the March at one of our get-togethers and told him that I wanted to do another test. The next thing I knew, I had bumped into Mike Riley in the foyer and he told me that this test would count if I failed it. You were only allowed three failures a year before being taken off the list. This would be my second and would increase the pressure on me for the final one in August that would decide if I would be offered a new contract or not. I could only defer to Mike, who insisted that there would be no special treatment for me as he had to be fair to other referees, but I was suddenly worried again. I went back to Simon Brevitt to inform him of what Mike had said and to tell him that I thought I should pull out. He told me not to worry, though – he would make sure it wouldn't count. He reminded me that I had passed one at the beginning of the season and had been through a life-threatening illness. It was good of him to be so encouraging.

With the pressure off, I went and did the test, Mark Clattenburg again accompanying me. And while I was running round a track with him, the lads were on the infield doing their training session, watching it all unfold.

I managed the sprints okay but then came the 150 metre runs.

The first three were okay, then I got to five. I was blowing now and the 50-metre walks between each were becoming more and more welcome.

I got to ten and could feel Clatts's hand on my back pushing me on as we did the walk in between. This was as tough a physical test as I had ever done.

By 15, I was done. I couldn't go on.

'Keep going,' Mark said. 'You're there.' I could also hear the lads on the infield shouting: 'Go on Tax!' The old nickname derived from the cab-driving days made me smile. I just had to keep going.

I got to 19 – and knew I had done it as you were allowed one failure. I was determined to finish, though. In the end, Clatts pushed me over the line for the 20th and all the lads came running over to congratulate me. I was spent, lying exhausted on the track. Steve Bennett came and picked me up to give me a hug. I wept as everyone cheered me.

Not everyone wanted to celebrate with me, though. As I got to my feet, I saw Keren Barratt, who had come to watch, walking away. He had not come over to congratulate me. Everyone noticed and pointed it out. That confirmed everything I was thinking and needed to know about how I was regarded.

It was bizarre. Football was welcoming me back. Around that time, Manchester United invited me to their Champions League home leg against Milan and the then chief executive of the FA, Ian Watmore, asked me down to Wembley for the England friendly against Egypt. My employers, though, did not seem to see me as an asset.

Watching Soccer Saturday on Sky with Jeff Stelling and his crew, who always made me laugh, gave me itchy feet and having passed the fitness test, I was ready to rock and roll.

I began my comeback at the end of March with a low-key reserve game at Hinckley between Leicester City and Scunthorpe United and it was all very emotional. Michelle came, as did Keith Hackett and Alan Wiley, and I had good support. Tears were shed in the dressing room before and after the game.

I enjoyed it but I was rusty and off the pace, by no means match fit. It was the same in another couple of reserve games I took in the next fortnight, one night game at Bloomfield Road between Blackpool and Rochdale and an afternoon game between Derby County and Sheffield United at Ilkeston. I was hoping that one might be off, with the pitch being so heavy.

Looking back, I was not ready, certainly not for the Premier League, but I was desperate to get back into a first-team match and I was badgering Dave Allison at the Football League for him to hand me a game.

It was due to be Accrington Stanley v Barnet in League Two but I had to call the game off shortly before kick-off, much to one of my old clubs' annoyance after they had already travelled up from Hertfordshire.

Finally, the big comeback – well, it felt big to me – was upon me.

Rotherham United 1 Port Vale 2
Coca-Cola Football League Two
Don Valley Stadium, Sheffield
Saturday, 3rd April, 2010

Michelle drove me over the Pennines, Lucy in the back of the car coming to watch me as well. Life felt good again this springtime.

There to support me were Keith Hackett and Howard Webb, a Rotherham season ticket holder, and it was good to see their smiling faces. Keren Barratt also came to check out my condition.

In the dressing room was a letter from the Rotherham manager Ronnie Moore expressing his delight at my return, which was a nice touch. I got a standing ovation from a crowd of 3,721 when I walked out for the game and I could hear the tannoy announcer urging them to give 'a fantastic welcome back for Mark Halsey'.

Every player also shook my hand before the game, expressing their good wishes for my return and it was very emotional. Players can be pains in the neck, but they can also be very generous.

It was a very enjoyable game, won by Port Vale with goals by Craig Davies and Marc Richards in three second half minutes, Josh Waller's late goal proving only consolation for the home side.

There were a couple of iffy challenges but I gave them the benefit of the doubt and I had no need to issue any cards. I was still struggling for some fitness on a heavy pitch, my legs feeling like lead, and I had to use all my experience to get through it but the Vale manager Mickey Adams was kind enough to say that I was still a different class even though I had been out for seven months.

My assessor was Stuart Martin, who showed me a lot of sympathy and empathy with a mark of 75. In all honesty, though, I knew there was still a lot of hard work to be done. This was nowhere near good enough for the Select Group and the Premier League.

I was shattered when I got home and spent the next day sprawled on the sofa but now there was a sense of satisfaction to the fatigue. I was back.

I was straight back on to Dave Allison at the Football League for games and he gave me three matches in eight days. First, I did Oldham Athletic v Bristol Rovers on a Saturday, with my assessor, Mike Ryan, saying I should have given a second yellow to a Rovers player. I didn't think so and Dave Allison didn't either. It was good to have a disagreement again.

Then it was another League One game on the Tuesday, Carlisle United v Leeds United, before Notts County v Rochdale in League Two the following Saturday. I got good receptions everywhere, my only concern being that I wasn't getting Select Group assistants, which I felt I should being Select Group myself. After asking for them, I did.

I was trying to test myself, to get back up to speed as I knew I was not quite there, behind the play a bit, using dead ball situations to get back into position. An abrupt end was put to that, however.

On the Monday after, I got a call from my friend Paul Rejer, who was in charge of the assistant referees in the Select Group, to say I would be down for Wycombe Wanderers v Swindon Town but when the appointments came out, I was not on the list. I rang Paul back to find out what could have happened. My suspicions were confirmed. Mike Riley took me off and put Stuart Attwell on the game, I was told. It would happen on other occasions too.

I immediately rang Mike to find out why. He said he had to be fair to all those on the National List who had been reffing all season, that it was not right that they should not be getting a game. He would never say that if dropping a ref from the Premier League to the Football League, mind. But, I said, I needed games under my belt. He then said that he didn't want to stress me, that he thought I might need a rest after four games in 18 days. Fair enough, I said, but why not ring me to discuss that?

He would not, he added, phone other refs to discuss that sort of thing and I was not a special case. I did not want special treatment, I said, but since they had never had a referee coming back from cancer, it was unavoidable that I was something of a special case. I felt I deserved a bit of communication. It was bad man management, I said. He took exception to that and I said I took exception to his treatment of me, knowing how much my comeback meant to me. 'Fine, thank you,' he said and put the phone down.

The next time the Select Group gathered at Warwick, I was called into a meeting with Mike, along with Alan Wiley and Pete Walton. The other most senior referee, Steve Bennett, was unable to attend that week and Mike said that he would be ringing him to have the same conversation with him that he did with us.

Mike made it plain that he no longer wanted us around. He couldn't enforce the retirement age due to Pete having invoked European legislation but he said he wanted to bring on younger referees and that we were blocking them. I think he was probably expecting us to quit there and then but there was no way I for one was going to.

I had worked too hard to get back from cancer, to pass the fitness test and return to the middle. I thought it unbelievably insensitive to say what he was saying to a man who had just come through such trauma but then I would grow to expect nothing better of Mike, who – from where I was standing – had few social skills and a confrontational style in managing men.

I have no idea whether his actions would have been legal, though there are plenty of rules about the treatment of people coming back to work after cancer. Maybe he would back off in the coming months because he had been advised that he was on dodgy ground and could face a serious lawsuit. Besides, I had experience and plenty still to offer. I still believed I was one of the best referees in the country.

When I was given Coventry City v Watford in early May, a Championship game with nothing on it, I made my feelings known to Keren Barratt, who had come to check me out again, possibly because he lived locally, about my conversation and meeting with Mike Riley. At least it meant they communicated with me the following week. I was called in at Warwick and told that I would not be assigned to a fixture on the last day of the season in the Premier League as I had hoped. The hits just kept on coming.

I was disappointed. I knew I was not quite physically right yet and not ready to take charge in the top flight and I understood their decision on that. I did think, however, that they could have given me a fourth official's role, perhaps at Everton for their game against Portsmouth, who were already relegated. I had started the season at Goodison Park and it would have been a nice way to end what had been a traumatic nine months.

But it was clear with the new regime that this was going to be a battle for me. That much became clear when I organised a fundraising dinner in the May for The Christie hospital at the Lancashire County Cricket Ground at Old Trafford. I wanted to give something back to the hospital that had given my life back to me and I had some profile to be able to do so.

It was an amazing night that raised around £70,000 and I was flattered and honoured that Sir Alex Ferguson, Roberto Mancini, David Moyes, Owen Coyle and Sam Allardyce all agreed to come and sit at the top table. José Mourinho did a video link that had the 1,000 guests entertained. Sir Alex gave a great speech mentioning his rivalry with José and just as he did, the marquee in which we were all dining began to shake and rattle in the wind. 'Bloody hell,' said Sir Alex. 'I can't even escape him here.'

There were some notable absentees, however – my fellow referees in the Select Group. There was a PGMOL block on them attending. They should not be socialising with managers, went the argument, but I thought it was petty and killjoy. They could have sat elsewhere in the room. It was an example to me of a new mood of miserable austerity coming down from the top. Of course there had to be professional distance on a match day, but what was wrong with everyone getting together now and then for charity?

I ended the season thinking I had come through an amazing period and experience – one that had taken me to the depths as well as lifting me to great heights of hope – but that I had a major problem with my job. My performances in my only six professional games that season had been acceptable, even if not yet up to Premier League standard, so they could not sack me on that. I had better pass that fitness test come pre-season, though.

It wasn't even that they needed to sack me, as that would have looked crass from the outside, but they could refuse to give me a new contract, citing an inability to keep pace with a top game and maintain standards. It certainly looked like they weren't going to encourage me to reach those standards again with an understanding of my condition, mental and physical. It was beginning to look as if they might even be trying to get me to quit.

15

BACK TO THE TOP

Michelle always had a routine at the end of the football season. On the Monday, she would wash all my kit and pack our clothes and on the Tuesday we would fly out to Spain for as much of the summer as we could. This year, the anxiety about my health had lessened, thankfully, but there was still a concern for this worrier: what about my career?

That meeting with Mike Riley in the spring when he talked of getting rid of us older referees had shaken me and I believed I was just one failed fitness test away from being dumped. I would have fought it through the courts, mind, and would have had plenty of sympathy, I felt sure, for what I had been through and what he was putting me through now.

I needed to pass that test again so I could remain on the Select Group and I embarked on another intense training regime, five days a week from 8.30am to 11.45am, running on beach and roads, doing spinning sessions, weights and bike rides. I had my next door neighbour in Spain and friend Fred Barber, goalkeeping coach at Bolton, geeing me on.

Usually I do nothing for the first two weeks of the time out there and drink some wine and eat well but this time I had to be dedicated non-stop. Michelle had strong words with me, trying to get me to loosen up especially after the year we had had, but I told her that she and Lucy would benefit if I extended my career, that I was doing it for them as well. I also felt very driven to be an inspiration for other cancer sufferers, to show them what was possible.

In all honesty, with no idea of what I might yet do out of football, we needed the job and the money. I also knew that I would be a misery around my family if refereeing was taken from me before I was ready to quit.

I popped back to England for a couple of days to attend the annual conference of the National Group referees, comprising both the Select and National List officials, at a hotel in Hinckley. And I noticed this year that now Mike Riley was head man, the after dinner entertainment on the Friday had been scrapped. I couldn't wait to get back to my training regime in Spain, though. I was a man possessed by now.

It was all worth it when I took the fitness test at the Pingles athletics track in Nuneaton on the Select Group's pre-season return in the August and passed comfortably. I felt really good and was touched when Howard Webb came up to me and said that he didn't know how I had done it, that it was inspiring how I had come through the last year.

I had an emotional echo of that time 12 months earlier when Everton requested me for a special pre-season friendly against Everton of Chile and the FA, who allocate referees for international meetings, kindly agreed.

It was eerie going back into the dressing room where I had felt so ill, where I had had my head in a towel a year earlier, but it was a great way to lay some ghosts.

There were 26,000 in the ground that night, including the people who meant most to me in Michelle, Lucy and Tim Illidge and I got a standing ovation just in the warm-up. When I came out for the match, which Everton won 2-0, Pete Walton, who was my fourth official that night, kept the players in the tunnel momentarily and allowed me to emerge on my own, to another moving reception.

186

It just went to show what a great club are Everton, who had struck a special commemorative plaque for me, and how much human kindness their supporters have. They can be volatile and demanding, mind, as are all fans with a passion for the game and know it inside out.

I would not be sent back to Goodison all season after that, though, and I was upset to discover later the reason why from Howard Webb, who was told by the PGMOL management. That night, Lucy was a toffee girl, that lovely Everton tradition of a young girl being chosen to throw toffees into the crowd. They had not liked that, apparently. The powers that be had clearly decided that I was too close to the club.

I couldn't help wondering if it was also to do with that charity dinner I had organised in the May because neither was I sent to officiate at a Premier League game all season at Old Trafford or Manchester City's Etihad Stadium. In fact, I wouldn't even do a Manchester United game away from home in that first full come-back season. It should have been a celebration of a good cause that you would have thought the PGMOL would have wanted to be associated with for some good publicity but instead it felt like I was being punished. I would end up being baffled and hurt.

Not that I knew any of this at the outset of the 2010-11 season. I was still trying to give Mike Riley some benefit of the doubt, despite being told I was yesterday's man, and I still thought I could do a job. Besides, they needed me, with none of those young bucks that Mike wanted to promote yet thrusting them-selves forward.

And I was grateful to him and the organisation for giving me a Premier League game on opening day. In fact, it delighted me when I found out on the Monday before it at 4pm, the time when the weekend appointments are announced – and are often on the internet before even referees hear about them. My return cap-tured some media attention in the week leading up, and I was even

187

allowed to do a couple of interviews – under the watchful eye of Phil Dorward, the Premier League press officer who had responsibility for the PGMOL, of course.

The middle of the week brought bad news with the death of the Exeter City player Adam Stansfield with colon cancer and it made me reflect on the random nature of this disease, when I survived and he didn't. I would later be happy to get involved in a foundation bearing his name.

For now, I was determined to treasure my own good fortune in being able to carry on in football in what would be a big occasion for me. It must have been something a bit special, in fact, as Mike Riley, who only goes to the big games, would even turn up. It would be the only match of mine he would ever attend as general manager.

Wigan Athletic 0 Blackpool 4
Barclays Premier League
DW Stadium
Saturday, August 14th, 2010

I was nervous the night before, nervous the morning of the match, nervous as Michelle drove me the 15 short miles to Wigan, nervous when I got in the dressing room, nervous in the warm-up and nervous when I blew the first whistle for kick-off. And I loved every moment of being nervous.

As I came out, I received another warm reception from the crowd and when I came over to hand the coin I had used for the toss to my fourth official, Martin Atkinson, the two managers Roberto Martinez and Ian Holloway shook my hand and wished me well. As had their assistants, Graham Jones and Steve Thompson respectively, when they came to hand over the team-sheets pre-match, telling me that it was good to see me back.

It probably helped that I had two first-year assistants in Paul Thompson and Billy Smallwood. While I needed their help, they needed mine too as they coped with their own nerves and it got me out of myself. I was certainly fortunate to have an understanding assessor in the great former referee George Courtney.

Paul actually got an offside wrong, and I mistakenly disallowed a Blackpool 'goal', but thankfully it didn't matter with the newly promoted club stunning the Premier League on opening day with a remarkable result. In fact, they were three up by half-time with two goals from Marlon Harewood and one by Gary Taylor-Fletcher. Alex Baptiste added a second half goal.

It all felt good. My fitness was good and my feel for the game was returning. There were no major problems in the game, thankfully as I just wanted a quiet afternoon free of controversy, with just two bookings in it, one for each side.

At the final whistle, drenched in sweat on a sunny day and emotionally and physically drained, I looked up to where my little knot of supporters was sitting – Michelle, Lucy, the now retired Keith Hackett, and Tim Illidge.

Later Tim would tell me that he had had stilted conversations with Mike Riley during the afternoon that revealed my boss's lack of understanding of what I had gone through and was still going through. Trying to be generous, this was new territory for the PGMOL, I guess, and they did not have precedent of how to treat someone with cancer.

I had hoped that speaking to Tim might have

opened Mike's eyes a little, and made him a little more tolerant, but it seemed not. While I might have thought I was back, he seemed to have other ideas.

The uplifting start was followed by a down-to-earth assignment – Aldershot v Stevenage in League Two. Now don't get me wrong. Every game is a big game for someone and teams at the bottom of the Football League deserve a good referee every bit as much as the top clubs in the Premier League. Besides, I always prepare the same each week wherever I am sent and a game at any level needs your full attention. I got on with it but did wonder why I wasn't back in the Premier League.

That feeling would grow over the coming weeks and months. I would be given a good game, like a TV match between Birmingham City and Liverpool or a derby that needed a firm hand like Wolves v Aston Villa, but then I would go three for four weeks without a game.

Worrying about being marginalised, I needed all the light relief I could get. I was invited to do Jamie Carragher's testimonial between Liverpool and Everton during the September international break and we had some fun.

One of my assistants, Bobby Pollock, was an Everton fan who ran the line with a replica shirt under his top until ten minutes from time when I gave him the signal. After removing the top, he proceeded to line in an Everton shirt, to the Kop's part amusement, part disgust, keeping his flag down for Liverpool offsides all the time. Jamie, an Everton fan as a boy, even took a penalty for them though in a red shirt and scored, nipping in as Yakubu stood back to take it.

By late September, I was ringing Keren Barratt to find out what was going on. I knew others did it regularly so I thought I might do it for a change. I told him that I was not just moaning about the quality of my appointments but pointing out that it was difficult to expect a referee to do a top game then not have another for another few weeks and immediately pick up the pace of it. The Premier League is an unforgiving arena and a referee needs to be up to speed with a run of games if he is to retain match fitness and thus the respect of the players.

Keren just told me to look at where I had been this time a year previously. My reply was that it shouldn't matter, given their own criteria. Yes, I hoped for some tolerance of my situation as I came back, but I had passed the fitness test and should be considered the same as all the other referees when it came to appointments. After all, at the end of the previous season, Mike Riley had said that I should be, hadn't he? Now they were treating me differently. How did that square?

I am guessing again – because no one ever told me – that they were trying to be gentle with me on my return to regular, full-time action. But then they should have been talking to me about these things, discussing, explaining. Perhaps if they had told me, for example, that there was nothing this week but that they had something good in mind for me next week, or that they wanted me to go and be fourth official to a young ref to help him out, I might have understood better. The lack of communication was frustrating.

At least I began to be treated as just another referee by people within the game, notably when I went to do Stoke City against Liverpool.

Stoke under Tony Pulis were always a tough team to referee, there was no getting away from that. They were physically strong, a tall, big side, and so much was going on in penalty areas around corners and free kicks – and from their trademark long throws – that you needed eyes in the back of your head.

You have to let games have some physicality and in all honesty, sometimes you have to ignore things, otherwise you would be blowing up every 30 seconds, which would be no fun for anybody involved, from players to supporters. It just turns the referee into the centre of attention and nobody wants that. The referee certainly shouldn't.

The atmosphere at the Britannia Stadium is also one of the loudest and most hostile in the country and I for one was caught between admiration for what Tony did in getting them into the Premier League – succeeding as an unfashionable manager at an unfashionable club – but staying alert to all the physical stuff.

Anyway, at half-time going down the tunnel, Tony was in my ear, as usual. 'Don't you be fucking bowing to them just because they are Liverpool,' he was saying. 'Tony,' I said, 'What are you talking about? Just shut up.' I don't know what he was moaning about. Stoke won 2-0 and I sent off Liverpool's Lucas Leiva, my only red card of that season.

It was actually nice to be normal, not to be treated with kid gloves. Once they were shouting at me, I knew I was back properly. I was Mark Halsey the referee and not the cancer sufferer. Players were soon back in the groove, too. I also had to learn not to play the cancer card myself when the going got tough, I have to admit.

I did Birmingham v Chelsea in the November and turned down a penalty claim by Chelsea. Ashley Cole was having a right go at me. In fact he spoke to me as if I was a piece of dirt on his shoe. I just lost it with him at half-time in the tunnel.

'After what I have been through, you fucking talk to me like that,' I said. 'Show some respect.'

I shouldn't have said it. Shouldn't have brought up my illness. He said that he did have respect for me and I apologised to him. To be fair, I never heard anyone, player or manager or even fan, say anything nasty in my vicinity or to my face. Now on social media, that would become a different story...

It was a season also tinged with poignancy. I was assigned to do Wolves v Spurs and it turned out to be a fixture that quickly followed the death of Dean Richards through a brain tumour. Dean had played as a centre back for both clubs and it was an emotional day at Molineux.

The players made sure that it was a rousing game as a fitting tribute and I was determined to let them get on with it, though that was not good enough for my assessor, Derek Bray. He came into the dressing room after the game and said I should have issued a red card to Alan Hutton early on for a foul on Matt Jarvis. I thought it was debatable whether it was denying a goalscoring opportunity or not but Derek said he would be marking me down, and I duly got 7.9, which meant that I would not be receiving bonus money, which was all totted up and awarded at the end of the season based on performance marks.

The next week at Warwick, the incident was shown to a group of referees from New Zealand over on a course. They all agreed with the yellow card I had shown. I always thought there was a maxim – if in doubt, don't show the red and I had a doubt.

Besides, if I sent somebody off early in the game, and the game became 11 v 10, would it have been the memorable 3-3 draw that everyone enjoyed? I suppose the Wolves fans would simply say that I should have applied the letter of the law – though, as I say, I had a doubt – but it is not always that simple in the context of games.

A referee always has to take into account whether a game is niggly, whether the players are nasty or not, and what the offence is. There are several factors that need to be considered before taking the ultimate sanction of a red card, in my view.

That game was in early March and my next Premier League game, bizarrely, was in mid-April – Liverpool v Manchester City. I had even had to ask to do a game during that period to keep my eye in so in international week I was sent by Keren Barratt to do Brighton v Swindon in League One, the home side then on their way to promotion on a long unbeaten run, in one of their last games at the Withdean Stadium. Again I got a good reception and recall a wag in the crowd berating me for giving a free kick when 'he hardly touched him'. Hardly was just enough, I said with a smile and he smiled back at me.

But Liverpool v Manchester City five weeks after not having done a Premier League game? And live on Sky on a Monday night? I couldn't believe a colleague who suggested that the powers that be might be setting me up to fail because they wanted me out of the business. Surely they wouldn't do that would they? I know our game is political but that was surely too Machiavellian. Too much was at stake for the two clubs for my bosses to be playing games like that. In the event, Liverpool won 3-0 and there were no problems, just one yellow card.

In fact, the following Sunday in his column in the *Mail on Sunday*, the Liverpool manager Kenny Dalglish said that he had been surprised that none of the journalists had asked him about my performance after the game because it had been so good. I was also told that season by the England physio Gary Lewin that I was the then national team manager Fabio Capello's favourite referee because I let the game flow.

Mike Riley and Keren Barratt would have hated Kenny's column. It was as if they simply did not like referees having profile and being in the media in any way, even if it was no fault of that referee. And it was probably best that Capello's comments did not reach them. They just didn't seem to like praise for referees from managers, who appeared to be the enemy rather than fellow contributors to the game.

There was one weekend when I didn't mind missing a Premier League game. It came when I took the Exeter City v Plymouth Argyle game in late April, which I asked to do as I had accepted a request to be a patron of the charity in the name of Adam Stansfield, the Exeter player who had died of colon cancer at the beginning of the season and whose funeral I attended.

The invitation came through an Exeter City employee Andy Cole but at first I told them that I couldn't do it, living so far away. I was still unsure when he said it was just to be a figurehead as if I get involved in something, I like to take proper part. But I was happy to lend my name to it and do what I could. It was all so sad. Adam had a wife, Marie, who was just 34, and three young children in Jay, ten, Taylor, seven, and Cody, four.

Michelle, Lucy and I went down to Devon for the week before the game and stayed in a caravan, and on the Saturday I refereed the League One game before taking part in the Great South West Run over five kilometres on the Sunday, then officiating a memorial game on the Monday between Exeter and a collection of players from Adam's previous clubs.

It was good to be there, to be alive, and do it, a special weekend that I recall with pride. I raised a good sum of money, including a few thousand pounds from the lads at Bolton and a cheque for £2,000, written straight away as soon as I asked him for a donation by a generous man called Sir Alex Ferguson.

Not, I should say, that my time in Devon was all sweetness and light. Plymouth lost 1-0 and were on their way out of League One. I commiserated with the Argyle manager Peter Reid but he had just two words for me, the second of which was 'off'. I understood his feelings.

I had a tough, but enjoyable, finish to the season with Stoke v Arsenal – always a volatile fixture, the more so since it was Aaron Ramsey's return to the Britannia 18 months after breaking his leg in the corresponding fixture the season before.

It all kicked off this time with Jack Wilshere involved in an altercation with Jermaine Pennant that warranted a yellow card for both.

Arsenal were in the process of losing 3-1 and with it seeing their title hopes disappear for that season, Jack was clearly frustrated. I managed to calm it down and it perhaps helped that

I had got to know him a little bit when he was on loan at Bolton and I trained at the club.

Those who think I might have got too close to some of the figures in the game should understand that often it helps with man and game management. In my opinion, referees need working relationships rather than distance that can be interpreted as an arrogance from the man in the middle. My assessor Uriah Rennie seemed to agree and gave me a good mark.

I finished the season with Newcastle 3 West Bromwich Albion 3, the home side pinching a point after being 3-0 down. It was a great way to end what was a successful year on and off the field, albeit one that had an undercurrent of mutual suspicion between me and my bosses at the PGMOL.

I was pleased to be alive and coming successfully through my three-monthly check-up visits back to see Tim Illidge, who would examine me, feel my throat and take blood tests that would show that my body was keeping the disease at bay. And I was lucky to be back doing what I loved and at the top of my profession again – if not as often as I would have wanted.

My body was still not quite there but I developed little coping strategies. For example, after all my treatment, my mouth would produce no saliva and I had to take plenty of fluid on board all the time. I would leave water bottles dotted around the pitch – on the halfway line, in the goals – ready to grab them when there was a break in play. Sometimes when players went down, I would playfully give them a little kick and say that they needed to stay down and bring the trainer on. Injuries to players always gave me the chance to rehydrate.

I worked my socks off that season to be there and deserved it. I felt proud of what I had achieved. I hoped I had also shown other cancer sufferers that this illness could be beaten and that with hard work, application and dedication, you could get back and do what you wanted to do with your life, not only functioning but achieving at a high standard. Bill Shankly once uttered the immortal sentiment that football is not a matter of life and death: it was much more important than that. Actually, I'm not sure he would have really believed it deep down but certain that he said it with tongue in cheek.

Still, my life had shown how significant the game was and there was more evidence to come. The sad events of the following season would certainly show how important it was to those of us who loved it, but that we needed to keep it in perspective.

16

FOOTBALL, LIFE AND DEATH

Strange as it may sound, as a referee, it is not always pleasing to receive compliments. Mostly they are gratifying, when sincere, whether from supporters, journalists, players or managers, and one such came my way on opening day of the 2011-12 season from the new Chelsea manager Andre Villas Boas for my handling of a tough game for his side at Stoke City. Perhaps he was trying to make a good first impression with referees, because I had turned down a penalty for his side when Frank Lampard fell over rather than being brought down and I was unsighted when Fernando Torres might well have been awarded one.

Sometimes, perversely, compliments can make you angry, however. How so? A few weeks later, I took charge of Norwich City v West Bromwich Albion. At the local airport afterwards, as I waited for my plane to Manchester, I ran into the West Brom party. Several of them came over to praise my performance and say 'well done' for my handling of a difficult game.

'Well done?' I said. 'Well done? I am pissed off with you lot. I am going to get done now.'

I guess Albion were happy because they had won 1-0 but my anger stemmed from one of their players, Gabriel Tamas, landing an elbow on James Vaughan off the ball a long way behind play and with my back turned. It left the Norwich player with blood streaming down his face and came in the 93rd minute, making it doubly ridiculous. I didn't see it – and if I had it would certainly have been a red card and a penalty to Norwich – but I knew I was in for trouble.

Afterwards, the Premier League match delegate Mick McGuire, a former player and PFA official, told me he had not seen it. When I spoke to James Vaughan later, he obviously knew he had been hit, but didn't even realise it was an elbow. And the referee, in the heat of the action, is expected to see all this?

Meanwhile, the assessor, Kelvin Morton, told me in the dressing room that he had seen it from the stands and that I should have done. I thought that was rubbish. Mick McGuire was also in the stand and hadn't seen it but Kelvin did? I sensed I could get taken off the next round of fixtures for this.

Normally, the delegate's report takes a week to arrive but the assessor's report comes to you by email within 24 hours, or Monday morning at the latest for a Saturday match. When mine took three days, I knew there was a problem. Had Kelvin consulted with management about what to put in the report?

In the meantime I received a text from Andy Gray at the talkSPORT radio station about the incident and I responded simply that I was gutted I hadn't seen it. When he read it out on air during his morning show that he and Richard Keys did after leaving Sky TV, I guessed I was in for more problems, for which Andy apologised when I rang him to say that I had expected the text to be private. I got over it, though. Richard and Andy have been good supporters of referees.

The following week, as demotion for missing the incident at Norwich, I was fourth official at a game then told at the next Select Group get-together at Warwick by Mike Riley and Keren Barratt that I would not be refereeing the following Saturday. It was for a breach of protocol in sending the text to Andy Gray, I was told. I felt they were looking for something against me and it was actually more down to the assessor's delayed report. There was a double punishment involved here.

I wondered quite how their reasoning squared with the referee who sent a text round all the Select Group of officials on the final day of a season when he was in charge of the biggest match, in which he said braggingly: 'I will decide the title today.' I suppose mine was made public while his remained private, even though I believed it was a dangerous overstatement of what his role in the game should be. He was called down to London and Premier League HQ and given a warning but there was no suspension.

I felt it depended on who you were and whether you were in favour with the current refereeing management. When I was again left off the fixtures for a second week, I was convinced I was being harshly treated. I did get a call from Roy Hodgson, the then West Brom manager, to apologise for the incident and I understand he also rang Mike Riley to say that there was no way I could have seen it but it cut no ice. Other referees would not be punished later in the season for missing things off the ball but I was. Howard Webb, for example, would miss a stamp on Scott Parker by Mario Balotelli in a Manchester City v Spurs match but he was supported by management. Some in the Select Group were asking why I was not similarly supported.

Later in the season, I had some harsh words with Kelvin Morton when he was my assessor for a game between Portsmouth and Millwall. I told him I was unhappy about him saying that I should have seen it and we argued. Neither of us held a grudge, though. Kelvin had been good to me during my illness and had often emailed me. That day at Fratton Park he would also give me a good mark.

My absence of three weeks from the middle and consequent rustiness may have had something to do with a couple of decisions I got wrong in the match between Wolves and Newcastle at the start of October.

When the Newcastle centre back Steven Taylor fouled Wolves' Jamie O'Hara on the edge of the penalty area, I gave a free kick outside the box. Later, on the replay I would see that the offence had started inside the box and should have been a penalty to Wolves.

Then, late on, with Newcastle 2-1 up, the ball came into their area from a corner and Wolves scored. I saw my assistant's flag go up and he indicated that the ball had gone out of play from the corner and so I disallowed the goal. Again with the benefit of a replay later, it looked inconclusive and I should have let it stand but you have to go with your assistant. He was the one in line.

Afterwards, Mick McCarthy came into our dressing room and had a go at the assistant, Ron Ganfield, and though I stood by Ron, I could only have sympathy for the Wolves manager. 'We make honest decisions,' I said to Mick, 'and if we have got it wrong, I apologise.'

In the aftermath, I served another suspension, this time for just one week, for missing the penalty and spent a Saturday with the family – nice as that can be on other days but a strange empty feeling for anyone involved in the game – but it would be more serious for Mick.

He would get the sack as Wolves failed to get themselves clear of relegation later in the season, and I felt for him, as I do with many managers who are victims of decisions. Who knows what might have happened if his team had taken that point, or even all three with an early penalty that might have changed the game? But then we didn't have technology. We are only human – like the strikers who missed the chances that might have also kept Wolves up if they had only scored.

I got hammered by the match delegate that day, Denis Smith, the former Stoke manager, with some justification and I asked him to apologise to Mick for me. The next time I saw Denis, he said he had since seen Mick, who was philosophical about it. That would be confirmed for me personally when I saw Mick at a dinner to celebrate Sir Alex Ferguson's 25th anniversary as Manchester

United manager and said sorry. 'These things happen,' he said.

Dave Allison, once my coach and really helpful to me as Football League referees' officer when I was making my comeback, rang me up as a friend to tell me not to worry about the Norwich and Wolves incidents. I was still a good referee, he told me. I also received texts and emails from managers like David Moyes, Owen Coyle and Alex McLeish telling me not to get down about it all but I was. I hated getting things wrong.

It was just a shame that nobody from my management at the PGMOL could do me the courtesy of ringing me up to reassure me and lift my mood. I was beginning to feel somewhat isolated, concerned that other referees were getting support in messages from management after certain games.

In fact, during my time under Mike Riley of more than three years, you could count on one hand the number of times I received any texts of support from him. I do recall one praising me for a penalty decision in a Sunderland v Chelsea game, and another to say I was right not to give a penalty for a handball where the ball had been blasted at a defender in a game between Sunderland and Fulham. Neither did he come to watch any of the big games – even if they were few under his leadership – that I took, where he did for other referees.

I complained after the Wolves suspension about the inconsistency of treatment that different referees were getting – and some of my colleagues were ringing me up about it – and lo and behold, I suddenly got assigned to a top game after three weekends in the Football League. It was strange to be brought back for Everton v Manchester United knowing how hard it can be to pick up the pace of the top flight. Your match fitness is inevitably going to be questionable. It was also nerve-racking. This was where I wanted to be but I was worried about getting big decisions wrong. I hoped I wasn't being set up to fail.

Michelle was in the stands that day with Lucy and gradually began to get fed up with two blokes nearby shouting that the referee was not fit, as they noticed I had to take a lot of water on board during breaks in play. Eventually she turned on them and announced that I had to take plenty of water on because I had just fought cancer to get back to the top and had no saliva in my mouth.

'How do you know that, love?' one of them asked her.

'Because he is my husband and this is his daughter,' she said.

It appeared to do the trick, Michelle later told me, and they soon shut up. I got through the game fine, with just three bookings, and there were no controversies as United won 1-0.

Actually, fitness seemed to be an issue as assessors would now often say to me that I did not look as fit as I used to. It riled me. Of course I wasn't as fit after what I had been through but I was starting from a high base as one of the fittest and I had still passed the fitness test to be here.

Besides, and despite all the concerns about match fitness and some of the treatment I thought I was getting, I knew in my own mind that I was still operating at a high level. David Maddock of the *Daily Mirror* newspaper even noted in a match report of the Everton v United match: 'So much to be admired in this game, not least from referee Mark Halsey, who allowed it to flow and allowed proper tackling. His performance should be videoed by the FA and distributed as a blueprint for the rest of their match officials.' Fat chance of that, I thought. They wouldn't want me shown in a good light.

Then came a November weekend that brought another controversy and problem for me but which paled into insignificance compared with some shocking news for football.

I refereed the Stoke v Blackburn game and thought all had gone well as the home side won 3-1. In fact, there was not one yellow card, which is extremely rare for a game at the Britannia Stadium.

Later I got a phone call from the assessor after *Match of the Day* had shown two supposed elbows by Blackburn's Steven Nzonzi on Ryan Shawcross and Greg Whelan. Peter Roberts, who had been an assistant but never a Premier League referee before becoming an assessor, said they were not red cards, though. Maybe one was a yellow. And so we had trial by television pundit again, when nobody else had noticed the offences, neither of which on replay I thought was a red card anyway. I knew that would not be the end of the matter, though. Not with Mark Halsey involved.

Events were overtaken the next day, however, when the football world was stunned by the announcement of the death of Gary Speed. I personally was numb all day. I had refereed Gary many times over the years during his playing days with Leeds, Newcastle and Bolton Wanderers and he was a pleasure to deal with. I then got to know him well at Bolton during my training there and also came to know his father Roger.

I phoned the assistant manager at Newcastle, John Carver, who had been with Gary at Sheffield United, and with whom I had become friendly over the years. John frequently used to phone me up for advice on refereeing – such as issues of whether his club should appeal certain decisions, for example. John hadn't heard and like me was stunned when I told him. So too Sam Allardyce and Sir Alex when I texted them. What made it all the more shocking was the manner of Gary's death, with him being found hanging, though an inquest would be unable to reach a verdict of suicide. Gary was a gent and a model professional, always first in the gym. He had come with Big Sam to open our restaurant, Sottovento, which by now we had finally sold, to our great relief, getting rid of the mortgage on it.

On the Monday at Warwick, the group agreed with my suggestion that we have a minute's silence. That came before a conversation with Mike Riley when he said I would be getting a phone call from Tarik Shamel, Head of On-Field Regulation at the FA, about the incidents involving Nzonzi, who would ironically later sign for Stoke.

When the call came, Tarik told me that Mike had told him there should have been a sending off. Not for me, there shouldn't, I said. Tarik left it up to me to decide the next step. Reluctantly, feeling under pressure to deliver the result Mike wanted, I agreed rather than cause a problem and have yet more bad blood with him. It would certainly have been interesting to see what would have happened to me had I not agreed. I told Tarik that I didn't really care, though, given Gary's death. There were more important things.

I was in the same boat as Lee Mason that time when Wayne Rooney swore into a TV camera in a game at West Ham. No referee would have sent off for that, but Lee came under pressure to report that he hadn't seen it but would have given a red card if he had seen it. That way, as in my case, the FA could take retrospective action, though with me it seemed that it was Mike who wanted Nzonzi punished rather than the FA.

On the following Saturday, I was sent to Newcastle v Chelsea as Mike Dean's fourth official and it was an especially emotional day. John Carver and I just embraced and burst into tears when we saw each other. He came to my house in Bolton before the funeral the following week and we drove over to North Wales together before going on to the reception.

After that Stoke game, I seemed to be out of favour again – surprise, surprise – and it would be another month before I got another Premier League match, just Portsmouth v Southampton in the Championship in between. Tough local derby? Pack your bags for the South Coast, Halsey.

It was indeed tough but there was some light relief. As a Southampton player went to collect the ball for a throw-in, a Portsmouth fan picked it up and rolled it down the line, forcing the player to fetch it. 'Bit daft,' I said to the fan. 'Your team's losing

1-0.' Cue a barrage of abuse from him and others around him. I had to smile. Pompey did force a 1-1 draw in the end though.

The next Premier game I did, almost four weeks after that Stoke game, was Fulham v Manchester United, and I admit I was lacking match fitness as United ran rampant on the break to win 5-0. Pete Walton, my fourth official, was in my earpiece about the fact that I was labouring. 'Come on, get up with it,' he was saying.

I did not appreciate being mucked about so much by my employers, and put in positions where I looked as if I was struggling, and was getting texts and calls from my fellow referees wondering why I was being treated so badly. One day, in a mood of frustration, I phoned Sir Dave Richards, chairman of the Premier League, and told him of my unhappiness at not getting games and not being given reasons why from my management.

The Premier League, after all, were the overall bosses of the Select Group as senior partners in the PGMOL. I guess I shouldn't have done it, but it was the action of a man who was hurt and frustrated at not being allowed to do the job he believed he was good at. I told him that if they didn't want me, they should pay me up.

I guess he told Mike Riley to start communicating with me as the next thing I knew I was getting a phone call to come and meet him in London. I immediately contacted my union, Prospect, and spoke to the head, Alan Leighton, and my representative, Pete Walton, to ask them I if I should get them involved. They advised that it was best to keep it informal for now and just to let Mike know my feelings without antagonising him.

It was an uncomfortable meeting with Mike, Keren Barratt and a Human Resources rep from the Premier League, Jenny Bhalla, and I wished I had had a representative with me. I told them that I felt marginalised and was not receiving any feedback or encouragement from them about my performances and the games I was being assigned to.

They soon turned it around and it emerged that they were actually unhappy with me because of a speech I had given at a Referees' Association dinner on the Isle of Man. Someone had complained to them regarding a light-hearted comment about sometimes wanting to shoot assessors that I had made during the talk, which was largely about the last year since my cancer treatment and getting back to refereeing. There seemed to be no problem at the time but apparently they took offence.

I was staggered, to be honest. I said similar things at the many refereeing functions and charity dinners I did without any trouble. Later, I would ring up the organiser in the Isle of Man, Tommy Crowe, to express my displeasure. I was not going to do dinners again if what I said was going to be taken out of context and relayed to my bosses.

Mike also told me that there had been complaints from some in the Select Group that at the Warwick weeks that I was not sociable enough and retired to bed too early. I told him that I had to get to bed early because my illness and the treatment meant that I got tired earlier in the evenings but I would try to integrate more with the group if they felt that. I was certain they didn't, though. I knew most of them well enough for them to tell me if they did and nobody had said anything. I think Mike was just trying to find things wrong.

I was still close to many of my colleagues, including Pete Walton, Mark Clattenburg and Howard Webb, and had good relationships with pretty much all of them. Howard was also having his own problems. He told me it had been suggested to him by the management that he might care to resign from his UEFA and FIFA positions – one year after taking the World Cup Final – because they believed it was time Martin Atkinson became our premier ref abroad. Howard refused.

In the end, Mike got round to admitting to me he was annoyed by my approach to Sir Dave Richards and that I should not have gone above his head. There would be formal proceedings if it happened again, he added. Fair enough, he was probably right and I was wrong.

I drove from the Premier League offices on that Friday to stay overnight near my game the following day musing about how petty I thought Mike and Keren were being. At least, I thought, I have cleared the air from my point of view and I hoped Mike would have seen where I was coming from – somebody passionate about what he did. I also hoped he might see that he might need to change a bit and become a bit more approachable to avert people feeling the need to go to an outside mediator. We would find out.

I had more immediate things to concentrate on. Someone was having a laugh with the FA Cup tie I was sent to referee on the first Saturday in January.

Gillingham 1 Stoke City 3
FA Cup 3rd Round
Priestfield Stadium
Saturday, 7th January, 2012

My first visit to Priestfield after that notorious play-off between Gillingham and Manchester City was against Burnley back in the 2005-06 season and I got fearful abuse, though was amused when the away fans started chanting: 'Mark Halsey, Lancashire.' Burnley won 3-0.

It would be no better this time. I came out on to the pitch to warm up to plenty of boos and as I was running around the perimeter of the pitch I came across the groundsman and the Stoke goalkeeping coach having a go at each other.

The goalkeepers have a set time before the game they are allowed to use the goalmouths before ending at 2.30pm and the groundsman was objecting that they were outside the time. The first problem to sort out, even before kick-off.

I then had a bucketful of abuse as I ran round some more – 'Halsey you twat,' 'You knob,' 'You cost us,' – the usual sort of pleasantries.

As I stood stretching, a group gathered to shout some more and I had a word with some stewards who moved them on. Fortunately, I heard nothing about the cancer and some good people behind the scenes even said that it was nice to see me recovering.

It was more of 'the referee's a wanker' when I walked out before kick-off, with Tony Pulis, in his usual fashion, telling me not to be influenced by the crowd. He was having a bad day of his own, mind   some time after that notorious play off when he was Gillingham manager, he had fallen out with the chairman Paul Scally, who childishly would now only allow Tony in certain areas of the ground.

Fortunately it all passed off peacefully, with just one yellow card for each side. It was heading for an upset when Gillingham took the lead through Danny Kedwell but three goals in 15 minutes by Jonathan Walters, Cameron Jerome and Robert Huth saw the Premier League side through.

At Gillingham, you have to go past the back of the main stand when you come out of the changing rooms to walk back to the car park and there were some home fans still milling around as there always are waiting for autographs – though not mine usually and certainly not on this occasion.

'Your watch working yet?' one of them wondered very loudly. 'Yes thanks,' I replied. 'I got a new one from Sir Alex Ferguson.'

Fortunately I had a more welcoming experience in the next round, after not originally being allocated a tie. I was having acupuncture on my back and hamstrings at Bolton when my phone rang with a call from Peter Elsworth, the Senior Referees Administration Manager at the FA. Martin Atkinson was injured; would I do Liverpool v Manchester United? I was taken aback, so out of favour was I with the FA. In fact, I thought they had deleted my name from their list of referees available for games beyond the third round.

Of course I would do it. And I would love going back to Anfield for my first visit since my illness. It was also the first encounter between the two clubs since Luis Suarez was banned for eight games after being found guilty by the FA of racially abusing Patrice Evra, who would be booed throughout the tie.

While there was always that undercurrent, fortunately there was no major incident and just one booking, Apart from that, all was quiet as Liverpool won 2-1. I like to think I contributed to nothing nasty happening with my handling of the game. It was strange that the high-up people at the FA who chose referees, Neale Barry and David Elleray, didn't seem to think so, however. I would not get another game in the FA Cup that season.

I seemed to be back in favour temporarily with Mike Riley, though, after our clear-the-air meetings. Perhaps he was aware that people at the Premier League like Sir Dave Richards were now watching. Whatever it was, I began to get some big games again.

I was sent back to Anfield in the March to do Liverpool against Arsenal, a game in which I gave a penalty for Suarez after he had been brought down by Woijtech Szczesny. Robin Van Persie scored an excellent winner for the away side. I then did Everton 1 Tottenham 0 and Fulham 0 Swansea 3.

Amazing – three Premier League games in three weeks. Mind you, Mike was getting a bit short of officials and by the end of the season, the Select Group would be down to just 16 full-time referees, so perhaps he didn't have a lot of choice in the matter.

After the Fulham game, I was waiting in the departure lounge at Heathrow to fly back to Manchester when I saw a picture of Fabrice Muamba on the news relating to Bolton's game at Tottenham. I knew him well from training at Bolton and thought to myself, 'Blimey, he doesn't score many goals. Well done, Fab.'

My mind went back to one he did score – when I was at the Reebok, during the treatment for my illness, for a game against Wigan. At training the previous day, I had told him that it was about time he scored a goal and he said he would score one for me. He did, in a 4-0 win, and ran over to where I was sitting to mouth: 'That was for you, Mark.' It was a big lift to me that day.

Gradually I grasped what the story was about, though – Fabrice had suffered a heart attack on the pitch. I was shocked. When I got back home, I phoned the Bolton chairman Phil Gartside, who told me that they were not holding out much hope for him. I couldn't believe it, though now seeing the TV pictures of the episode, I could see how frightening it all was.

I decided to travel down to London to see Fab in University College Hospital but was not allowed by the PGMOL management to go on the Tuesday as I was apparently needed at the Warwick get-together. And so I went on the Wednesday.

I was shocked when I entered the room, his father at his bedside, to see such a magnificent athlete laid low. He had regained consciousness early in the week but was now dozing.

'Fab, it's Mark,' I said a few times. Suddenly he opened his eyes and his father and I looked at each other, tears welling up.

'Thank you for coming Mark,' he replied softly. He began to talk slowly and recalled that goal against Wigan. I stayed 15 minutes, not wishing to stay longer and tire him out. It was moving and uplifting, a miracle that he had survived, really, and now beginning to come through it. Later I would be on Sky Sports News coming out of the hospital, the reporter's voiceover noting that I was used to hospitals. I would get used to more hospital visits in another couple of weeks over Easter. As well as going back to see Fab, who by now looked fab, to give him a hug, I called in on the Aston Villa player Stan Petrov who had been diagnosed with leukaemia earlier in this sad season and was having treatment at a cancer hospital near UCH. He was looking better, though it was clear to me that, like Fabrice, his playing career was over.

The hospital visits probably counted against me, especially being shown on TV, with my closeness to people within the game being resented, as I continued to be messed about for the remainder of the season. I didn't care though. It was more important to show solidarity on a human level with people I cared about rather than worry about what they thought at the PGMOL.

I did do some good games, officiating as Suarez recorded a wonderful hat-trick for Liverpool at Norwich and Demba Ba scored with an amazing shot from wide for Newcastle at Chelsea – another like that Alan Shearer volley that I loved being close to – but I was also seeing some strange decisions around me or being on the end of them.

My great friend Pete Walton asked for me as his fourth official at his final game before he took up a new job as head of referees at America's Major League Soccer, Everton against West Bromwich Albion, and Pete also wanted Dave Bryan and Glenn Turner, one of Graham Poll's assistants for that fateful World Cup match, as his two men running the lines.

In a typically small-minded gesture, Pete was denied Glenn, however. Glenn and Mike Riley had fallen out after Glenn had been stood down from matches following Glenn's refusal to accept what he considered to be an unfair and inaccurate assessment by Kelvin Morton at an MK Dons match.

After absence for a while, Glenn instigated grievance procedures that would not be upheld. He argued that Kelvin had said one thing to him after the assessment then another at the grievance meeting, which Kelvin denied. It led to Glenn walking away from the game that season, disillusioned. It was sad. We could hardly afford to lose such good men.

At least Everton proved they had some class that day of Pete's retirement. They presented him with signed shirts and a decanter in David Moyes's office. Probably best nobody told Mike Riley who might well have put a block on it.

During the second half of the season, I found myself fourth official three weeks in a row and my own unhappiness at my bosses was resurfacing. My only consolation during what was a disappointing period was being José Mourinho's guest at the home and away legs in Munich and Madrid of the Champions League semi-final between Bayern and Real. José was always the perfect host, though his side were eliminated.

After doing a Championship play-off game between Birmingham City and Blackpool, I was told by Paul Rejer at the PGMOL office that I had been taken off a game on the final week of the season and made a fourth official and wanted to know why from Keren Barratt. 'I am one of your most experienced referees,' I said, but he simply wondered why I was moaning. I wasn't, I said, I just wanted to let him know I was disappointed. Any good professional, especially a senior one, should be disappointed by being omitted. It was the same for referees as players.

In the event, I was switched to take Swansea v Liverpool after Mark Clattenburg cried off with an injury. But I continued to feel that my life was being made difficult. That was to be confirmed by something that happened at the end of the season.

I asked to be allowed to officiate at a charity fun day at Manchester City's Etihad Stadium where teams were paying to play, with children's cancer research benefiting. I was told, though, that instead I had to attend the referees' end-of-season golf day and dinner, even though several referees had been given permission to miss Warwick meetings during the season. I appealed to the management, saying that this was good public relations for referees. In the end they relented but it was a struggle I didn't think I should have had to endure.

Their attitude to me was also shown when it came to my end-of-season bonus, an award to the Select Group worked out by Mike Riley. It was determined by two factors, on-field and off, along with Mike's discretionary input.

On-field involved the number of games and quality of performances, and the top man could get up to £15,000 depending on the marks he had received from delegates and assessors during the season. Mine was a middling £7,000. I felt I was punished twice for that suspension following the talkSPORT text – denial of a match fee as well as low bonus.

Off-field was about what you contributed as a referee and involved such things as talks to referees' associations and charity appearances. It went from a scale of zero to six and it could be worth up to £1,000 and more.

I thought I deserved something decent as I had done 17 referees' association functions and many cancer charity appearances, along with officiating at a tournament representing the Premier League. My rating was zero, according to Mike, however. The Isle of Man counted for too much against me, it seemed, unjustly in my eyes.

I was disappointed, angry even. I could sense which way the wind was blowing. My professional life was becoming more and more difficult and the time was coming for me to reconsider my position and what now to do with the rest of the life that had been given back to me.

I was now in my 50s and was the longest serving and most experienced referee in the Select Group. Those might have been seen as assets in some professions. In mine, with the bosses I had, it seemed to me they were being viewed as defects. Contemplating my future, indeed, was probably exactly what they wanted.

17

THE FINAL INSULTS...

I knew my time was coming to an end and sensed that 2012-2013 might well be my final season as a referee. There was the lack of support and concern from my bosses at the PGMOL, Mike Riley and Keren Barratt – what felt like their barely concealed desire for me to quit, indeed – which was draining my spirit and morale.

It had started even before the season began when someone in the know said that I could expect a diet of one Premier League game a month and plenty of fourth official and Football League appointments, a strategy designed to get me to walk away. I didn't believe them. At that time.

There was also a series of unsavoury events that were to come to pass in a shocking season for all referees and which duly proved why my instincts were right. It was time to get out.

The cause of my disillusion came from the sorry aftermath of two Premier League matches that I refereed on live television at either end of the season. In between was scarcely any better with a host of incidents that illustrated how sick football had become, notably one that involved my good friend Mark Clattenburg and brought one of our best referees to tears and the verge of a nervous breakdown as he was unable to defend himself publicly.

For me, the season started badly with the repercussions of my sending off of Tottenham's Tom Huddlestone in a 1-1 draw against Norwich City. From my angle it looked like serious foul play as Huddlestone slid in on Jonny Howson with his foot raised.

My decision to award a red card was supported by the match delegate – Peter Shreeves, my old Spurs junior team coach who had let me go all those years ago. Finally I got to go back to White Hart Lane as a professional with him there.

This season, however, the PGMOL had a new system in place. Instead of the assessor system of ex-referees assigned to the match to write a report on you, we now had evaluators who did not attend the game. There were seven of them appointed, each paid £14,000 a year, and their job was to sit down with a DVD of the game in their homes and study it minute by minute.

They would go through every play, every free kick, goal kick, corner, every challenge. They would assess your yellow cards to decide if they were right or wrong and they would point out where you should have given cards if you didn't. You received their evaluation by email within two days of the game.

Clearly my evaluator decided by watching the DVD that I should not have issued a red card to Huddlestone and it was withdrawn. I am all for admitting mistakes but this wasn't one and the FA set a bad marker down for the season. It happened to Howard Webb as well, when they overturned his red card for Wigan's Jordi Gomez against Sunderland.

They almost seemed to be saying: We will not back our referees but have the right to change their decisions – except when it suits us to say we can't re-referee games. That would be seen some months later.

For now I shrugged my shoulders and got on with it. Except that they didn't give me much to get on with. I did Nottingham Forest v Birmingham City a fortnight later then drove up to the north east to do the Great North Run the next day with Mark Clattenburg. We ran for the Sara's Hope Foundation, a charity that sends sick children and their parents on much-needed holidays, part of my sponsorship money also going towards the children's cancer unit at The Christie. Sir Alex contributed a cheque for

£3,000 and José one for £2,000. It was a good day and I ran the half marathon in a reasonable one hour and 52 minutes, though the last four miles seemed to take forever. Mark and I had plenty of time to notice a few Geordies having a laugh by waving red cards at us as we struggled on.

My spell on the naughty step for my own red for Tom Huddlestone came to an end the following week and I would see why. It was one of the most sensitive fixtures in the English game at the most sensitive of times. Mark Halsey was seen as a referee who would not inflame a delicate situation.

First, there was a fourth official's role to fulfill the day before, at Wigan v Fulham. During the match, I was horrified when referee Lee Probert went down with an injury after a hefty challenge from Steve Sidwell that had me wondering if Lee had upset the player. 'Get up you softie,' I was shouting into his carpiece. If I had had to go on and take over from him, it would have meant not being able to take my big game the next day.

Liverpool 1, Manchester United 2
Barclays Premier League
Anfield
Sunday, 23rd September, 2012

I was really relishing this one. It would be my first Premier League game for three weeks and I always loved going to Anfield, especially for such a big game between two giants with long histories, the two highest number of titles, and a fierce rivalry. I texted Sir Alex after learning of my assignment to the game.

'See you Sunday,' I said.

'How emotional is that going to be?' he texted back.

The reason for that emotion was that at last the Hillsborough report into the tragedy of 1989 when 96

Liverpool fans lost their lives at an FA Cup semi-final had finally been released and confirmed at last that the fans themselves were not to blame but were instead the victims of bad policing and safety at the Sheffield Wednesday ground.

We all remember where we were on hearing the news that day. Me? I was refereeing Potters Bar v Evergreen in the Herts County League reserve division and watching events unfold on television as mine was a 4pm kick-off. Like the rest of the country, I was stunned.

In the background to this as a sub-plot was also an enduring hostility between Liverpool's Luis Suarez and Patrice Evra of United. As managers try to get players to do, I told myself that it was just another football match. Except it wasn't. It was the highest category of safety for the police. But I knew I was capable of handling it. Certain other people may have not had faith in me any more but I did.

Later, in his report, the match delegate Denis Smith would note that I gave a very brief but to-the-point pre-match talk to the captains and team officials making sure that everyone was in no doubt about what was expected of them. 'The atmosphere at the ground created its own pressure on this very special day,' he said. 'The officials were very aware of this before they stepped on to the pitch.'

Before kick-off, United's great ambassador Sir Bobby Charlton presented Liverpool's record scorer Ian Rush with flowers and the two captains released 96 balloons into the air. The atmosphere was a poignant mixture of sadness, relief and anticipation – and anger at the sheer length of time at 23 years it had taken to get justice. The Manchester United supporters behaved themselves well, Sir Alex having done a good job during the week of impressing on them the need for respect.

It was a game when you just wanted everything to go smoothly. Some hope. Football refuses to be sanitised sometimes.

There were a couple of early challenges that might have warranted yellow cards but I opted to issue stern warnings. One was by Jonjo Shelvey for the home side, the other by Evra. After that latter one, Steven Gerrard came up to me and insisted that it should have been a yellow card.

'So should Shelvey's,' I said.

'Fair enough,' said Steven. 'That's one-all then.'

The evaluator's report that came in the cold light of day 48 hours later would say that I should have booked both Shelvey and Evra early on but the evaluator was not trying to manage a game in the heat of battle. I had to take the context and mood into account. This was why I was given the game, after all. I was a referee with experience and a reputation for defusing explosive situations rather than a stickler who might antagonise.

I did not want to create early problems for myself nor inflame the game but in truth, the game needed no help with that. When Shelvey and Johnny Evans went into a challenge together midway through the first half, I immediately thought that Shelvey had gone in higher and it was a red card. When I saw the gash on Evans's leg and Shelvey run off, it confirmed what I had to do.

I wanted to give myself thinking time, though, and walked away from the incident. It also has the effect of players following you and drawing them away from the incident so that injured players can get treatment with space around them, and a clutch of players is not concentrated in one small area. My body language probably said that I did not need this now but the red card for Shelvey was necessary and justified.

Afterwards, Brendan Rodgers would say that I should have sent both players off but Shelvey's offence was worse, even if Evans had also shown studs and warranted a yellow card. As his early challenge showed, Shelvey was a loose cannon, had lost his head. If he had stayed down, I might just have shown both players a yellow but Shelvey knew what he was doing, in my opinion, which took the offence from a yellow for reckless play to a red for serious foul play endangering a player's safety.

I also annoyed Brendan by not giving a penalty for a claim on Suarez then giving one for United when Glen Johnson clipped Antonio Valencia. But Johnson didn't argue. It was a penalty. I was later disappointed when Brendan went off on one after the game in interviews. He is not usually like that.

But then, I tried to put it down to a disappointed manager who had seen his side lead through Steven Gerrard's volley early in the second, only to concede to Rafael Da Silva and Robin Van Persie, with that penalty, for a 2-1 defeat.

I was relieved when it was all over, satisfied that I had had a good game, something which would be confirmed by the delegate's honest report, that also highlighted the fact that I was not as young as I once was – though I believe if there were any shortcomings, they were also down to not being match fit due to lack of regular Premier League games.

'Mark Halsey was excellent in handling the players, talking to them throughout and doing his best to keep the game flowing,' Denis Smith said. 'Although he isn't as mobile as he once was, his reading of the game meant that he was always in a credible position to make his calls.'

It confirmed to me what Denis told me in the dressing room afterwards he would be saying and his report would also discuss the three key match incidents: the Shelvey sending off, the Suarez penalty appeal I turned down, and the penalty for Valencia I did give. Denis said that he believed I got all those incidents right and they were confirmed by the DVD. He would give me a mark of 27 out of 30.

I had been given the game because I was a peacemaker and despite the potential of the occasion, the game had passed off peacefully. I would be far from blessed, however.

Driving home, my phone rang. It was my son Jason, asking if I had heard about the stuff on Twitter. I had heard of Twitter but never paid it any attention. Being on the internet and on social messaging forums wasn't my thing and I wasn't on it. I had seen how plenty of footballing people had got in trouble with comments that were picked up by all the news media outlets. Besides, we wouldn't be allowed to as referees.

Jason started reading out some of the postings on there about me and my performance in the game. It was disturbing and frightening. They were saying things like, 'I hope your cancer comes back,' and 'I hope your wife dies of her leukaemia and your daughter too,' and 'If I had a bullet I would use it on you.'

When I got home, Michelle was even angrier than I was, having looked up the stuff for herself on the computer. She phoned Greater Manchester police to register a complaint and then Phil Dorward, the press officer assigned to the referees at the Premier League, to tell him what she had done. His reaction surprised us. He told us that it was a waste of time and we would be better just forgetting about it. I couldn't talk to him as I was so upset. I wondered how he might have reacted if it had been his family.

I'm told that the papers monitor Twitter all the time now and so they had noticed it themselves. The following morning it duly came out that I had been the subject of death threats following the game. I started to get calls from journalists and TV and radio stations for comments. I simply confirmed when asked that, yes, we had made a complaint and left it at that.

Soon I got a call from Dorward wanting to know why I had made it all public. I told him it had been nothing to do with me but when people ring me up, I am not going to lie about having made a complaint. I insisted I gave out no quotes but when you have been threatened and your family involved – and your little daughter is asking you, 'Daddy, why do people want us to die?', you tend to get a bit upset.

I was disappointed when he said that by confirming the story I had given a quote and him adding: 'I can't help you if you don't help me.'

I was determined to carry on and flew down to referee Southampton v Sheffield Wednesday in a Capital One Cup tie on the Tuesday and the police came round on the Wednesday. They told me that the Tweet mentioning the bullet in it had come from a young girl in North Wales who supported Liverpool. She had closed her account quickly and her local police had been around to warn her about the episode. That was good enough for me and I told them I didn't want to press the matter against a kid.

The stuff about my cancer was more upsetting and the police tracked down the man who had made the comments. A Liverpool fan, he worked in a health club in the north east, where he was also a coach at his local football club, and was in danger of losing his job as a result of being exposed in the newspapers. Soon, via the Premier League, I received a letter of apology from him.

'The comment I made on Twitter on Sunday was disgraceful, vile, disrespectful and in extremely poor taste,' it said. 'I have shamed and embarrassed myself and ruined my reputation in one horrid act of spitefulness.'

It stretched to two pages of A4 and he sounded genuine in his regret and fulsome apology. He added that he had two grandparents and an uncle who had died with cancer. He didn't know what came over him in the heat of the moment, he said. Since he had not offended before, I decided not to follow this through and I accepted the apology. I rang his boss at the health club and his football club and asked them not to sack him.

I also had a letter from the Liverpool managing director, Ian Ayre, 'to pass on my sincere regrets for the vile and disgusting treatment that I believe you have received on various social media outlets following our match on Sunday.

'I'm sure like me you know these idiots are a minority and certainly do not represent the view of our fanbase,' he added. 'I hope that these sad individuals have not caused you too much personal distress and I hope you know you are always welcome at Liverpool Football Club in a professional and personal capacity.'

What disappointed me was that although I got plenty of support and communication from around football and outside, managers at the Select Group were largely silent, apart from Phil Dorward in his attempts to keep a lid on everything.

I received plenty of texts from managers in the Premier League and other contacts and friends saying I had refereed the game well, Sir Alex Ferguson even saying in the media that my performance had been one of the best and bravest by a referee in all his years of going to Anfield. I got nothing from my bosses, however, apart from a brief call from Mike Riley on the Tuesday and one from Keren Barratt asking if I wanted to come off the game at Southampton. He did say that he didn't blame me for making a complaint to the police.

Such lack of understanding and backing would be a hallmark of the Mark Clattenburg affair that came to dominate a season that was turning into a nightmare from a refereeing point of view.

After the league game between Chelsea and Manchester United at Stamford Bridge, Mark was scandalously accused by some of the home players of calling Juan Mata a 'Spanish twat' and then by Ramires of telling their Nigerian midfield player John Obi Mikel to 'shut up you monkey'.

Whether Chelsea were upset with Mark at the 3-2 defeat along with decisions in it when a controversial goal by Javier Hernandez was allowed and Fernando Torres sent off for an apparent simulation in going over without being touched, I do not know. I do know, from first-hand communication on a daily basis with him as I tried to support my friend and colleague, that Mark and his family suffered a month of torment.

Chelsea very quickly issued a statement that Sunday night accusing him of the comments and I spoke to Mark on his way home to the north east, and the next day. He was adamant he had said neither of those things and was mortified that people would even think it of him. Anyone who knew him in the slightest would know that he would never utter them.

But Chelsea made a formal complaint and Mark was taken off the fixtures while an FA investigation took place. He would miss four weekends, in fact. Chelsea soon dropped the Mata claims because none of their players would corroborate them – and I personally knew of at least one Chelsea player who was put under pressure to do so. I understand some players were also asked to back up the allegation about what Mark had supposedly said to Mikel, even though Mikel himself had not even heard it, by his own admission.

My information was that Mikel stormed into Mark's dressing room when he was told about the remark after the game, shouting: 'I'm going to break your legs. You called me a fucking monkey.' He tried several times to land punches on Mark but was pulled away by a combination of the Chelsea manager Roberto Di Matteo and assistant Eddie Newton, and Mark's three fellow officials, fourth official Mike Jones and assistants Mick McDonough and Simon Long.

Even before Mark had left Stamford Bridge that night, the press were knocking on the door of his home, waking up his frightened baby girl Mia and worrying his wife Claire. The problem was that he could say nothing in his defence as part of legal advice and clauses in our contracts. He was also worried that it might all get covered up, so powerful were Chelsea as one of the Premier League's 'stakeholders'.

In the days following, many in the Select Group felt that Mark was not getting the support he deserved from his own management, who were embarrassingly silent publicly. We felt that under the Riley-Barratt regime we lacked backing in controversial matters and this case was no exception.

And so, unbeknown to anyone, I took matters in my own hands and rang Sir Alex Ferguson, asking him to speak out. He agreed and used his Friday press conference ahead of a Manchester United game to say that he could not conceive of Mark Clattenburg saying such things. It helped the situation a great deal.

In the end, the FA agreed that Mark had no case to answer and Mikel was found guilty of misconduct, banned for three games and fined £60,000. It was nowhere near enough for all of us in the Select Group and we were outraged. Mark – quite rightly deemed blameless in the whole affair – was sidelined for longer than that.

A Brighton player, Ashley Barnes would get seven matches later in the season for a second sending off and tripping up a referee and if Luis Suarez had got an eight-match ban for his alleged racial comments towards Patrice Evra – followed by a ten-match ban for biting the Chelsea player Branislav Ivanovic – then Mikel should certainly have got a multi-game suspension.

Even that would have been lenient. If a Sunday League player had done what Mikel did after the game, then they would have been banned '*sine die*' – literally 'without day' in Latin – and not been allowed an appeal for five years. His only mitigation was that he had been misinformed by a team-mate.

We were unhappy that Mikel's behaviour had not been made public and we were not impressed by Chelsea's feeble admission that they could have handled the situation better. We wanted a proper apology. I accept their assertion that they were duty bound to report the allegations of an employee but at the end of it all, they should have been big enough to apologise and have words with that employee when nothing was proven. In fact, their mealy mouthed ending to the whole sordid episode typified how distasteful it all was.

We were all, as a group of referees, speaking on the phone regularly and at our next get-together at Burton – our headquarters now being the newly opened national football centre at St George's Park – Mark came down to talk to us all in our own private meeting separate from our bosses.

The mood was for a strike. At first it was just to refuse to officiate at Chelsea matches unless Mark got a proper apology. That action was not deemed to be feasible, though – after all, what about the effect on the innocent opponents they were playing? – so we contemplated an all-out strike for one or two weeks.

The Premier League knew that while our morale may have been low, we were still in fighting mood, which was why their chief executive Richard Scudamore and the Chelsea chairman Bruce Buck came up to Burton to talk to us. It felt very stage-managed and I guess we were never going to get a proper apology, for legal reasons, even though Mark was willing to say he would not sue them for defamation of his character.

All we got from Buck was a repeat of the Chelsea belief that they had to back their player – again fair enough, but they could have condemned his actions – and their 'regret' at the way they had handled the episode. I think he was a bit taken aback that we were ordinary people, had mortgages and didn't live in gated communities. Out of a sense of duty, we decided in the end against a strike having at least seen one or two people eating some humble pie. An unprecedented strike of English referees was a close-run thing, though, such was the depth of feeling about how Mark had been treated.

Some months later at St George's Park, England were staying there at the same time as us ahead of their internationals in San Marino and Montenegro. Frank Lampard approached me asking if Mark Clattenburg was around. When I told him he was absent, Frank said: 'Just tell him I felt for him.' It said much about how some good people within Chelsea at least were uncomfortable with the episode.

Mark was also involved in something else controversial, though not so serious, this time behind the scenes, during the course of the season.

There was an incident when Mike Dean gave a goal against Manchester United, in a game against Newcastle, involving an offside interpretation. Mike decided that Papiss Cisse was not actively interfering with play when Johnny Evans turned in an own goal.

Before the start of the second half, probably having seen a replay, Sir Alex Ferguson strode on to the field to berate Mike in front of everybody, leading to calls for a ban on Sir Alex. It looked bad and led to more debate about football's image but there was no disciplinary action against Sir Alex because Mike, privately, did not report the incident as he did not feel intimidated by it and it came outside of the play. And although Sir Alex jabbed his finger, Mike said he was not abusive.

Soon after, in a game between Norwich and Southampton, Mark Clattenburg found himself surrounded by players at the end of a game and Mike Riley suggested he should file a report to the FA about the role in it of the new Southampton manager Mauricio Pochettino. Mark said he did not wish to as again he did not feel intimidated. There shouldn't be one rule for Sir Alex and another for Mauricio Pochettino, Mark felt.

In the end, Mark was finally sent back to Stamford Bridge the following April, six months after the Mikel episode, to take Chelsea v Swansea City – watched by Riley and Barratt – and all passed off peacefully. Mikel was left on the bench and Ramires was forced off the field after 24 minutes with an injury. A modest amount of justice for his role in it all, perhaps. Mark was relieved there was no chanting against him from the home supporters and grateful for kind comments from Lampard and John Terry.

From my own point of view, given what happened in the Liverpool aftermath and to Mark at Chelsea, I was beginning to wonder more and more often if I needed all this any more. It seemed almost weekly that we were getting grief – both external and internal.

I was sent to do another of the Halsey specials again – Millwall v Leeds in the Championship – and had to send off the Leeds striker Luke Varney for an elbow. While it was missable, it was definitely a red card and I was pleased I had a good view of it. The Leeds players were no problem at the end, they knew the score, and many came to shake hands.

The Leeds manager Neil Warnock, though, came over and pulled them away, shouting at them: 'Don't shake his fucking hand.' It upset me. I had made the right decision but even if I hadn't, that is no way to behave at the end of a game.

I sent a misconduct report to the FA, saying to the head of on-field regulation, Tarik Shamel: 'You talk about respect in the game? There is none any more.' Tarik replied that he wished more referees would report such events. I was pleased that Neil was later fined £2,000 for misconduct at a time when we were all supposed to be preaching the FIFA campaign of Respect. I like the bloke off the field, but that was out of order.

If I hadn't been so angry, I would have been amused a while later when the reports of the two sides on the referee's performance came through. Leeds awarded me 20 out of 20 for general control of the game but one out of 60 for my judgment. Millwall gave me 45 out of 60 for that.

Neil's mark was at odds with the match assessor, Dermot Gallagher – my referee on my first trip abroad, to Vladikavkaz, as a fourth official. In the 'Management of the Game and Players' category, he said: 'I feel this referee is the best within this category.'

Dermot added that I had made the correct call on the Varney red card, noting also: 'I feel it is to his credit also that on the request from the visiting manager to visit him post-match, he declined knowing that he had already slagged him off on television and was brewing for a fight which the referee negated.' He gave me a mark of 8.6 out of ten.

But while I might still have had faith in myself and the majority of my peers and those in the know, beating the slings and arrows fired at me from others was getting harder and harder, as was the uphill task of trying to control players who were deliberately attempting to get away with things behind your back or cheat you.

I did Stoke v Everton in the December and from the outset the visiting side were determined to match the home side in the physical battles. You needed eyes in the back of your head, mainly at corners and free kicks because there was so much pushing and shoving. Personally, I think defenders are more likely to concede goals when they are grappling with attackers instead of attacking the ball but then good defence was beginning to be one of the fading arts of the English game.

When a Stoke corner came in, I was watching all the tussles on the goal line. As the ball was cleared I turned round to see Stoke's Ryan Shawcross lying on the ground, clutching his head. 'He's done me,' he said of a clash with Marouane Fellaini. 'Didn't see it,' I replied. 'But if he has, he'll get done on retrospective action.'

As a referee, you are often the last to know. Phil Henson, the match delegate, said nothing in the debrief. I only realised the seriousness of it when I got into the people carrier after the game to be driven back to the Holiday Inn to pick up my car and the driver said he had seen it on TV. Fellaini had headbutted Shawcross, he said.

Later that night, I watched the DVD provided by the home club, and noted that Fellaini had even looked to see where my attention was before butting Shawcross. I was furious with him. I rang up Tarik Shamel at the FA and told him that if I had seen it, it would have been a red card. That left them free for retrospective action, which they would indeed implement with a three-match ban.

I texted David Moyes to tell him I was upset and to be fair, the Everton manager replied that he knew I wouldn't have been able to see it and he was sorry for his player's behaviour. He said he thought I had had a good game.

The next time I saw Fellaini, when I was doing Manchester United v Everton in the February, I went up to him before kick-off and told him that he had let me down at Stoke. He apologised, but I added: 'I've got my eyes on you today.' Leon Osman came over to urge me not to pick on him but that is the way of the world – if players are going to do that to me, I am going to show them that they will not make a mug out of me.

I had a similar situation with Southampton striker Jay Rodriguez in the January in a crucial relegation game at Villa Park. When Rodriguez went down in the penalty area as Enda Stevens slid in, it looked a nailed-on penalty. Rickie Lambert duly converted for what would prove to be the winning goal.

Some of the Aston Villa defenders complained but then again, they would, wouldn't they? Players don't realise that their cases often go unheard because of all the times they complain without any justification. Nothing was said as we went up the tunnel at half-time.

It was a different story on the way back out for the second half, though. The Villa manager Paul Lambert and his coaches had clearly seen the incident on the TV by now and they were having a right good go at me. There was nothing I could do then except concentrate on the second half. We had no way of watching things at half-time nor would we want to as it might undermine confidence for the task still ahead.

When Lambert knocked on my door at the end of the game – not waiting the prescribed 30 minutes – I asked him to give me 15 minutes while I spoke to the assessor. But he persisted with the knocking every two minutes and I gave in. He told me that I would be embarrassed when I saw the incident on TV. Rodriguez had clearly dived, he reckoned. I told him that from my angle, it looked like the player had been brought down but that if I had got it wrong I would ring him and apologise. He just had to leave me his number.

That would translate in his press conference as me having admitted to getting the decision wrong and him saying I had guessed at it. His opposite number Nigel Adkins – in his last game before being sacked as Southampton manager – conceded that there had been no contact on Rodriguez but there would have been if he hadn't gone down. I couldn't work that one out.

The simple fact is that I made a mistake but then so did most in the ground who thought it a penalty without the benefit of TV replay and so did the majority of TV pundits who needed the replay to determine that it wasn't.

But the whole scenario showed what we as referees were up against. You had a player who had been guilty of simulation and defenders who might have been crying wolf. Then one manager who blamed you and another seeking to justify his player's action. Among all that, the ref was the easy target, the fall guy.

When I was fourth official at Reading v Villa later in the season, I went to Lambert and told him that, yes, I had made a mistake but that I was not embarrassed by it because plenty would have given it. He, after all, had only complained after seeing it on TV and not before as we went up the tunnel at half-time. He said I had not phoned him. But then, he had not left his number. He was not the most gracious of guys.

Soon after, I also saw Jay Rodriguez again when I was fourth at Newcastle v Southampton and told him I felt he had undermined me. He insisted he had not dived intentionally. I wasn't sure what an unintentional dive was, mind. I just wanted to let him know, as with Fellaini, that I was aware of what he had done for future reference.

All of that paled into insignificance with the events that would unfold at Wigan in the March in their game at home to Newcastle, a match that was pretty much the final straw for me.

Early in the game, there was a clash between Wigan youngster Callum McManaman and Newcastle's Massadio Haidara, who had just come on as a substitute. It looked just like a coming together – I couldn't tell any more than that because as the incident occurred, a Newcastle player – Mapou Yanga-Mbiwa – ran right across my line of sight. As Haidara lay writhing on the ground in agony, I could tell something was wrong, however.

Later, when I saw the incident on DVD, it was clear that while McManaman had got a touch on the ball, his right foot was danger-ously high and he had followed through to catch Haidara around the knee. It was a shocking tackle, I have to admit, but I didn't have a clear view of the incident on the pitch.

At half-time John Carver, the Newcastle assistant manager, confronted McManaman as he came off the pitch and the Wigan assistant Graham Barrow intervened. I sent them both to the stand for the second half.

When Wigan scored a late goal from a corner that Maynor Figueroa had helped on with a hand at the near post to win 2-1, something I couldn't make out amid all the jumping bodies, it compounded my role as the villain of the piece – this despite McManaman having been the one who perpetrated the tackle. A supportive email from José Mourinho would later make that very point: yes, I had made a mistake but I had not made the tackle.

I noted in my report that if I had had a clear view, I would have issued a red card, which should have left the FA free to charge McManaman. However, it was pointed out that my assistant Matthew Wilkes had a line of sight to the tackle but had not alerted me to anything wrong with it. The FA said that they had entered into an agreement the previous summer with the 'stakeholders' – Premier League, Football League, players and managers' unions, the PFA and LMA respectively – that if one official has seen an incident, no retrospective action can be taken.

I was just a foot soldier, forced to comply with the bidding of the stakeholders. I was no longer the man who should be having the last word on discipline and decisions. The new law had to be obeyed but everyone knew that in this case, the law was an ass. Later, the agreement would be rescinded so that retrospective action could be taken even if one official had a line of sight to the incident.

But it was me in the firing line again. On Twitter it began anew – one person wondered if anyone had an address for me where they could send a death threat. The hope that my cancer came back, and that my family should suffer, resurfaced.

And of course Graham Poll had to have his say. The next day, he went on talkSPORT to say that I was now too old and unfit and should be retiring.

He was wrong about the first two but maybe right about the

third. I felt far from old and far from unfit but I was ready to quit. I may have been frightened about the future and losing the income of around £100,000 that came from basic salary, match fees and bonuses, but all this was starting to make me ill and I worried about the implications of that for my cancer. The time, my time, had come.

18

...AND THE FINAL WHISTLE

After the unhappy start to the season that saw the overturning of a red card at Tottenham, the death threats following the Liverpool v Manchester United game and the abuse from Neil Warnock in the Millwall v Leeds United match, I first mooted my retirement with Mike Riley in the November of 2012. I asked him if he could prepare a severance package for me. He said to leave things with him.

I knew Mike wanted me out from that meeting with him soon after he had taken over but he had no grounds to sack me as I kept passing the fitness tests and receiving decent marks for my performances. So I reckoned if he did want me out, I was owed some sort of exit deal for the 14 seasons I had given to the Select Group, which made me the longest serving on the list. After all, there were no pension arrangements and I would have to find work again at the age of 51. Besides, my friend and colleague Pete Walton had been paid up the previous year.

It felt the right time to go. It wasn't just the increased amount of grief that came with the job. I could have handled that if I felt valued. I was also depressed at the lack of support from my superiors and the irregular appointments I was receiving. I would do only 30 games all season, the joint fewest of the Select Group with Lee Mason, and just 18 of them in the Premier League. I would not do a tie beyond the third round of the FA Cup. This despite finishing in the top six of the delegate's merit list.

I did not want to become angry and bitter. I wanted to be left with memories of good times, not bad. I had had some really good games in this season of 2012-13 but they often were over-looked amid the controversies and I did not want those to be what I was remembered for,

I heard nothing back from Mike, however. Instead, some five months later, I had a call from Alan Leighton, the National Secretary of the union the referees were attached to, Prospect. Mike had seen on the internet that I was going to be bringing out an autobiography and he wanted to see me in London.

I duly went to see him, to be told that I had to seek his permission for any book. I told him that it would not be coming out until I had quit and my contract had expired but even then he tried to tell me what it should and shouldn't contain and talk about.

That attitude, coupled with the Wigan v Newcastle game and that Callum McManaman episode, convinced me that even if I were to go on another season, I would have more, and worse, of the treatment I had had this season. Mike was now clearly not going to offer me a deal to go, with my relationship with him now shifting from chilly to frozen so I went straight to the top.

I phoned Peter Heard, the chairman of the PGMOL and someone I had always got on well with, and he agreed to offer me an exit deal. I was hopeful for the first time in months. When it arrived in the post, however, the contract was basically offering me money to shut up about my career and my views on certain people. I could not have that. I would not be gagged.

It would drag on for a few months as we sought to find a solution but there would be none. I felt it was not only a bullying tactic trying to suppress my free speech but also a restraint of trade with the book not coming out until after I had retired and my contract was no longer applicable. Someone had to speak out about what was going on inside the PGMOL – and my fellow referees were urging me to do so. I also had a living to earn.

Their treatment of me remained mixed while all that was going on. They gave me a mid-table game between Swansea and Southampton – my first Premier League game for four weeks after the Wigan incident – and although I refereed well, while others made mistakes that weekend, I was back as a fourth official the following weekend.

Normally, for their final appearance, referees are assigned to games they request that have a sentimental attachment for them. I would have to do what I was told, however.

I had long since given up hoping that I would be awarded the FA Cup final as a last, joyful, hurrah. This season, that would go to Andre Marriner, who was a good man and I did not begrudge him the accolade. I did hope, though, that I might have a request honoured for Manchester United v Swansea City on the penultimate weekend to coincide with Sir Alex Ferguson's last home game before his retirement but it went to Jon Moss instead. Jon knew I wanted that one and even came up to me at Burton to apologise, which was good of him, but it was not his fault and I was not upset with him.

Instead, I was sent to Fulham v Liverpool, which was a good game, but I was worried that it would be my last match since I had not had back-to-back Premier League games since Christmas. I wanted to know if I would be getting another on the last day as I wanted Michelle and Lucy and friends there.

I asked Keren Barratt, who told me that nobody at the PGMOL knew for certain if I was retiring or not. I found that hard to understand, I said, since I had long ago asked Mike Riley about a severance package and Peter Heard had agreed one, even if I was not going to accept the gagging clauses in it. In which case, Keren said, to be fair to him, that I would be getting a game on the last day.

I still hoped I might get Sir Alex's last match, at West Bromwich Albion, but at least when the appointments came out on the

Wednesday ahead of the Sunday finale, as my swansong they sent me to a club with whom I had a good relationship and history.

Manchester City 2 Norwich City 3
Barclays Premier League
Etihad Stadium
Sunday, May 19th 2013

They were all there, all the people who meant so much to me – Michelle and Lucy, my old boss Keith Hackett, who had brought a promising young referee from Sheffield with him because, he said, he wanted to show him how a top pro did it. Touchingly, Pete Walton also flew in from New York and came with his wife Jo. I got the fourth official I asked for in Mark Clattenburg and my two assistants were Ron Ganfield and Mick McDonough, good men all.

I knew it would be emotional and it was, from the moment City's long serving secretary Bernard Halford came to the dressing room to bring me a club tie, as he said he did for all officials who had had their last game officiating City down the years. Players were coming up to me and wishing me well and I would leave that night with about a dozen signed shirts.

By now Roberto Mancini had departed City and the caretaker manager Brian Kidd came to the dressing room to pay his respects, as did Norwich's Chris Hughton. Chris almost had me in tears, as he came with a signed shirt and told me I had been a good referee and an inspiration to people.

As Norwich captain, Grant Holt arrived at the pre-match briefing joking that he was glad I was going – at least I think he was joking. He smiled when I said in riposte: 'At least I won't have to deal with you any more, you fat bastard.'

'Pride in Battle' it says over the tunnel at the entrance to the pitch in the dressing room area but I wanted no battles today and told the captains and coaches so. City were confirmed as runners-up and Norwich were safe from relegation. I wanted us all to enjoy our Sunday. It was certainly enjoyable walking out to the middle with Lucy holding my hand.

I could have booked a Norwich player, Anthony Pilkington, early on for pulling back Edin Dzeko but gave him the benefit of the doubt, which prompted a City fan to shout 'You're rubbish Halsey.' That sort of abuse I could take. People around him were laughing. I had no choice but to show the game's only yellow card to Joleon Lescott, however, when he blatantly held back Robert Snodgrass in midfield. It was ironic, given that Joleon had played such a part in my last game before my break for cancer treatment.

It was a good, flowing game. Jack Rodwell scored two nice goals for City but Norwich, relaxed in their safety, responded with goals by Anthony Pilkington, Holt and a lovely solo effort from Johnny Howson. I was tempted to play five minutes of added time in memory of 1999 and that play-off final but resisted it. There were three instead.

When I blew the final whistle, I was moved by the reception I received from the Etihad stadium as the tannoy announcer reminded them it was my last game. In fact, Chris Wheeler wrote in his match report in the *Daily Mail*: 'After referee Mark Halsey called time on the season and his own career, the Bolton official was given as warm an ovation as any of the City players who traipsed around the pitch on a rather forlorn lap of honour.'

I was asked by Sky Sports and *Match of the Day* to do an interview and I now broke my rule never to do another after that Fulham v Arsenal debacle years earlier. There was plenty I wanted to tell them... and I wanted to finish by saying that at least I had got through my career without showing three yellow cards to the same player in the same match.

But Mark Clattenburg prevailed on me, quite rightly in hindsight, to keep my dignity. He told me just to say that it had been a great career, that I was grateful to the PGMOL for the chance I had been given and that I hoped other cancer sufferers and survivors could take heart from my fight back to the top.

All of that was true, anyway, and I choked back tears as I did the Sky and BBC interviews. They both used nice little quotes from me, notably on *Match of the Day*, about inspiring other people with cancer. That, after all, was the important message rather than any personal grievances I might have. In the end, I departed the stadium on a good note, which was how it should be.

I have to be honest, though. There was something that still rankled...

In the run-up to the game, I had received a lot of goodwill messages from my colleagues and people in football and I was touched by all of them.

'Enjoy your last game at Man City today,' wrote Alan Wiley. 'Your family and friends are very proud of your refereeing career but we also know the potential you possessed was not truly recognised by the powers that be. But you can look back on refereeing for 14 years on the best league in the world, gaining respect of the best players, managers and your colleagues. You could not have done any more and you can feel immensely proud of what you have done. Once the game is over, don't look back but look forward with excitement to a new chapter in your career.'

This came from Chris Foy: 'In the summer of 1994 I undertook a fitness test as a brand new linesman on the Football League. It was then I met a bloke who did level 16 in a QPR kit. "Who's this lunatic, I thought," and you will have guessed it was you!

'Who would have thought that some 19 years later you would be walking into the professional arena for the last time. A truly amazing feat. You have been through the mill in football and in life but tomorrow you walk out with your head held high – a top ref who I have had the pleasure of working with both on and off the field.

'Enjoy the day and remember to stay focused and go out with your reputation intact. Going to miss you.'

There were cards from other fellow officials – even dear old Roy Williams from my mid-Herts days, who said how many in the game had told him I was their favourite referee – wishing me well.

I also had an email from Ben Thaler, a Rugby League referee who trains young referees.

'As a group of referees in the gym on a Monday morning, we can't believe some of the stuff that has been said and the obvious lack of support you've received,' he wrote.

'How you've not ever been appointed to an FA Cup final is mind boggling, but in saying that, you've achieved probably more than any other by the respect you have gained from the players, which is what I think officiating is all about – talking and man management.'

I was also surprised to receive an email from Joe Guest from the FA. 'I have just read that you will officiate in your last PL game this weekend,' he said.

'Congratulations on reaching this historic milestone. You have been an excellent ambassador for the sport and refereeing. Your triumph over adversity during the period of your cancer shows what a special person you are. Moreover the support of Michelle and that which you have given her provides further proof if it were needed.'

It was good of him, I guess, but I thought it a bit rich given my treatment by the FA, in which he had played his part. I tried to be restrained in my reply.

'Hi Joe,' I said. 'Really appreciate your comments. Just disappointed the FA never saw fit to give me the FA Cup final in the last couple of years. What a message that would have sent out to all those men, women and children living with cancer.'

Then, in the aftermath of the game, I really appreciated this from Keith Hackett: 'It was a real pleasure to see a master at work in his last Premier League game. Mark, I hope that you have a happy retirement away from the politics of appointments etc.'

In the *Racing Post*, their columnist Kevin Pullein described me as 'quite simply the most accomplished of all English officials. Halsey tried to help players produce the best spectacle of which they were capable – intervening when necessary to protect the safety of players but otherwise allowing the action to flow... The affection in which he is held by a great many supporters only increased after his brave fight against cancer... Since then, he tried to use his experience to encourage and raise funds for others struck by the disease.'

What was sad – though I suppose I didn't expect anything else – was that I did not receive one word of thanks or support from any of my bosses or those high up at the PGMOL, Premier League or FA, just a brief 'good luck' in a phone call from Keren Barratt.

I also found out from a Manchester City official in the tunnel after the game that the club had wanted to present me with a signed shirt on the pitch but were instructed not to do so. I was hurt when I discovered that, as I was when informed that Phil Dorward, the league's press officer assigned to the PGMOL, had gone on Twitter to note the retirement of an assistant referee Ceri Richards but could say nothing about mine.

Michelle too was hurt, so much so that she even phoned up Richard Scudamore, the Premier League chief executive and a former PGMOL board member, to say how upset she was about how it was ending for me. She was a bit taken aback to be told that I should not have been 'a silly boy' in doing my autobiography.

I wondered how that all squared with Graham Poll doing a book published soon after his retirement and nobody complaining about that, nor threatening the legal action they had with me. Also, in his last season, he had secretly filmed a fly-on-the-wall TV documentary for the BBC about his life, not telling the PGMOL about it, but received no sanction for that, still being awarded the play-off final.

He even recorded on film during the season his decision to retire, which he did not inform the PGMOL about. That came out in a newspaper about a month before the end of the season. He got none of the grief from the bosses about not informing them formally that I would get, however. Faces fitting, and all that.

The pettiness did not end with that banned City presentation. In previous years we had taken Lucy out of school at the end of the season for a much-needed holiday and Mike Riley had provided a letter of authority for her head teacher. This year he declined to do so.

Michelle emailed this to Mike: 'I cannot understand why this year you are taking an extremely different approach to my request when it has never been a problem for the past two years but I am not surprised given the way Mark is being treated.'

Given attitudes to me, I was worried that they might not pay the last few months of my contract if I did not continue to comply with their rules and so I reported as required to a venue near Warwick to take a fitness test for the following season two days after the Manchester City game, even though I was retiring. I passed it easily. Funny how some referees who knew they would fail did not show, however.

I was also told that once back from my holiday in Spain, I would have to come down to London to explain those tickets for the Real Madrid v Manchester United game that José Mourinho had given me. In fact, he came to the dressing room at Old Trafford when I was taking the Everton v United game the weekend before and he was there scouting his opponents. At least now, with José back at Chelsea to my great delight, I could enjoy his company without worrying about risking ridiculous disciplinary procedure for it.

I was also asked to explain why I had been refereeing at an event hosted by Delta Airlines without permission. Delta were a sponsor of Chelsea, it was pointed out to me, but it was all above board and I was retiring anyway. In the end, the meeting never took place as my barrister John Cooper finally negotiated my release but without the financial exit package that had been accorded my mate Pete Walton the previous year. It was a lot of money, and would have almost paid off my mortgage, but I preferred to retain my integrity and freedom of speech.

What was sad was that usually when a referee retires, his colleagues honour him and make a presentation to him at the annual conference of referees on the National List and in the Select Group. This year, though, I was told my presence was not required. It hurt me.

Like me, Michelle grew sick of it all. I wondered whether I should have sued my employers for constructive dismissal. They might have been in breach of employment law in the way they treated a cancer survivor.

But I just wanted to get away to Spain for a few weeks then

start a new chapter in my life and did not want to risk damaging my health and Michelle's in going through prolonged legal procedures. From my point of view, I did not want to sour my career.

Because it had been a great career, from Sunday League to Premier League and beyond into European football, with great characters and great games along the way. I wanted to remember those people and those occasions fondly.

I knew also that I still had much to offer the game in a variety of ways. I had a story and skills that could benefit others. I could mentor and coach young referees coming through – and I believe there is a dearth of those with potential to get to the top. I could share my experiences of recovering from cancer to give people hope. I had experience of managing some of the most difficult people in the most intense of circumstances.

I also believed that the game and refereeing was in crisis and wanted to have my say on that in an attempt to improve the experience of spectators and viewers as well as the lot of the modern referee.

19

DUG-OUTS AND DRESSING ROOMS

There are probably two schools of thoughts among the refereeing fraternity about relationships with managers and players. There are those who believe that refs should keep their distance, that they should not risk being compromised by any human contact with those they have to deal with on match day. Then there are those like me.

I always considered it part of the job to establish working relationships and tried to get on well with them, even to get close to them, so that I understood where they were coming from, and for them to understand me, my decisions and why I made them. We should be in this together, not on opposite sides – that was my philosophy. In my view, it helped in keeping a game flowing and improving the experience for those involved and the spectacle for those watching. It didn't mean I was not going to give the decisions I had to give.

But, it was football and supposed to be enjoyable, wasn't it? Why have hostility when you could have harmony? Of course you were going to fall out with people, going to make wrong decisions, but if they knew you, they were going to tolerate those mistakes better and have more respect for the job you were trying to do.

I am sure that attitude and closeness counted against me, though, as did my training at Bolton Wanderers, or at least that is what I was told by some of my colleagues. Personally, I thought it helped me understand professionals and thus become a better referee. I also had the medical expertise and back-up on site. I think my thinking about the game was out of fashion with certain people in key positions at certain crucial times of my career, however. They preferred the sticklers, the referees who obeyed edicts without question and who almost seemed to treat players with an arrogant disdain that, in my view, riles managers and players.

My face and style not fitting with certain uptight individuals was the major reason, I am convinced, why I did not get as far in my European career as I hoped and in latter years was not assigned to the biggest of domestic games. Not getting the FA Cup final, when I have watched as younger – and I believe less talented – referees did so, was a particular source of sadness.

A Select Group referee of my standing and longevity would have definitely been allocated a final had two of the key figures who decided the cup final ref, Mike Riley and David Elleray, not been so hostile towards me. 'I'm afraid your face doesn't fit at the FA,' my old coach and head of Football League referees Dave Allison told me. As it went, the closest I got was a sixth round tie between Everton and Middlesbrough in 2009.

In fact, I did not even get an FA Vase, FA Trophy or FA Youth Cup final, a decision that many of my colleagues have told me they find baffling. Some have even called it a disgrace. There were times when I certainly could, maybe should, have been given the cup final. I was unlucky a couple of times, notably in 2007 when Steve Bennett got it. He finished third in the merit list that season and I finished fourth. I didn't begrudge Steve, as he was a friend.

So too Mike Dean, but I was more annoyed when he got it in 2008, much as I rated him as a ref. I finished fifth that season, Mike much lower down, but it was his reward for having had it taken off him in 2006 because he was from the Wirral and Liverpool got to the final.

It certainly rankled on other occasions seeing referees sometimes lower than me in the merit list getting the FA Cup final. This for a man Philip Don believed for a time was the best referee in England.

He wasn't the only one. In my final season, when my morale was low, I was grateful for the comments of Glenn Turner, one of our top assistants who walked away after that disagreement with Mike Riley, on Richard Keys and Andy Gray's talkSPORT show.

'Mark Halsey,' Glenn said, 'was the most naturally gifted referee I ever witnessed. He was born to do it.'

In a brave interview, Glenn said many of the things that I have been unable until now to say. He worried that the current PGMOL management wanted robotic referees who would 'park' their natural personalities.

'Mike Riley came in saying he was going to take the fear out of refereeing but it has got worse,' Glenn added. He also said that a lot of officials were ringing and emailing him – not on official phones and addresses because they were so worried about being monitored – to say that they knew they would get punished and disciplined for mistakes, rather than be helped through them and backed.

'Mike Riley,' he continued, 'has been over-promoted.' Riley had brought unnecessary pressure on officials and hung them out to dry instead of getting them in and talking to them properly.

It all echoed my experiences and I could only shout 'well done' at the radio as Glenn was saying it. I knew plenty of my colleagues who were doing so as well. Mike had taken over with a fanfare, saying that he wanted to bring back transparency and fairness to refereeing. Instead, the opposite happened.

Despite all that, and my regret that I didn't get to take charge of a Champions League match beyond a qualifying round, go to a European Championship or World Cup, or get that FA Cup final that I might have done, I developed relationships and friendships with people in the game that will last beyond my retirement and into a new working life. For that reason alone, it has been a

marvellous career. Above all, I will always treasure my friendship with José Mourinho, which grew after my illness to the point
where he would invite me and Michelle out to Portugal, Milan
and Madrid for holidays and he would put us up in hotels. Mike
Riley didn't like that, illustrated by that summons to London – in a
letter signed by Keren Barratt while Mike was away on holiday – to
explain why I accepted complimentary tickets from José for the
Real Madrid v Manchester United game in my final season. As if it
compromised me in any way. It was after he left England and there
was no conflict of interest.

What amused me about it was not only that Mike had known
for three years that I went to Real Madrid games but that Keren
Barratt had even once given me a book to take out there for José
to sign. By then, though, rightly or wrongly it felt that Mike was
looking for any stick to beat me with, trying to get me to resign
without a pay-off, in my opinion.

I wondered, after all, why he took an interest in something
like that but not an incident at one of our get-togethers in my
last season. During a light-hearted five-a-side game, two of our
number got into an argument over a penalty and a bout of pushing each other developed. One referee then pushed his head into
the other's face. You've seen it between players on the TV.

On the surface, this was quite funny and ironic – referees who
are supposed to clamp down on this sort of thing getting involved
in it themselves. Actually, it was quite nasty for a moment and
underneath that, if we were supposed to clamp down on players, why were our bosses not summoning those two supposed to
implement the laws and good behaviour on the field to London
to explain themselves and discipline them? Accepting a couple of
Real Madrid tickets was the more damaging crime, it seemed.

Besides José, many others were also kind and helpful, and not
only sent me text messages and were warm to me on my return to
refereeing, but also gave their time and money to help my cancer

charity work, as shown by that dinner with Sir Alex Ferguson, David Moyes, Roberto Mancini, Sam Allardyce, Owen Coyle and Martin O'Neill.

One thing should be made clear, though, and was shown in my relationship with Sir Alex. I may have spoken to him a lot and shared text messages, but he knew that when I crossed that white line, there would be no favours. Players and managers wouldn't respect you if you did give decisions based on any relationship or friendship. They respect honesty and incorruptibility.

Many did see me, though, as a referee with whom they could have a dialogue and seek advice. As such, I would sometimes speak to them over refereeing decisions, to develop a better understanding of decisions with them, for their benefit and ours as referees so we might not get grief off them in the future. Mind you, they did not always appreciate it.

I once texted a manager after a red card for one of his players to say that on TV, it looked like a decision that he might be able to appeal.

'Fuck off,' came the reply. 'I'm finished with all you wankers.'

Shocked, I phoned him up and he started laughing. 'I didn't mean it,' he said. 'I was just so pissed off.'

The fact that Martin O'Neill – whose own wife had had cancer – agreed to come to that dinner shows that you don't always get on with people during matches, and in the time before and after them, but you separate the professional from the personal. Some things are just more important. Football is a great game for accepting that things are said and done in the heat of the moment but then not holding grudges but instead getting on with life.

I saw that early on and it was confirmed when I had my run-in with Gary Megson but became friendly with him later. It was the same with Neil Warnock. There were all sorts of problems down the years on the field but he was a different man away from the heat of battle.

Martin, in fact, could be obnoxious at times because he got so wrapped up in the game. I recall being a fourth official when his Leicester City lost 4-1 to Liverpool in his first season at Filbert Street and getting a right volley of abuse.

Then, when he was in charge of Aston Villa, I did their opening game of one season at Manchester City and I gave a penalty against Villa in the first half. Martin and his assistant John Robertson gave me all sorts of verbals. At half-time, there was a knock on my dressing room door and John was asking if he could come in. I didn't want him in there but he said that they had seen the incident on replay and that I was right to give the penalty and they wanted to apologise. I should have reported them but I didn't, probably because of that apology. Maybe they were being clever and heading off later action against them.

I had something similar with Martin in the 2012-13 season after the Sunderland v Fulham game when he came banging on my dressing room door, claiming that Sunderland should have had a penalty for handball. I let him in and told him that it was ball to hand in my opinion and not deliberate – handball being the only part of the laws where intent still counted. It didn't calm him down, though, and soon I had to throw him out.

A few months later, he would lose his job at the Stadium of Light, which explained why he might have been upset – due to the pressure he was under rather than anything I had done wrong.

Sometimes as referees we are our own worst enemies because we take stuff like that. If we didn't, and couldn't get over it, we wouldn't have been at that level.

How come? Well, lower down the scale if you developed bad relationships with people and complained about the abuse or reported it, then clubs would give you bad marks, which meant you were less likely to progress. It is one of the problems of the system. A referee can have a great game but if he gives a last-minute penalty against a team, he is going to get marked down. As

I said, in this profession, the cream doesn't always rise to the top due to politics and personal relationships.

Then at Premier League level, if you complained about a manager or a player, you were unlikely to get sent back to that ground, back into the firing line, for a good while. And referees want to do the big games at Old Trafford, Anfield, Stamford Bridge, the Etihad and the Emirates, just like players who want to perform at those big venues, so they are often going to just bite the bullet.

Not that I ever had too much trouble at the Emirates with Arsene Wenger. The only problem with him was when he gets agitated, which was more often in my later years, I have to admit, as his team went longer and longer without a trophy. Otherwise, I found him to be a gentleman, as shown by him contacting me during my illness to wish me well.

I always texted him at the beginning of a season to say 'good luck' and he texted back. He always asked after Michelle, too. During my cancer treatment, I went to see Bolton v Arsenal and met him in the dressing room area. When I told him Michelle was upstairs in the players' wives lounge, he asked me to take him up and, to everyone's astonishment in there, strode through to have a conversation with her.

Naturally, managers are different personalities. I was once fourth official for a West Bromwich Albion v Manchester United match and the then Albion manager Roberto Di Matteo complained about a Gary Neville tackle on one of his players that referee Chris Foy did not give a penalty – or a red card – for.

'Eh, Roberto,' I said. 'It could be worse. Look at what I've been through.'

'That's true. You are right,' he replied and smiled. After that, he always reminded me of that conversation.

Then there is Paul Lambert. I recall pre-game between his Aston Villa and Manchester United when Sir Alex shook my hand but Lambert just walked straight past me. I just thought that was ignorant. He seemed fine when he was at Norwich, always polite, but it changed when he went to Villa. I was fourth official at a Villa game at Manchester City and he called the referee Jon Moss 'a fucking cheat' for giving two penalties against his side. Then there were the run-ins with him after that Jay Rodriguez simulation for Southampton. I guess it shows the increased strain of being at a bigger club.

Some who you might expect to be hard work are not always so. I had episodes, for example, with Tony Pulis, who was always in my ear, but he was fighting his side's corner and I understood his passion. He would always tolerate you having a go back, as well. Outside of the game itself, he is a calmer character altogether, one who I admired as having come up through the ranks to show younger, home-grown managers that it was possible.

Otherwise, most managers in the Premier League were respectful by and large, and they included some real gents like Gerard Houllier, who would invite me and Michelle to his home in Paris some years later, Roberto Martinez and Chris Hughton. Harry Redknapp always came for a chat when he was at Spurs, though I never reffed his QPR side, for obvious reasons.

I guess if I had to name my three favourite managers, it would be José, followed by Sir Alex, then joint third would be David Moyes and Sam Allardyce, who was marvellous to me through my illness.

Least favourite? I find myself able to forgive Neil Warnock and Martin O'Neill for my bad days with them because of their good natures in other ways but there was one controversial character from the lower divisions who I just cannot look back on with any fondness. His name: Steve Evans.

Evans took Boston United up into the Football League from the Conference but had to serve a suspension of 20 months, also incurring an £8,000 fine in the process, for his part in contract irregularities at the club. He also has a history of suspensions for berating officials in a career which has also taken in Crawley Town and Rotherham United.

I did Boston's game at Wrexham in 2007, which would decide who would be relegated from the Football League. It was a sell-out and an intense atmosphere – I wonder why they might have sent Halsey? – and when I gave Wrexham a penalty in the second half, from which they equalised, Evans had a right go. I should have put him in the stand but was willing to give him a second chance.

Later after Boston had lost 3-1 – filing for administration as they were going down – I saw him in the corridor. I had Lucy with me but it didn't stop him having another go and I told him to shut his mouth. I didn't want my young daughter hearing all that. He did stop and actually wished me all the best, saying I had controlled the game well but he would be at it again when I later did a Boston v Mansfield game. Leopards and spots.

I just thought he was a loud-mouthed piece of work who brought no credit to professional football. You have got to think of kids and the Respect campaign.

The curious thing is that just as some of the biggest name managers can be the easiest to deal with, so the players with difficult reputations could be pussycats. And I like to think my experience of them was actually down to the way I handled them.

Take El Hadji Diouf, who once spat at a spectator when at Celtic and has had numerous episodes down the years that have made him unpopular with fans. I got to know him well during his time at Bolton and could have a laugh with him. Again though, as with managers, once you cross that white line, it is a professional working relationship.

To be honest, there were times when I gave soft free kicks for him just to appease him, to keep control of the game. That's game management. It is a similar situation to pre-season games involving overseas teams when you would give free kicks that aren't so clear-cut in the more lenient Premier League. But then, if Diouf was at me, I would not give him other free kicks that he perhaps merited. That to me was how you managed a tricky player, kept him under control for his and the game's sake, as you showed him who was boss. I took decisions based on the context of the game, so as to not inflame situations.

It was Bill Shankly who once said: 'I treat my players like men because I am going to have to ask them to play like men,' and I hoped I refereed them in a similar way.

Men like Joey Barton and Lee Bowyer were always seen as problem players and they did indeed do some daft, even nasty things. I can only speak as I find, however, and when I took their games, they were usually respectful towards me, mainly because, I believe, I talked to them like grown-ups rather than naughty kids. You just had to keep on top of them – use prevention rather than punishment.

I hope people remember that of referees who are seen as not issuing enough cards. It is an art of refereeing to keep the card count down if at all possible, rather than strutting around showing them all the time. The times a whole clutch of them are needed to control a game should be few and far between.

I also always got on with Roy Keane. With him, as with all players who were known to be tough, I would say before the game in the tunnel: 'Right, don't be stupid today. Nothing fucking silly from you.' I just tried to talk to them as a human being in the same language as they used, for which football is known.

Then, if they executed a bad tackle, it would be: 'Right, no more.' And usually they would agree. Some players would answer back at United, such as Rio Ferdinand, who was fond of a 'fuck off,' as was Wayne Rooney. My response was a simple 'you fuck off' and they would retreat.

I didn't do that all the time and it's not the style of other referees but I used it when I needed to and it has always worked for me as my way of handling players. I always went to them and admitted it if I made a mistake – even if the refereeing authorities did not like you showing any form of weakness, though I saw it as a strength – and they appreciated that.

Patrick Vieira was always one who did. I recall an Arsenal game when I gave a free kick and he queried it, I told him to get on with the effing game. 'You are a funny guy,' he said. 'You make me laugh the way you talk to me.' When he was later at Inter Milan and José told him about my cancer, he was one of the first to come and ask after me upon his return to England with Manchester City. After I did a City FA Cup tie, he came into our dressing room and gave me his signed shirt.

I had a similar relationship with Robbie Savage, a notoriously fiery character with plenty to say for himself. I once told him – jokingly – that I would always look after him on the pitch because I was amused by his action in once defecating in Graham Poll's toilet in the referee's dressing room as a comment on what he thought of him.

Apart from the odd curser, mostly Manchester United's players were very quiet. I think Sir Alex instilled in them not to talk to referees unless decisions were not going their way. Then you would know about it and it made them a hard side to referee. Gary Neville and Jaap Stam were always at you. You couldn't have a conversation with them.

Not that Gary seemed to hold anything against me, asking me to do that testimonial of his before he retired from the game and became a very good TV pundit. It was strange that when United players went to other clubs, suddenly you could talk to them. Gary's brother Phil was an example. He became a changed character when he went to Everton.

Apart from my run-ins with Danny Mills, one player I always found difficult was Ashley Cole. He often spoke to me very nastily but during my illness, he was sympathetic to me, as also were John Terry and Frank Lampard, the latter a really fine character.

Often more than the hard ones, it is the 'gobby' ones who give referees the most problems. Dean Windass, the old Bradford City and Hull player was one, though a smashing lad off the pitch, and Sebastian Larsson of Sunderland another. He was constantly in my ear, forever moaning.

There was one Sunderland game where I gave a penalty for Chelsea to prompt all sorts of abuse from Larsson. After the game, Martin O'Neill showed him the incident on a laptop to prove that it was a penalty – quite something, Martin agreeing with one of my decisions – which calmed the player down and he apologised to me, to be fair.

Another great whinger was Fernando Torres, and it seemed to increase with his form dipping and his frustration at that. In a Chelsea game against Reading, I blew the whistle for a head injury to Gary Cahill – one of his own players – and Torres was furious. He was then even angrier when I asked for the ball to be kicked back to Reading from the drop ball.

At this point, I lost it with him and shouted: 'Will you shut up?' prompting new abuse, this time in Spanish. 'I wouldn't worry,' said Frank Lampard. 'He's always like this.'

Overseas players always understand English on the field, by the way, no matter what they profess. They certainly all seem to get to know 'fuck off' pretty quickly. And though they speak their own language to curse you sometimes, you get the gist pretty easily. When I did Swansea against Aston Villa, I spoke a bit of my pidgin Spanish to the home side's striker Michu just to let him know that I had an idea of what he might be saying to or about me.

The player who gave me most grief in my career was Craig Bellamy, right from his early time at Norwich and it got worse as he went on to bigger clubs, from Liverpool to West Ham. He was an earworm – burying himself into your ears about everything. Telling him to fuck off did not work the way it did with Ferdinand or Rooney. You could never shut him up.

But he could also be very funny. During a game when he was playing for West Ham against Aston Villa, he gave me grief because Villa broke away to score a winner and he thought I should have given a free kick on the half way line. I gave him a yellow card and told him to shut up. He put his arm round me, thanking me for not making it red.

Off the pitch, he seemed fine. At Gary Speed's funeral, I got talking to him with Michelle and he was polite and charming, no doubt partly due to the subdued occasion. Then, next time on the pitch, he was off again, straight into me.

'Gary's watching us both from up there,' I said, 'and I think he would want you to shut up.' At that, finally, Craig smiled and calmed down.

He would still top my list of players I didn't like dealing with, though, with Danny Mills second and Ashley Cole third. As for those I got on best with, there were plenty. I loved Steven Gerrard for his attitude to the game and it was a privilege to be asked to referee his testimonial against Olympiacos as a sort of encore at the end of my career. I also got on well with Lampard, Rooney, Vieira and Speed while Matty Holland of Ipswich Town and Charlton Athletic was also a gent.

I wouldn't have changed too much of it, I guess. You take the good, the bad and the ugly as representative of human life and part of the appeal of the game. There was also the beautiful. I got to be on the same pitch as some wonderful footballers and not many people can say that. My favourites close up? Zinedine Zidane, David Beckham – the best crosser of a ball I ever saw – Thierry Henry and Steven Gerrard. Robin Van Persie in full flow was also a delight.

I'll miss them, players and managers – well most of them – and I'll also miss all those special rituals of match days, if not their aftermath.

20

DAY OF THE MATCH

Sometimes I think back to that first time it hit me what a lonely job refereeing can be, when I made the change from being a player to an official and sat alone in that dressing room for a Herts County League game, listening to players laughing and joking in adjacent rooms just the way I did when I was a goalkeeper.

Then I think of the career I have had, thinking I might make the Football League one day but going on to exceed that by making the Premier League, where refereeing in front of 75,000 at Old Trafford could not have contrasted more starkly with a field in Borehamwood. You were never alone, what with your co-officials, all the people behind the scenes working at football clubs, managers, players and those vast numbers in the crowds down the years.

Despite that, the loneliness never leaves you. In the end, you know that it will be you in the middle, on your own, standing or falling by your decisions. That feeling started the moment I got up on match day. I needed to be alone to acclimatise myself to it, packing my kit, soaking in a hot bath contemplating what was to come, getting my head straight.

Living in Bolton, I could often stay at home on a Friday night before a game then meet up on a Saturday morning at the Suites at Knowsley for a match on Merseyside, the Holiday Inn at Haydock Park for a game up at Wigan and other places in the north west or the Radisson Blu at the airport if it was Manchester.

Overnighters would be Ramside Hall near Durham for the north east, the Crowne Plaza in Birmingham for the Midlands and the Radisson at Heathrow for the south east. I preferred to take the train or fly, rather than drive.

Wherever I was, though, my matchday routine would be the same, getting up at 8am and breakfasting on porridge, two poached eggs on toast, then toast and jam, all washed down with tea and a mixed fruits smoothie. That, apart from the supplements and small snacks, would be all I would eat all day. After breakfast, I would take a sports hydration tablet designed to prevent cramp.

As a group of officials, we would meet in the reception areas of our designated hotel at around 11.30am for a 3pm kick-off. After a cup of tea, a biscuit and usually some football and refereeing discussion, we would leave together for the game in our assigned people carrier from the First Class Events company at around 12.30pm. Usually you were just 20 minutes or so from the stadium.

Why the travelling together? Well, I guess it was to make sure we arrived as a unit, as a team, but also there were security implications. It meant that there was less scope for anyone to influence us but most important was that we were dropped, and picked up afterwards, right outside entrances to grounds to minimise any likelihood of being attacked or assaulted. In a way, it was a sad statement of where we had got to in the modern game.

The drive to the ground would be when the butterflies came to the stomach, when the feeling was a mixture of excitement at the day ahead and the fear of making an error. Towards the end, I have to confess, I remained nervous but not like previous years when it was more of an adventure and less of the job it became.

After dropping off kit in the dressing room, it was then up to the lounge to meet any guests we may have and the match delegate, who is either an ex-player, manager or administrator appointed by the Premier League. They are there to mark your performance from the perspective of a professional observer of the game.

I used to go down to the dressing room at ten past one, mix myself up a sports drink and start getting changed. These days, there is an email early in the week from the PGMOL to tell a referee which of the four colour shirts – green, red, yellow or black – they have to wear for that game.

I also liked to put my music on, which after my illness became a compilation of inspirational songs. Give me easy listening all the time. Can't stand all that boom-boom stuff.

I particularly liked The World's Greatest by R Kelly and Hero by Mariah Carey. I also loved Bobby McFerrin's Don't Worry Be Happy – I know the irony of the title is that he committed suicide but I admire the sentiment. Also on the playlist was Enjoy Yourself by Paolo Nutini, Rise by Gabrielle, I've Got A Feeling by the Black Eyed Peas, The Best Things in Life Are Free by Janet Jackson, The Living Years by Mike and the Mechanics and You Raise Me Up by Westlife.

It might sound a bit corny and emotional but they helped me feel grateful simply for being there and to inspire me for the job ahead. I played Perry Como singing Magic Moments because these were. And I played a Huey Lewis song for a laugh with my assistants – Stuck With You.

Last tune before walking out would always be Robert Goulet and The Impossible Dream. There were definitely times during my chemotherapy and radiotherapy when getting back to refereeing, certainly at the top, looked like it would be an impossible dream.

The routine was that at 1.45pm, the officials received briefings from the police and the stadium's safety officers. We were informed about what size of crowd was expected, the procedure for an emergency and what to do if we got a runner on the pitch – leave to the police and stewards, basically, and make sure the players were safe. We also discussed how to handle crowd trouble, including racist abuse. Personally, I could not say that I encountered that towards any players during my career but then I was so bound up in my own world out there that I might have missed anything directed from the stands or even opponents. If I had heard anything, I most certainly would have reported it to the FA, the police and the stadium manager. I would then have asked the player or players concerned what they wanted to do about it and would have supported them if they wanted to walk off and have the game halted, including their statements in my report. There is no place for any racism in the game, by word or deed.

I did get a call from Mike Riley after a Millwall v Leeds game when TV cameras for an undercover documentary had picked up a home fan spouting racist abuse. I gather they got the fan concerned and banned him but I didn't hear it and the police didn't contact me.

At 2pm, the managers or their assistants and captains would arrive to hand over the team sheets. At this point I would talk to them, my speech normally just consisting of a request for them to work with the officials, not against them, and for the captains to get their teams to behave and not risk cheap yellow cards.

Above all, I always told the players to enjoy it because life was too short not to and you never knew what was round the corner. Keep smiling, I would say. It normally ended with smiles and handshakes.

It did seem that the bigger the club, the less likely the manager was to attend personally. Sir Alex, Arsene, whoever happened to be at Chelsea and Brendan Rogers didn't, though he did at Swansea before he went to Liverpool. Roberto Mancini sent Brian Kidd, Steve Round came from Everton and Steve Walford appeared on behalf of Martin O'Neill. Alan Pardew used to send Steve Stone but in my later days took to coming himself, as did Paul Lambert. The one who always came was Harry Redknapp. He liked a bit of a chat.

If I saw players and managers I knew in the dressing room area or in the corridors, I would always say hello but I never went to seek anyone out. Personally, I think all managers should come to meet the officials to hand over the team sheet and hear the briefing as a mark of respect. They were always quick enough in your dressing room afterwards if they felt hard done by.

I wanted my assistants to be ready by 2.20pm for our warm-up, which was never too strenuous. I didn't believe in too much – I trained hard and was fit enough; this was just about loosening muscles for a 15-minute routine. If I was fourth official, I didn't do the warm-up. I just stood in the dug-out area chatting to people. If I was refereeing, I would ask my fourth official to have a water bottle ready for when there was a break in play to ease the dryness in my mouth due to the lack of saliva after the cancer treatment. If I was too far away, I would prevail on the goalkeeper to lend me his. I tried not to make it too obvious.

After the warm-up, it was back into the dressing room to take in my caffeine gel and make the final visit to the toilet of four of five I made in the two hours before kick-off. I then took five caffeine tablets and had a good swig of water. By now my mouth was as dry as a bone.

Referees nowadays have to have the teams in the tunnel at 2.52pm to make sure of a 3pm sharp kick-off. The Premier League insists on it these days, what with all the live TV feeds around the world. We were kicking off at one and two minutes past and the broadcasters were complaining. Referees can be reprimanded for a late kick-off but if it is shown to be a team's fault, they are fined heavily.

I did get an email from the Premier League after a Newcastle v Wigan game had kicked off a couple of minutes late asking for an explanation. I said that it was my fault, due to a need for the toilet, rather than the clubs. I didn't want to dob them in it.

It is rare to come under any pressure from managers, coaches or players as you are going about your business in the run-up to kick-off but at this point in the tunnel somebody might say something to you, such as: 'Watch him today ref,' of an opponent, pointing at him. Other comments might include: 'He's a diver, this one.' Or, 'Keep track, Mark, that one's a time waster.' Most players were fully focussed by now, though. Little was usually said.

You would also get remarks when coming off at half-time, about your performance or a decision, but I usually told them to get on with analysing their own performance – which their manager would be doing pretty soon anyway. The most memorable interval discussion was that one at Aston Villa, in the game against Southampton when nobody said a word going up the tunnel but had plenty of comments as we came out of it having seen that Jay Rodriguez simulation.

At half-time, I would take on board a sachet of caffeine gel and maybe a caffeine sweet for an energy boost and after a 12-minute break, would press the bell in our dressing room that has a line to the home and away dressing rooms and rings to alert the players that they have three minutes to be back out on the pitch.

The pressure does not always relent at the final whistle, what with managers banging on your door. They are supposed to wait 30 minutes but sometimes just can't. If they wanted an explanation, that would be one thing but often they just wanted to scream in your face. You were the softest target if things had gone against their side.

If I thought they would be reasonable, like Mick McCarthy would be, I agreed to them coming in but if they got aggressive, out they went. I refused entry to Neil Warnock that time at Millwall not only because I was so disgusted by him telling his players not to shake my hand. To be honest, if he had come in, I didn't trust myself not to thump him if he kicked off at me, so upset was I. It would have meant a premature end to my career.

It was certainly the angriest I have ever been after a game.

Referees can get angry too as we are only human but there would be hell to pay if we showed that anger the way that managers do, or said some of the things they do. It is a one-way street.

The delegate would be in quite shortly after the final whistle, just to give you his initial impressions of your performance. I preferred the delegate's assessment to any assessor's – which you still get in the Football League though no longer the Premier, having been replaced by the new evaluations – as I was never the most technical of referees.

After that, and picking up the match DVD from the home club's secretary, I was usually out of there pretty quickly, unless invited for a quick glass of red by Sir Alex or David Moyes. I liked to get home. It was a job of work and I wanted to get back to my family. We would leave as officials together back in the people carrier at about 5.30pm, an earlier time than in the past when there were assessors to be heard too. At that time, it was a case of braving the traffic along with everybody else to pick up our cars back at the hotel.

Quite often I would speak to fellow referees on my way home to see how their match had gone. Once in, I did my report, which in later years took only ten minutes rather than the hour of the old handwritten days. It is filled in on a template on a laptop now, with sections for misconduct – cautions and red cards – and nuts and bolts information like the score and kick off times. You also had to comment on breaches of league rules and extraordinary incidents. It has to be in by midday on a Monday for a weekend game or midday the day after a night game.

If it was a weekend, after filling that out, I would be with the family and no distractions. I ended up not watching *Match of the Day* and would usually be fast asleep by the time it started, though I used have trouble getting off before 1am if it had been a night game. I knew I would get stick from within my profession if I had got something wrong and I didn't need to hear it broadcast to the nation by those who had never refereed themselves.

I didn't mind taking criticism if I genuinely got something wrong, and had respect for pundits who had some experience of refereeing – as long as they didn't have an axe to grind with me from the past. Some pundits, however, do not even know the laws of the game and are unable even to differentiate between careless and reckless tackling and violent play, between what is a yellow and a red card.

For a referee, the game is far from over on the day it is played. There might be complaints to address by the clubs concerned. One such arrived with me, via my bosses, from Nottingham Forest, who complained that I appeared to be waving to Leeds supporters in the crowd before a game at Elland Road between the two clubs I was taking. I had to email them to say I was waving to Michelle and Lucy, who were coming to all my games at that time after my illness.

I did wonder that time I shook Alan Shearer by the hand after his wonder volley for Newcastle whether I might be the subject of a complaint but I got away with it. The precedent was Mike Reed punching the air back in 2000 after Liverpool had scored a goal against Leeds. He was actually celebrating playing a good advantage. Mike is an Aston Villa fan.

Actually, the game these days lasts ten days for a Premier League referee, with the controversial new match evaluation introduced for the 2012-13 season arriving first by email within two or three days to be followed a week later by the delegate's report. I was happy to receive criticism from delegates when it came with all the things you do right in a game as well. I wish the same could be said of the evaluations which so upset pretty much all of us in the Select Group.

The system used by the evaluators – ex-referees in their homes working with a DVD on the game, though we never knew the person concerned doing it – was devised by a company in the

United States for analysis of American football and basketball but I have to say that those sports lend themselves more to a play-by-play assessment, given all the stoppages in the game. When the evaluation dropped in your email, you logged on and a few clicks later you could see the blow-by-blow report.

We used to complain about assessors and their inconsistencies, but this system was something else. We were being told every week that we were all missing too many yellow and red cards. Some refs would be getting a mark of 79 per cent, others 100 one week, and it could be reversed the next week.

There were times when I thought I had an average game and got 100 per cent, but then a good one that only brought me 90 per cent. The evaluation took no account of mood and difficulty of game. We had a meeting with Mike Riley about it and he told us not to worry, just to keep managing games rather than issuing cards for borderline decisions.

But then at a meeting at Burton late in my final season, we were shown 39 incidents where red cards should have been issued, apparently, but only seven had been. That meant we had missed 32 red cards between us. I know that English football's card count was down due to a reputation for letting games flow – an average of one red card every 8.6 games compared with one every 2.6 in Spain – but that was ridiculous.

I wondered how it squared with what Mike Riley told *The Independent* for an article: 'The Select Group refs go in to clubs twice a season,' he said. 'It used to be once but this season we introduced a second one where referees take a training session and they have time away from the pitch to talk with the players about law and decision making.'

I, incidentally, was never asked by Mike to take one of these sessions – the only one in the Select Group not to be.

'There's the pre-season managers' meeting, the exchange of team sheet between the officials, captains and managers before every match,' Mike added. 'We also have quarterly meetings with the PFA and the LMA, so there's constant dialogue going on. It's not a coincidence that things are improving.'

And yet we were being told to issue more reds? It was all very confusing. I think the aim was to provide Mike with statistics that he could take to the Premier League to measure performance but the problem with that was that the system was being used to award marks to referees that, coupled with the delegate's marks, went towards deciding a merit list at the end of the season.

Although never published, it counted towards your performance data and you could be sacked on only two things: failing the fitness test and performance issues. It also affected the bonuses you might be paid.

The evaluations had been used before in football, in the Japanese A League, I was told by a senior administrator, but only as a training tool and not a marking system. I was all for technology as an aid to refereeing. The way this was being implemented, though, was a hindrance to it.

At first, I pored over the evaluations, took everything on board. And I was baffled by all the things I was supposed to be missing. On the screen, next to a description of each movement came one of three judgements about you: CD – Exp: Correct decision, expected; Develop: You can improve this decision; ID: Incorrect decision. It was decision-making by numbers.

You could respond to each comment in writing and I did after receiving plenty I disagreed with in a game between Stoke and Sunderland.

Against one decision, the evaluator had instructed me not to allow players to place their arms on my shoulders during the cautioning process. I thought this was ridiculous. No harm had been done. The player was just making a human gesture, not threatening me in any way.

I was also told that I should have booked a player for dissent but wrote back in an email saying that: 'As part of my player management skills, I chose to give the player a public admonishment rather than a caution. The player apologised for his initial reaction.'

Then the evaulator took me to task for not giving a yellow for a reckless challenge. 'From my position, it was just a careless tackle,' I wrote. In a nice irony for a referee who liked the game to flow, I was also accused of not letting an attack develop but giving a free kick instead. 'I did not break up a promising attack,' I replied, 'as the player was heading to the corner flag with no support from his team-mates.' That was the trouble. The evaluator was seeing the picture on screen. I was in the middle of the bigger picture.

After that, hearing nothing back, I decided it was a waste of time to defend my decisions and only once more in the season replied to an evaluation. It came after that Wigan v Newcastle, Callum McManaman, game when I felt the evaluator had made some personal remarks. I hope my comments were passed on to him.

In the beginning, it also dented my confidence in my ability and my game-management – and I was not alone as other refs told me they felt the process was flawed. Like me, they also gave up responding. For me, the best solution to that was simply not to place too much store in the views of people who were not even at the game and not experiencing the atmosphere of it.

If you did, it might drive you nuts. I knew of one referee in the 2012-13 season who sustained a convenient injury ahead of a Manchester United game because he was so worried about making mistakes and wanted a break from all the criticism that came with the evaluations. That couldn't be right. Surely when a referee passed up a chance to take a match at Old Trafford, it showed there was something wrong with both the system and the people administering it.

We asked Mike if we could go back to the old assessors – and we had been critical of the disparity in their marking, so that told you how seriously troubled the Select Group were – but it cut no ice with him.

At least the delegate's report – that arrived seven to ten days after the game – was usually supportive of me, as they came from people who had had careers in the game and appreciated referees who played advantage and ran matches without being too demonstrative. My spirits always lifted if I saw understanding men like Peter Shreeves and Kenny Hibbert at my game. Depending on the attitudes of certain delegates, you could get between 22 and 26 out of 30 for a performance.

Some were known to be high markers, some were known to be hard. There was a feeling among referees that if the bosses liked you they would send you a high marker. And if they didn't, a hard one. I remember one time during the 2012-13 season when I watched Mark Clattenburg have a great game doing Spurs v Arsenal but he got a mark of 23 when another delegate might have given him 25 or 26.

The delegate focuses on three main areas: key match incidents, decision-making and game management. Each will carry a mark out of ten. I was usually in the Q1 bracket of delegate marks, which meant top four in the Select Group, and I often did well in the eyes of the professional, but non-technical, assessor for my handling of matches.

Taking one from the 2012-13 season as an example, for the Manchester United v Everton match, it showed that I received seven for key match incidents, nine for decision-making and nine for game management, totalling a high mark of 25 out of 30.

The delegate noted in his introductory remarks about my pre-match briefing that my team talk was very brief and no more than a personal message to both teams. He would add that though I had given a professional performance on the field, my approach missed a good opportunity to pass across points which could assist my management on the field to both captains and officials.

Fair enough. It is a constructive comment and the delegate was also positive in the report on the match analysis. My movement, he said, was of a high quality, showing intelligent positioning. He noted, though, that in giving a couple of fouls against Da Silva and Rooney, I could have squeezed closer to 'sell' – a technical word that means had I been nearer, the players would have accepted it better. But it was not always wise to be too close and so not have a wide view of an incident. I could, he added, also have been closer to a penalty decision – though rightly not given.

I also began to tire about the 70-minute mark and there might also have been validity to that, though not because of my age. After all, I was not getting regular Premier League games and I always maintained match fitness would suffer. He noted that I used the advantage rule well because I had a desire to let the game flow and that I had an empathy with the game.

He remarked on a key physical clash in the game, Phil Jones's man-marking job on Marouane Fellaini, with its potential for physical problems that never arose due to my man-management, which, he said, was of a very high standard throughout.

The delegate continued that I had the respect from the players from the outset for the way I managed and had an authority and a maturity. I talked to the players all game to quieten down, he said, to check on fitness, to advise of decisions or advantage and noted that I warned Rooney and Evans to calm down.

Overall, he concluded, 'The referee gave an accomplished performance, underpinned by good positioning through intelligent reading of the game... A quality performance... He has a calm persona and body language and a smiling face... A man who clearly looks like he is still enjoying his work and the players responded positively to this.'

The delegate, by the way, is also supposed to ring the managers on the Monday after a weekend game for their verdict. On this occasion, he noted, Sir Alex Ferguson was abroad in the Champions League while David Moyes didn't want to make any comment on the referee's performance. I knew privately that David was so concerned about standards that he preferred to keep his own counsel on all of us.

I too was worried about standards as I made my exit to take up new, exciting opportunities. I questioned how Mike Riley was administering a Select Group that was low on morale. I wondered where the young referees were coming from to augment a group that was getting dangerously low on numbers of high-quality referees. And I worried about where the game itself, with all the madness around it, was heading.

21

...AND THE DAY AFTER

That final season made me feel something I never wanted to feel and never thought I would. I loved refereeing, loved the people I met and the places it took me to, but many of the events, from the death threat I received to what happened to Mark Clattenburg, made me wonder what was happening to football. To be honest, I think the game is in the gutter.

A referee, particularly at the top in the Select Group, is under scrutiny as never before and while I am all for people being accountable, the ignorance of some of the criticism and the rise in social media, with its unmonitored vilification, almost makes it impossible to referee Premier League matches these days.

That is without all the media attention through press, radio and, above all, television that analyses every move you make, every decision you take. They want you, for example, to crack down on pulling and pushing in penalty areas. Then when you do and award a penalty, you are criticised for a 'soft' decision.

Opinions are like backsides, they say. Everybody's got one. But so many are ill-informed and not worth a light. Those judging you are usually seeing incidents from ten different camera angles and in slow-motion. Referees see them from one and in real time. On top of that, there is the internal scrutiny you have to undergo, from delegates at the game, your line manager, the head of the referees, the governing bodies and the detailed evaluations of every match.

Wherever referees go, when people recognise you on trains and in taxis or at airports or on holiday, they want to talk about games, decisions, personalities in the game and their own team. Most of that is nice and enjoyable, because I am a sociable kind of person, but the problem is that we signed contracts that meant we were unable to say much while we were active as referees.

Sometimes people think you are being stand-offish but if you were too forthcoming, you always worried about your private thoughts becoming public. I had an instance, for example, of my immediate boss, Keren Barratt, ringing me up saying I had been spotted on a train when I shouldn't be there. Not quite Sir Alex Ferguson once getting a call from a member of the public to say – untruthfully – that David Beckham, while a Manchester United player, had been spotted at Barcelona airport on his day off but sad nonetheless. Certainly saying something public could lead to repercussions, meaning that you had to just take all the mud that was hurled at you.

Take Mark Clattenburg. I believe Mark should have been allowed to come out and say what he needed to say to vindicate himself, certainly once the whole affair was over. It was not like that time at Fulham for me when it was all about a decision, serious as that might have felt to me. This was about a man's livelihood and his health. In many ways, he was being denied his human rights by not being allowed to speak in his own defence while his accusers did. His career could have been over just on the word of others.

As it is, the episode will always stick with him and be mentioned, rightly or wrongly. I just hope it didn't damage his chances of going to the World Cup in Brazil in 2014. It would be between him and Howard Webb to be England's representative, with Howard the favourite.

Those of us close to Mark knew the truth and stayed in contact with him to keep his spirits up but he experienced a miserable month when he couldn't fight back and that is not right. The fortunate thing in the end was that I am sure that people believed him and that public opinion was in his favour. I am not saying referees – or anybody – should have to explain and justify themselves all the time but there is such a thing as fairness and people should know what we have to put up with.

I admire Richard Bevan, the chief executive of the League Managers' Association, who is a passionate spokesman on behalf of his members. He stands up for their rights and makes sure they are properly compensated when sacked, and also talks so much sense about managerial issues.

I don't always agree with him, and would like to hear some admission from managers about when they get things wrong, but I would have liked someone like that in my corner. Compare and contrast with Mike Riley. I can't remember him saying a word in support of a Select Group referee when controversy arose and he was shamefully silent over the Clattenburg affair.

I do think the game's authorities had a great chance to make a statement by appointing Mark the FA Cup final referee in 2013. Andre Marriner is a good man, but the FA could have reasserted some control by saying in effect that after all the Chelsea shenanigans, they backed Mark Clattenburg and were demonstrating it by giving him the showpiece occasion.

I guess Mike's silence was because he was more concerned about what his paymasters at the Premier League might do or say to him, rather than the welfare of his own referees, who would love some support in the face of the unjustified barbs from certain managers. Imagine if we said about them what they say about us and questioned them the way they do us.

Now and then I would have enjoyed saying that a manager had made a shocking mistake with their team selection, that their striker was incompetent for missing an open goal or that their goalkeeper should not be playing at that level after making a howler.

I saw Rio Ferdinand sarcastically applaud the Turkish referee at the end of Manchester United's Champions League defeat by Real Madrid at Old Trafford in the 2012-13 season after the official had sent off Nani for serious foul play and I couldn't help wondering: how might Rio react if the ref sarcastically applauded the player after he had missed a tackle that led to a goal? I could understand Rio's frustration but I think he would have come to be embarrassed by his reaction.

Incidentally, the UEFA match assessor, the former Italian referee Pierluigi Collina, awarded Cuneyt Cakir a low mark of 8.2 that night, about 0.3 below average. The reason was not the red card, which Collina saw as justified, but because Cakir declined to punish Rio for his show of dissent at the end of the game.

The Nani incident illustrated a gulf in interpretation of the laws of the game, that may well have contributed to England, certainly the national team if not its clubs, failing to achieve what they might have done at international tournaments.

Raising feet and catching an opponent, even if the player is unaware of the other in the vicinity, is seen as a red card offence by the Elite Group of European referees. Top players should know that, and know that there is greater indulgence shown in the Premier League by Select Group referees. It is why I was criticised for giving that red card for Mido for his high foot for Middlesbrough against Arsenal that time, though was backed by the FA.

Why the disparity? In my opinion, one reason could well be because the Premier League want fast, furious and physical games. It is also what the world wants and television pays huge sums of money for. Fabio Capello, when manager of England, said that English referees are the best and I agree but you do wonder if we are doing a disservice sometimes by being different and letting the game flow more than our colleagues abroad. Then again, I doubt if fans would stand for stop-start games.

I think, for example, of England being disallowed what would have been a winning goal in a World Cup game against Argentina in 1998 for a foul by Alan Shearer at a corner that would probably not have been seen as an offence in the Premier League. But English players will continue to commit them, and be baffled if they are then given, if they do not adapt properly. Many of our clubs now have, so regularly do they play in Europe.

Unfortunately, there is also a culture of overturning red cards in England that happens in Europe only if it is a case of mistaken identity, and not a questionable decision, as over here. I had that one in my final season for Tom Huddlestone.

It is curious, though, how the FA said they didn't want to re-referee games when it came to punishing Callum McManaman of Wigan in retrospect, even though I admitted I had not seen that foul against Massadio Haidara of Newcastle. That is just a blatant contradiction.

The FA said the disparity came because of a loophole agreed the previous summer between themselves, the Premier League, the LMA and the PFA – 'the stakeholders' – that if one of the officials had a clear view of an incident, there could be no retrospective punishment. Now I don't recall being asked my opinion as a senior referee. I would have thought the PGMOL might also have had an input. In the event, that loophole soon got closed.

It was an example of how the FA no longer run the game as they once used to, but mostly just administer it. They have to consult with all the interested parties fighting their corners before they can govern, which might sound democratic in principle, but in reality means they are forced to compromise their standards, in my view.

It is interesting to note again that in all other footballing nations, it is the national federations who control refereeing, not their main league. La Liga, Serie A and the Bundesliga are servants, not masters.

One of the problems in our current system is that it is the

Premier League funding the PGMOL, along with the FA and Football League to a lesser extent. The offices of the PGMOL are, in fact, in the same London building as the Premier League.

In effect, these organisations are paying the wages of referees. There is clearly potential for conflict and vested interest here, with the people who administer our own organisation vulnerable to pressure from the Premier League, who have their ideas on how games should be handled, and that filters down to us.

You could see down the years with what happened to Philip Don that certain managers can put pressure on the Premier League to make sure the PGMOL is run a certain way and games refereed under that system. And, for example, we knew we weren't going to get a proper apology from Chelsea for the way Mark Clattenburg was treated. The Premier League was always going to side with the stakeholders; that is, the clubs.

I know it is a relationship that has concerned the FA, who have wanted to take more control of refereeing. But whether that would make a huge amount of difference, I am not sure. What might make refereeing much more independent is if the money that goes into the PGMOL from the Premier League came straight out of the television deal. That way, they could operate in conjunction and consultation with the Premier League and the FA but not be beholden to them, certainly financially with the sense of obligation that brings. I also think they should have their own offices away from any of the governing bodies.

If that makes the game better off the field, then what will improve it on the pitch in my view is the introduction of technology – and not just for the goal-line, as was introduced for the 2013-14 season. Trust me, referees at the highest level want it and do not see it as undermining their authority. Rather, it is an aid to getting things right so that they don't have to go through the grief they get.

I have always been in favour of goal-line technology to

determine a goal. It would have meant Cristiano Ronaldo was awarded that goal I could not have given in the Portugal versus Azerbaijan game, and that Pedro Mendez would have got his just deserts that time for Spurs at Old Trafford, where I was the fourth official and knew from a replay it had gone over the line but could not intervene because it was beyond my remit. And who will forget that Frank Lampard goal for England against Germany in the 2010 World Cup that should have been given?

On top of that, I would have it for everything, from contentious penalties to offside – every significant decision, in fact. As referees, we could go to the video official, as they do in Rugby League and Union and cricket, if we are unsure of anything. If we let play go when the managers think we have missed something, then they should be allowed one challenge each per half, as with similar systems in tennis and American football.

People point out all sorts of potential pitfalls – such as delaying a game that is essentially about action being continuous. But there are plenty of stoppages already and these can be sorted out quickly. We have an adage in refereeing: better to be slow and right than quick and wrong with a decision. Besides, if there were breaks like that, maybe players wouldn't go down for an injury so often when all they really want is a breather.

How then would you restart the game after a video decision? Well if the pictures showed that it was not a goal or free kick, then it would have to be with a drop ball, with possession going to the goalkeeper of the team who were in possession when the incident occurred. It is the same system as now when the players agree to concede possession after an injury.

As for the argument that human error is part of the game and makes for lively taking points, I don't buy that. People are going to talk about the game whatever the decisions and it might mean that pundits on TV analyse the actual play better and look at the referee's role in facilitating that, rather than focus on the negatives.

Human error is for players. That is what makes the game so interesting – as somebody once said, games are not won, they are lost; meaning that it is all about the fallibility of its players – and there is no reason when technology exists not to use it. I certainly know that there have been things I have missed but been picked up by cameras – such as Marouane Fellaini's head butt on Ryan Shawcross in that Everton match at Stoke – and I would be happy for that omission to be rectified.

I don't believe referees would be reduced to mere 'clerks' out on the field. We would still be in control of players and the game. But quite simply, as referees, we are assessed by technology and therefore should be allowed to have access to it. That way, too, we also might put an end to one of the curses of the modern game – diving, or simulation to give it the technical term.

I have always liked teams who simply get on with the game rather than cheat or look to con a referee, as my enjoyment of lower league games shows. In the Premier League, though, it is getting harder and harder to spot what is a penalty and what is simulation, what with the speed of the game and the sleight of foot of some modern strikers.

To be honest, it has been a nightmare in the Premier League, as that dive by Jay Rodriguez for Southampton at Aston Villa showed to me. Whether you give it or don't, you are going to get grief from one set of supporters. You have to ride that, without fear or favour, but it can grind us all down.

Until my final season when I succumbed and gave a yellow card to Cesar Azpilicueta of Chelsea in a game at Reading for throwing himself to the ground, I never cautioned a player for simulation, which may be another reason I didn't endear myself to the powers that be sometimes. I think you have to be certain it is a clear act. There are often shades of grey, with players stumbling for example, and even if there is contact, it doesn't mean it is a foul or a dive. That is where some pundits get it wrong in my view, thinking that contact is an automatic penalty. It may be the striker who has instigated the contact or perhaps it is a simple collision of two players arriving at the same time.

In my time, there was often much debate about Gareth Bale and all his yellow cards for simulation at Tottenham. At the pace he was going, the slightest bit of contact might bring him down so I would have given him the benefit of the doubt most of the time. It can become about reputations, though. For his future career, I would have urged him to stay on his feet wherever possible because then he will get the penalties he deserves rather than them being turned down. There can be rough justice if referees feel they have been conned and they may not give the next one. My wariness of Jay Rodriguez after his simulation should be a warning about that.

The best thing, in all honesty, was often to give nothing and just get the hell out of the situation. You just couldn't tell a lot of the time, given the speed of the game, which means that referees are bound to get some things wrong. Again, this is where technology would help.

And being closer to incidents doesn't always help. We did a training exercise at Burton where we were asked to look at a picture from various distances. Too close, and the brain can't cope with all the information. Sometimes you see more of what is going on by stepping back. Pundits should remember that rather than criticising referees for apparently not being up with play. Referees don't have eyesight tests by the way, despite fans urging us to, but in the Select Group we did have reaction tests, touching lights on a board as they flash on.

Actually, it has been proved that the brain simply cannot cope with too much data or certain types of it. How can an assistant, for example, be expected to watch when the ball is kicked then change his line of sight to know whether a player was offside 40 yards away when it was launched? It is educated guesswork some of the time. Another argument for technology.

There are arguments, too, for other innovations, some loopy, some helpful.

I dismiss the two referee system that was once trialled many years ago and which involves having a referee in both halves of the field controlling just their area. Arsene Wenger was once an advocate of that.

The problem is that the complaints now are about inconsistency from referee to referee, from game to game, so how might that be with two men having differing opinions in the same game? After all, sometimes at refereeing summits, officials themselves can't agree on decisions in the cold light of day, let alone heat of battle. One man, one job, I say.

Wenger, a great thinker on the game I have to admit, has also suggested that referees should not be named on a Monday, as now, in order to avert pressure on them in wars of words between managers and players before games. Instead, he reckons, it should be done by a draw, allocating a ref to a Premier League match randomly from the Select Group on a Thursday and the result not made public till Saturday morning.

I understand where he is coming from and don't object to the idea of a draw but the problem is making all the logistical arrangements to get refs to games, all the needs of such peripheral things as printing the matchday programme, so late in the week. Besides, do you think in the leaky world of English football, you would be able to keep refs a secret until the day of the game?

There have also been suggestions for a three card system, with one between red and yellow. It comes because it looks on the surface that a technical offence such as delay of game – that is, time-wasting –should not be as serious as something like a reckless tackle. But then, some referees have had enough trouble with two cards, let alone three, haven't they?

Where I do see a potential change for the better is in the

introduction of a sin bin. I do think it unfair that a player can be sent off for two technical offences, such as not being back ten yards and kicking the ball away. Instead, I think if a second yellow is a technical offence, then a more appropriate punishment might be to spend ten minutes in the sin bin rather than give someone a red card. If it is not, and is a bad tackle, then of course they should still go. And if the offence occurs in the last ten minutes, they simply miss the rest of the game. It all seems to work in the rugby codes.

It may be one more thing to think about for a ref but should be simple enough, especially if we are going to make more use of technology in the future, as I hope we will.

Something certainly needs to be done to ease the burden on officials because the demands are relentless, be they on referee, assistant or a fourth official – a position of responsibility without power. 'Holding the board up' as refs call it. The pressure is ever greater in that area between the two dug-outs from managers, coaches and from fans in the vicinity. Often it seems as if your only real function is to be the butt of the abuse, thereby diverting it away from the referee out on the field. As a ref, I always liked my fourth official in my ear with words of encouragement. It gave you a real lift to hear 'great decision' on my headset. I would always thank them for that afterwards.

Otherwise, it is a thankless task, containing and controlling all the coaches who also turn to you whenever the man in the middle makes a decision they don't like. As if I was going be able to change it. I suppose they were wanting me to forward their comments to the referee if it happened before half-time but it still goes on in the second, even though nothing will be changed.

But then, as I have indicated, we have often been our own worst enemies, taking all this simply because we want to get sent back to these big grounds to officiate rather than being kept away from them till situations die down. You put up with it because you wouldn't get an appointment there for a while otherwise.

The whole atmosphere led to the shocking fall in morale among Select Group referees and if I am honest, in talking to them during my final season, I don't think there were many among them who wouldn't have resigned if they had had something else to go to that paid them the same money to pay off their mortgages. Even the best, who remain at the peak of their careers.

The two best, in my view, remain Howard Webb and Mark Clattenburg, though both have also had their own reasons for being disillusioned. Both have the right personalities for the job, a mix of carrot and stick, tolerance and firmness, and a good understanding of players and what they go through as well as the ability to interpret instantly the laws of the game so that they by and large get the big decisions right.

Mike Dean is right up there, too, but has taken a long time to get over – in the eyes of the bosses that is – a three-month suspension for his association with a business venture involving horse racing ownership. I think a friendship with Graham Poll also counted against him in the eyes of the new management. Mike could well have been one of England's Elite Group officials and should have got more of the bigger games. Somehow his face didn't fit as well as others, however. I know the feeling.

Of the new breed, Michael Oliver and Anthony Taylor are very promising but there are just not enough young English referees coming through.

I guess the best English referees of my whole era have been Graham Poll, despite my reservations about him as a man, and Paul Durkin, who both had the added skill of knowing how to play the system. As for the best from overseas, it would have to be the Italian Pierluigi Collina. He was a great referee who made his reputation and then lived on it – and I don't mean that in a derogatory manner.

What happens is that once you establish your style and earn

some respect, you have it from then on in your dealings with players and managers. Collina did that. He frightened the life out of players, just by the way he looked with those intense eyes and bald head. Perhaps I should have kept my head shaved after the chemotherapy instead of letting the hair grow back.

I wonder, in England at least, where the next wave of high quality referees are going to come from. We began the full-time professional Select Group with 24 referees. In my last season, there were just 16, with two of those part-time. The group could hardly afford to lose other experienced referees like Chris Foy and Phil Dowd. I also knew that Howard Webb was contemplating going back to the South Yorkshire Police as he was growing concerned about his prospects at the top.

I have great respect for the PGMOL as an organisation, and reason to be grateful to them because they treated me with great respect through my illness. But, with the current set-up in personnel, it means that the young referees coming through are not up to the required Premier League standard, in my view.

I don't think there is enough good quality coaching going on at the lower levels and enough good assessors to ensure a production line. In trying to get referees into the business younger, they are producing people without enough experience of playing and working so that they develop man-management skills that enable you to empathise with players.

In effect, they are trying to manufacture referees who do it by numbers, rather than helping to bring natural ability to maturity. You have to feel refereeing. You have to smell it.

I would be all for more players becoming referees at the end of their career but such is the money in the game – and their intimate knowledge of what referees are put through on the pitch – that very few want to do the training and spend time coming through the ranks, even if they are fast-tracked.

We did have Steve Baines, a former Chesterfield player, who

went on until the then retirement age of 48 and he was decent but he upset the powers that be. They considered that he refereed the game his own way and was too lenient. It is always about striking the balance between letting the game flow and applying the laws.

Not enough women have made it through either and it is probably down to the severity of the fitness test that even strong men have had trouble with. Wendy Toms had a good run but then failed the test. We now have Sian Massey who is an excellent assistant and takes charge of non-league games but it will be a question as she goes higher of meeting the increasing fitness requirements.

There is simply no way of getting away from the physical fact of life that the same fitness test is – more often that not – going to be harder for a woman than a man. It doesn't mean they are worse referees, just that they may struggle to last the pace in the physical hothouse that is the Premier League today.

Another of Mike Riley's changes for the worse, by the way – quite apart from clamping down on the petty things like getting signed shirts (even though it is permitted by UEFA in European games) and being able to communicate with managers and players by phone and text – was making the Select Group take the fitness test for a forthcoming season at the end of a previous season rather than in the August at the start of one.

It meant that a ref could come back for a new season out of condition after passing the test three months earlier, which struck me as a recipe for disaster. In fact, I am not quite sure how it has been allowed to happen given a UEFA edict that fitness tests should be taken less than six weeks before the start of a league season.

Anyway, in many ways, I would like to see more women coming through, not just to be politically correct, but because their approach might civilise some of the less well behaved players. First they have to pass that test, though. It is only right if there is to be an equality. And the Premier League is an unforgiving world that

286

all aspiring referees have to learn to cope with.

I would be more than happy to be involved in helping to coach and mentor young referees now I am retired but given the people in charge currently, it is unlikely to happen, however much experience and knowledge I might have to bring. I could certainly tell them all about trying to cope with the pressures at the top. Going from Football League to Premier League is just the same as it is for players and clubs, and only the strong survive.

There is no hiding place on the field and you have to be mentally tough. It also follows you off the field more and more these days, which is one reason why it is advisable not to read the newspapers or watch the analysis of games on TV. It can destroy you.

I do feel that referees should get more help to cope with the increasing level of mental strain. The Select Group do have a sports psychologist available in Sheffield, Ian Maynard, but I would like to see a counsellor in attendance at the fortnightly get-togethers at Burton for those who would like to talk things through.

With the referees coming through younger and younger, I do fear that they could suffer from burn-out due to the intensity of the modern game and all the media – mass and social – they are subjected to, quite apart from the strains of match day itself.

In my view, given some of the episodes of recent seasons, it will not be long before a referee has a nervous breakdown and that emerges into the public domain. I also believe that if we do not do something to help referees with mental health and stress issues, then we could even see a suicide.

It almost happened in Germany a few years ago. Luckily the Bundesliga referee Babak Rafati was found in the bath of his hotel room with his wrists slit just in time to be saved and he underwent treatment for depression.

I say this all this for those who will follow me because I am seeing the job getting tougher and tougher – and if you don't have the life experience to cope, it can be overwhelming. In recent years, there has been a welcome increase in the number of grass-roots referees, with more than 28,000 active, up by five per cent on 2010 and 20 per cent on 2008.

That is partly due to the Respect campaign organised by the game's governing bodies urging the players to behave themselves better and also to local football leagues having made punishment for misbehaving players much more serious so that referees are supported more. It may also be down to there being a bit of pin money to be made in these days of high unemployment.

There will always be those among young referees who, like I did, had a feel for it and aimed for the Football League, then the Premier League. But I am wondering if so many fall by the wayside or don't want to progress to the top level because they see on television what they would have to go through and just don't want that grief?

In some ways, I was fortunate that my perspective on the game changed with my illness when I became less intense about the game – not less concerned about my performances but less worried when I got things wrong. I also became less frustrated by the politics of refereeing and the way I was treated by my bosses after my cancer, even if some of the injustices continued to upset me.

I never issued a big spiel to my assistants in the dressing room before the game. 'Just enjoy it. Let's keep a smile on our faces,' I would say. I simply wanted to do the game to the best of my ability and go home to my family.

As the Liverpool v Manchester United game and that Twitter nonsense showed, it is not always easy to let things wash over you. Liverpool supporters vilified me at the same time as I received a text from a colleague who was at a conference of European referees in Zurich who had been watching the game. 'Class red card,' it said. Some solace, but it could not make up for how much I – and Michelle and Lucy – had been affected by the whole episode.

Thus did I need a new challenge. José Mourinho always said to enjoy the game with a passion and a little bit of that left me towards the end. Don't get me wrong. I still enjoyed the 90 minutes on the field absorbed in a game I had loved since kicking about on the playing fields of Welwyn Garden City. It was just all the rubbish around it that started to get me down. I wanted to go out with my enjoyment intact, rather than become bitter.

Now it became all about finding a new way to stay involved in the game and making the most of my talents and experience. I had the recovery from cancer to pass on to people, to offer fellow sufferers hope, and I had the experience of handling pressurised situations and environments, after all.

I wanted to put back something into my profession, if refereeing still wanted me that was, and I wanted to work for cancer charities to inspire people in their own recoveries. I wanted to do motivational talks to companies and sporting bodies as I felt I had so much to pass on from my life and my story.

I was fortunate enough that the new BT Sport set-up that had bought rights to 38 games a season in the Premier League, and was creating some exceptional programming on their sports channel around those games, recruited me to be one of their pundits.

Now, I know I have had my complaints about pundits, but I hoped I could bring some insight and perception of what a referee goes through from my experience and my actual knowledge of the laws. It was a great opportunity and one that BT Sport were being clever about in having a ref there on their panel for the first time to give instant reaction, that I hoped would be fair and honest, to events on the field.

Let's face it, pretty much every TV game has a major decision and talking point that impacts on the match result and it made sense finally to have a qualified official at hand.

One of the ironies was that one of my colleagues on the new channel was... Neil Warnock. I was sure we would be fine as long as he didn't question my authority.

It would be strange, and something of a wrench, to quit and not be involved as the new season of 2013-14 kicked off. But I have to be honest: all the rubbish around being a referee, if not the actual game itself, had got me down and I was not expecting to miss it as I might have done had I been forced to retire at the age of 48. I was going when I was ready.

I just did not want the modern stress to get either myself or Michelle down any more and have any impact on our cancers returning. Besides, exciting times were on the horizon, with the new BT job and any other opportunities that life might throw up.

Endings, they say, also mean beginnings.

ACKNOWLEDGEMENTS
MARK HALSEY

There can only be one place to begin my thanks to people for their help and support for me before my cancer, during my treatment for it, and the trials and tribulations after it, along with their backing of me during my refereeing career. That is with my wonderful wife Michelle and loving daughter Lucy. Their life-enhancing love has kept me going and kept me sane during some tough times and also helped me savour the good times even more. I love them to bits.

After them, I need to thank Professor Tim Illidge, my consultant at The Christie Hospital in Manchester. Quite simply, without him and his expertise, I would not be here. I am also beholden to the marvellous care of the staff at the Christie who helped Tim get me through.

Then there is my back-up team of mine and Michelle's family. Thanks to my Mum Shirley, brother Paul and son Jason, along with Michelle's Mum and Dad, Lorraine and Peter and sister Angela and her husband Dennis. They have given me much.

I have also valued greatly the close friendship of Fred Barber, former goalkeeping coach at Bolton Wanderers, and his wife Christine. My big mate and refereeing colleague Pete Walton has also been a tower of strength.

I would also like to pay tribute to other referees who have been there for me, notably my former boss Keith Hackett, along with Lee Mason, Alan Wiley, Mark Clattenburg, Howard Webb, Steve

Bennett and Barry Knight. Indeed, the whole of the current Select Group have been very supportive.

Kelly Wright at the Professional Game Match Officials Board Ltd was also a great help, as was the sports scientist there, Simon Brevik. I have always been able to rely on Jimmy Martin, kit man at Everton. I would also like to thank the kit man at Arsenal, Vic Akers.

The former fitness coach at Bolton, Jimmy Barrow, has also been good to me, professionally and personally, as were the managers of the club who allowed me to train there, in Sam Allardyce, Gary Megson and Owen Coyle.

Two other managers especially deserve my thanks, in José Mourinho and Sir Alex Ferguson. I have particularly valued the friendship of José and am grateful to both for their ready backing of my charity work for cancer organisations.

Roberto Mancini, David Moyes and Martin O'Neill also gave their time freely to back a fundraiser for The Christie, as did Geoff Shreeves and John Gwynne of Sky. Ed Chamberlain at Sky has also supported me, as have Richard Keys and Andy Gray of talk-SPORT. I am grateful too to Ian Dennis of BBC Radio 5 Live.

My appreciation goes to all those people who sent me messages of support — not just referees, players and managers but members of the public. You are too numerous to thank individually and by name but I remain grateful for your touching words and gestures during my illness. Each little act of kindness played a part in helping me to survive then prosper again and I thank you one and all.

Finally, thanks to my writer Ian Ridley who has brought his dedication and skill to this book and become part of our family. He has fought his own battles with cancer and so understood what I have gone through. It was a pleasure to have him at my final game.

Mark Halsey, Bolton, August 2013

Mark Halsey was the longest-serving full-time professional referee in the English game when he retired at the end of the 2012-13 season after a 20-year career that took in three seasons officiating in non-league, another three in the Football League and a remarkable 14 in the Premier League. An inspiring survivor of throat cancer, he lives with wife Michelle and daughter Lucy near Bolton, Lancashire, and is now a refereeing pundit with the BT Sport television station.

Ian Ridley is the author of ten football books, including the number one best-selling *Addicted* with the former Arsenal and England captain, Tony Adams, which was nominated for the William Hill Sports Book of the Year. Over a 35-year career, he has written on the game for newspapers including *The Guardian*, *The Daily Telegraph*, *The Independent on Sunday*, *The Observer* and *The Mail on Sunday*, for whom he was Chief Football Writer. He was named Sports Journalist of the Year in the British Press Awards for 2007.

Also by Ian Ridley

Season In The Cold: A Journey Through English Football
Cantona: The Red and The Black
Tales From the Boot Camps – with Steve Claridge
Addicted – with Tony Adams
Hero and Villain – with Paul Merson
Floodlit Dreams: How to Save a Football Club
Kevin Keegan: An Intimate Portrait of Football's Last Romantic
Beyond The Boot Camps – with Steve Claridge
There's A Golden Sky: How 20 Years of the Premier League
Have Changed Football Forever